STEVE EMANUEL'S
BOOTCAMP FOR THE MBE: TORTS

EMANUEL BAR REVIEW ADVISORS

emanuel®
BAR REVIEW

STEVE EMANUEL'S

Bootcamp for the MBE

TORTS

STEVEN L. EMANUEL

Founder & Editor-in-Chief,
Emanuel Bar Review
Member, NY, CT, MD and VA bars

www.aspenlaw.com

Wolters Kluwer Law & Business | Aspen Publishers

Emanuel Bar Review is a division of Aspen Publishers, a Wolters Kluwer company.

Aspen Publishers
Attn: Permissions Department
76 Ninth Avenue, 7th Floor
New York, NY 10011-5201

For information about Emanuel Bar Review (including Emanuel Multistate Review), contact:

email: info@emanuelbarprep.com
phone: 1-888-MBE-PREP
fax: 781-207-5815
website: www.emanuelbarprep.com

Printed in the United States of America.

1 2 3 4 5 6 7 8 9 0

ISBN 978-0-7355-9737-2

TABLE OF CONTENTS

PREFACE

Dear *Bootcamp* enrollee:

This book consists mainly of a short outline on Torts. I hope that you'll read the outline before you watch the online substantive lecture that's part of Steve Emanuel's Bootcamp for the MBE. If you can't read the outline before watching the online lecture, read it by way of review afterwards.

The outline section of this book does not contain any MBE-format questions — that's what we'll be doing in the 2-volume "*Emanuel's Essentials*" set of multi-choice questions and answers in context, which is part of your materials.

I have written the outline in an attempt to cover virtually all the substantive rules of law that the MBE examiners test in their Torts questions, and to highlight the traps they set. I've tried to omit any topic or rule of law that doesn't seem to pop up on the MBE, no matter how important that topic may have been in your law school Torts course.

The last part of the book consists of the 33 questions on Torts extracted from our 200-Question Self-Assessment Test, together with our model answers to those questions. I hope that you will first take the Self-Assessment Test on a stand-alone basis, and that you will only consult the Torts questions in this book as a means of reviewing after you've taken the Self Assessment Test.

Good luck, and see you online soon!

Steve Emanuel

Larchmont, NY

April 2010

TORTS OUTLINE

TABLE OF CONTENTS
TORTS OUTLINE

Chapter 1
INTRODUCTION

Chapter 2
INTENTIONAL TORTS AGAINST THE PERSON

Chapter 3
INTENTIONAL INTERFERENCE WITH PROPERTY

Chapter 4
DEFENSES TO INTENTIONAL TORTS

Chapter 5
NEGLIGENCE GENERALLY

Chapter 6
ACTUAL AND PROXIMATE CAUSE

Chapter 7
JOINT TORTFEASORS

Chapter 8
DUTY

Chapter 9

OWNERS AND OCCUPIERS OF LAND

Chapter 10

DAMAGES

Chapter 11

DEFENSES IN NEGLIGENCE ACTIONS

Chapter 12

VICARIOUS LIABILITY

Chapter 13

STRICT LIABILITY

Chapter 14

PRODUCTS LIABILITY

Chapter 15

NUISANCE

Chapter 16

MISREPRESENTATION

Chapter 17

DEFAMATION

Chapter 18

INVASION OF PRIVACY

TORTS OUTLINE

This outline attempts to cover only topics that have been repeatedly tested on actual MBE exams. "Rest. 2d" refers to the Second Restatement of Torts. "Rest. 3d (Apport.)" refers to Restatement Third, Apportionment of Liability. "Rest. 3d (P.L.)" refers to Restatement Third, Products Liability. "Rest. 3d (P.H.)" refers to Restatement Third, Liability for Physical Harm. "Dobbs" refers to Dan Dobbs, *The Law of Torts* Hornbook (West, 2000). "P&K" refers to *Prosser & Keeton on Torts* Hornbook (West, 1984).

This outline generally assumes, as does the MBE, that the jurisdiction applies pure comparative fault and common-law joint-and-several liability.

CHAPTER 1

INTRODUCTION

I. GENERAL INTRODUCTION

A. Definition of "tort": There is no single definition of "tort." The most we can say is that: (1) a tort is a *civil wrong* committed by one person against another; and (2) torts can and usually do arise *outside of any agreement* between the parties.

B. Categories: There are three broad categories of torts, and there are individually-named torts within each category:

1. **Intentional torts:** First, *intentional* torts are ones where the defendant desires to bring about a particular result. At least for MBE purposes, the main intentional torts are:

   a. *Battery;*

   b. *Assault;* and

   c. *Intentional infliction of emotional distress.*

2. **Negligence:** The next category is the generic tort of *"negligence."* Here, the defendant has not intended to bring about a certain result, but has merely behaved *carelessly*. There are no individually-named torts in this category, merely the general concept of "negligence."

3. **Strict liability:** Finally, there is the least culpable category, *"strict liability."* Here, the defendant is held liable even though he did not intend to bring about the undesirable result, and even though he behaved with utmost carefulness. There are three main individually-named torts that apply strict liability:

   a. The keeping of *wild or dangerous animals*;

   b. The conducting of *abnormally dangerous activities* (e.g., blasting); and

   c. The *selling* of a *defective product* which causes personal injury or property damage.

C. Significance of categories: There are two main consequences that turn on which of the three above categories a particular tort falls into:

1. **Scope of liability:** The three categories differ concerning D's liability for *far-reaching, unexpected consequences*. The more *culpable* D's conduct, the more *far-reaching* her liabil-

ity for unexpected consequences — so an intentional tortfeasor is liable for a wider range of unexpected consequences than is a negligent tortfeasor. (For more about this, see p. 11 *infra*.)

2. **Damages:** The *measure of damages* is generally broader for the more culpable categories. In particular, D is more likely to be required to pay *punitive damages* when he is an intentional tortfeasor than when he is negligent or strictly liable.

CHAPTER 2

INTENTIONAL TORTS AGAINST THE PERSON

I. "INTENT" DEFINED

A. Meaning of intent: There is no general meaning of "intent" when discussing intentional torts. For each individual intentional tort, you have to memorize a different definition of "intent." All that the intentional torts have in common is that D must have intended to bring about some sort of physical or mental effect upon another person.

1. **No intent to harm:** The intentional torts generally are *not* defined in such a way as to require D to have intended to *harm* the plaintiff.

Example: D points a water gun at P, making it seem like a robbery, when in fact it is a practical joke. If D has intended to put P in fear of imminent harmful bodily contact, the "intent" for assault is present, even though D intended no "harm" to P.

2. **Substantial certainty:** If D *knows with substantial certainty* that a particular effect will occur as a result of her action, she is *deemed to have intended that result.*

Example 1: D pulls a chair out from under P as she is sitting down. If D knew with "substantial certainty" that P would hit the ground, D meets the intent requirement for battery, even if he did not desire that she do so. [*Garratt v. Dailey*]

Example 2: While P, a cheerleader, has a megaphone near her lips, D pushes the megaphone towards P, hitting P's teeth. Even if D didn't intend to cause the contact between the megaphone and P's teeth or other body part, if D knew to a substantial certainty that such a contact would occur, he will be deemed to have intended the harmful contact (thus meeting the intent requirement for battery).

a. **High likelihood:** But if it is merely "highly likely," not "substantially certain," that the bad consequences will occur, then the act is not an intentional tort. "Recklessness" by D is not enough.

3. **Act distinguished from consequences:** Distinguish D's act from the *consequences* of that act. The act must be intentional or substantially certain, but the consequences need not be.

Example: D intends to tap P lightly on the chin to annoy him. If P has a "glass jaw," which is broken by the light blow, D has still "intended" to cause the contact, and the intentional tort of battery has taken place, even though the consequences — broken jaw — were not intended.

B. Transferred intent: Under the doctrine of *"transferred intent,"* if D held the necessary intent with respect to person *A*, he will be held to have committed an intentional tort against *any other person* who happens to be injured.

Example: D shoots at *A*, and accidentally hits *B*. D is liable to *B* for the intentional tort of battery.

II. SCOPE OF LIABILITY

A. Distinction: An important consequence of the distinction between intentional torts and negligence has to do with liability for *unexpected results*. Whereas the negligence defendant will generally be held liable only for those consequences which were at least somewhat foreseeable, the intentional tortfeasor will be liable for *virtually every result stemming directly or even somewhat indirectly from his conduct*, however unlikely it might have seemed at the time of his act that this result would follow. Rest. 2d, §435B.

> **Example:** D intentionally hits P on the head intending merely to annoy him. P is slightly injured, and is taken to the hospital. There, by a gross and completely unforeseeable error, a nurse gives him poison instead of medicine, and P dies. D will be liable for P's death, not just the minor injury. But if D had merely negligently given P the same minor injury, he would not be liable for the unanticipated death. Rest. 2d, §435B, Illustr. 1.

III. BATTERY

A. Definition: Battery is the *intentional infliction of a harmful or offensive bodily contact.*

> **Example:** *A* intentionally punches *B* in the nose. *A* has committed battery.

B. Intent: It is not necessary that D desires to physically *harm* P. D has the necessary intent for battery if it is the case *either* that:

[1] D intended to *cause a harmful or offensive bodily contact; or*

[2] D intended to cause an *imminent apprehension* on P's part of a harmful or offensive bodily contact (even if D did not intend to cause the contact itself).

> **Example of [1]:** D shoots at P, intending to hit him with the bullet. D has the necessary intent for battery.

> **Example of [2]:** D shoots at P, while facing him, intending to miss P, but also intending to make P think that P would be hit. D has the intent needed for battery. That is, the "intent to commit an assault" (see *infra*, p. 13) suffices as the intent for battery.

1. Intent to create apprehension of contact: Alternative [2] above means that an *"intent to commit an assault"* will suffice as the intent for battery. That is, if D intends merely to *put P in fear of an imminent harmful or offensive contact*, that's a sufficient intent for battery, and it doesn't matter that D does not intend that such a contact actually occur.

a. Prank gone bad: Therefore, on the MBE be on the lookout for a *"prank gone bad,"* where D tries to trick P into thinking that P will undergo an imminent harmful or offensive contact, but D doesn't intend the contact to actually occur. If something goes wrong and a harmful contact occurs, that's battery of the "intent to commit assault" (i.e., intent to create an imminent apprehension of harmful or offensive contact) variety.

> **Example:** D and P are golfing together. As a prank, D swings his club toward P's head, desiring to make P think (falsely) that the club will strike P. D holds up his swing at the last instant, but due to a hidden defect in the club the clubhead flies off and strikes P in the face, injuring him. This is battery, because: (1) D intended to create in P an apprehension of an imminent harmful or offensive contact; and (2) an actual harmful or offensive contact ensued.

2. D must intend contact: Don't forget that battery is an intentional tort, and the intent is to make a harmful/offensive contact (or induce an apprehension of such a contact). You may see a fact pattern in which D performs an intentional *act without intending a contact*, but a harmful contact ensues. That's *not* battery.

Example: In a one-mile race, D attempts to cut in front of P, not intending to make contact with P. D negligently fails to leave adequate clearance, and P's foot hits the back of D's leg, causing P to fall. This is not battery — D attempted to cut in, but did not intend a bodily contact (let alone a harmful or offensive one), so the intent requirement for battery is not met.

3. **Must intend contact with a "person":** The defendant must intend a contact with what the defendant *believes is a person.* So if D intends to bring about contact with what D thinks is an *inanimate object* or an *animal*, that won't suffice, even if D is wrong and a contact with a person results.

Example: D, walking in the dark while carrying a cane, swings at a shape near the sidewalk that D thinks is a bag of leaves. It's in fact a homeless person in a sleeping bag, who is injured. Even if D was negligent in believing that this was a bag of leaves, D has not committed battery, because he did not intend to make a harmful or offensive contact with a human.

C. **Harmful or offensive contact:** If the contact is "harmful" — i.e., it causes pain or bodily damage — this qualifies. But battery also covers contacts which are merely *"offensive,"* i.e., damaging to a *"reasonable sense of dignity."*

Example: D spits on P. Even if P is not "harmed" in the sense of being caused physical pain or physical injury, a battery has occurred because a person of average sensitivity in P's position would have her dignity offended.

1. **Reasonableness standard for "offensive" contact:** In determining whether a particular contact is "offensive," the standard is not whether the particular plaintiff was offended, but whether "an *ordinary person not unduly sensitive* as to his *dignity*" would have been offended. P&K, p. 42.

2. **Ordinary and reasonable contacts:** Thus if *A* gently pushes past *B* in a crowded public place, or taps him on the shoulder to ask directions, no battery will be found even if: (1) it turns out that *B* is unduly sensitive and was in fact offended by the touching; or (2) *B* is startled, and moves in a way that injures himself.

Example: On a crowded subway platform, D's access to the entry door to a waiting subway is blocked by P. D, coming up from behind, gently taps P on the shoulder to let him know that D wishes to get by. P is startled, spins around, and in so doing trips and falls, injuring his head. Assume that D did not behave negligently in touching P.

D has not committed battery of P, because D did not make an "offensive" contact with P's body. D did not intend to offend, and an ordinary person not unduly sensitive as to his own dignity would not have been offended.

3. **Contact beyond level consented to:** Battery can occur where the plaintiff *consents* to a certain level of bodily contact (see *infra*, p. 23), but the defendant *goes beyond the consented-to level* of contact. At that point, the consent becomes invalid, and battery results. Look for this "beyond the consented-to level of contact" scenario on the MBE when the facts involve either a *sporting event* or a *medical/surgical procedure.*

Example 1: In a pick-up ice hockey game in a park, P and D are skirmishing for the puck near the side wall of the rink. D intentionally delivers a hard body check that throws P into the wall, and the collision between P and the wall badly injures P. P sues D for battery.

If the level of contact between P and D was within the level to which players in this pick-up game would be found to have impliedly consented (based on past practices, actual words, etc.), then consent would be a complete defense to P's claim. But if D intentionally delivered a body check (a body contact) that went beyond the level or type of contact D knew or should have known P was consenting to, then it would constitute battery.

Example 2: D, a surgeon, agrees to perform liposuction on P's thighs. While P is under anesthesia, D decides that P could benefit from liposuction on P's arms. Assuming that P is not found to have impliedly consented in advance to the procedure on the arms, that procedure was battery, because it went beyond the scope of the bodily contact to which P consented.

D. Extends to personal effects: A battery may be committed not only by a contact with the plaintiff's body but also by a contact with her *clothing*, an *object she is holding*, or anything else that is *so closely identified with her body* that contact with it is as offensive as contact with the body would be. The idea is that contact with the plaintiff's *"person"* is enough, and things closely identified with the plaintiff's body count as being part of her "person." See Rest. 2d, §18, Comment c.

Example 1: P is a waiter at a restaurant, who is holding a plate. D snatches the plate from P's hand, and shouts a racial epithet at P. The plate would likely be held to be part of P's "person," in which case this would be an intentional offensive contact, and thus battery. [Cf. *Fisher v. Carrousel Motor Hotel*]

Example 2: P is horseback riding. Without justification, D takes a stick and hits P's horse. This is battery: (1) the horse is part of P's "person," so when D struck it this was as if D struck P's body; and (2) the touching of P's horse was an "offensive" touching in the circumstances.

1. **Indirect contact:** It is not necessary that the defendant touch the plaintiff with his own body. It is sufficient if he causes the contact *indirectly*. See Rest. 2d, §18, Comment c.

Example 1: P is standing in the street with a bullhorn to his lips. D, who is sitting nearby in his car, opens the door so that the door hits the bullhorn. If D intended for his door to hit the bullhorn, D has intended to cause a harmful or offensive bodily contact, even though the intended contact was indirect (i.e., between an object held by D and an object held by P).

Example 2: As a prank, D mails P a box of home-made cookies containing peanuts, to which D knows P is highly allergic. P eats a cookie (not thinking it contains peanuts), and suffers severe hives, necessitating a hospital stay. D has committed battery, since he knew with substantial certainty that a harmful contact between the object and P's body would occur. The fact that the contact was indirect (from an object mailed by D instead of from D's body or an object held by D) is irrelevant.

E. P need not be aware: It is *not* necessary that P have *actual awareness* of the contact at the time it occurs.

Example: D kisses P while she is asleep. D has committed a battery.

IV. ASSAULT

A. Definition: Assault is the intentional causing of an *apprehension* of *harmful or offensive contact.*

Example: D, a bill collector, threatens to punch P in the face if P does not pay a bill immediately. P fears being hit. Since D has intended to put P in imminent apprehension of a harmful bodily contact, this is assault, whether D intends to in fact hit P or not.

B. Intent: There are two different intents, either of which will suffice for assault:

1. **Intent to create apprehension:** First, D intends to put P in *imminent apprehension* of the harmful or offensive contact, even if D does not intend to follow through (e.g., D threatens to shoot P, but does not intend to actually shoot P); or

2. **Intent to make contact:** Alternatively, D intends to *cause* a harmful or offensive bodily contact.

   Example: D shoots a gun at P, trying to hit him. D hopes P won't see him, but P does. P is frightened, but the shot misses. This is assault.

3. **Summary:** So D has the requisite intent for assault if D either "intends to commit an assault" or "intends to commit a battery."

C. No hostility: It is not necessary that D bear malice towards P, or intend to *harm* her. All that's required is that D want to induce in P an "*apprehension*" (i.e., a belief, not necessarily even a "fear") that a harmful or offensive contact will *imminently occur*.

   Example: D as a practical joke points a toy pistol at P, hoping that P will falsely think that P is about to be shot. D has one of the two alternative intents required for assault — the intent to put P in imminent apprehension of a harmful or offensive contact — so the fact that D does not desire to "harm" P is irrelevant. Therefore, as long as P actually believes that D will fire a bullet at him, the tort of assault has immediately occurred, even if D never fires or otherwise brings about any harmful or offensive contact.

1. **MBE tip about pranks:** On the MBE, you'll often see a *"prank"* situation, in which D tries to induce in P an apprehension of an imminent harmful or offensive contact, without intending to cause an actual contact; then, something goes wrong, and an unintended harmful or offensive contact ensues. This is battery (see *supra*, p. 11), but it's *also assault*, if P was placed in apprehension of an actual harmful-or-offensive contact, however briefly. So the correct MBE choice in this kind of fact pattern will typically be that *both* assault and battery have been committed.

   Example: D, intending as a prank to cause P to think P is about to be hit in the head (but not intending to make contact), swings a golf club toward P's head. P momentarily thinks that he'll be hit. Then, due to a manufacturing defect, the head of the club flies off, hitting P in the head. Not only is this battery (see *supra*, p. 11), it's also assault, because P momentarily was in apprehension that he'd be hit, and D intended to cause this apprehension. (Indeed, this would be assault even if the head never flew off — once D succeeded in his intent to make P believe he was about to be hit, the tort of assault was complete.)

D. Actual contact or apprehension required: Apart from the defendant's intent, the tort of assault requires an *effect*. P must either actually *undergo* a harmful or offensive contact, or be put in *immediate apprehension* of such a contact.

1. **Unsuccessful prank or bluff:** So where D is pulling a *prank or making a bluff*, if P believes or knows that no imminent harmful or offensive contact will really occur, and none does occur, there is no assault.

   Example: P has been having sex with D's wife, W, and P knows that D knows this. D, holding a revolver, walks into P's office and says, "I know you've been having sex with my wife, and I'm gonna blow your head off." The particular gun that D is holding is a toy replica that cannot fire anything, and P knows this because W has told him so. D has not committed assault — even though D intended to put P in fear of an imminent harmful contact (a bullet fired at him), the "result" requirement for assault has not been met because P has not in fact been put in apprehension of such contact.

2. **Feared contact with ground or independent object suffices:** The harmful or offensive contact of which P is placed in apprehension does not have to be with D or an instrumentality under D's control — it can be with the *ground* or some other *free-standing object.*

    Example: While P is driving along a narrow two-lane road which has a stone wall to P's right, D drives up behind P from the same direction. D wants to frighten P into thinking that D will force P's car into the stone wall. D therefore comes up even with the left side of P's car, and veers rightward until there is just one inch between the right side of his car and the left side of P's. P believes, for an instant, that P will be forced into contact with the wall. Then D veers away, laughs, and drives off. P's car never touches either the wall or D's car. This is assault — D intended to make P believe that P's car (which is part of his person for this purpose) would touch the wall, and D succeeded in that goal, so the tort was complete at the moment P had the "I'm about to hit the wall" belief.

E. Imminence: It must appear to P that the harm being threatened is *imminent*, and that D has the *present ability* to carry out the threat.

Example 1: D learns that her employee P has agreed to start work for a competitor in two weeks. D fires P, and says, "If you're not off the premises with all of your possessions in ten minutes, I'll have security handcuff you and carry you out." This is not assault for two reasons. First, the threatened bodily contact is not imminent (ten minutes is too far away). Second, the threatened contact is conditional — it will occur only if P doesn't take an act (leaving) that P has the power to take (and that D has the legal right to insist that P take).

Example 2: D threatens to shoot P, and leaves the room for the stated purpose of getting his revolver. D has not committed an assault on P, because the harm is not imminent.

F. P unaware of danger: P must be *aware* of the threatened contact.

G. Threat to third persons: P must have an apprehension that *she herself* will be subjected to a bodily contact. She may not recover for her apprehension that *someone else* will be so touched.

Example: P sees D raise a pistol at P's husband. D shoots and misses. P cannot recover for assault, because she did not fear a contact with her own body.

H. Conditional threat: Where D threatens the harm only if P does not obey D's demands, the existence of an assault depends on whether D had the *legal right* to compel P to perform the act in question. If D had the legal right to compel P to perform the act, then there is no assault; if D didn't, then there is.

Example: P, a burglar, breaks into D's house. D says, "If you don't get out, I'll throw you out." There is no assault on P, since D has the legal right to force P to leave.

V. INTENTIONAL INFLICTION OF EMOTIONAL DISTRESS ("IIED")

A. Definition: There is a separate tort of "intentional infliction of emotional distress." It occurs when D intentionally or recklessly inflicts, by *extreme and outrageous conduct, severe emotional or mental distress*, even in the absence of physical harm. We'll abbreviate it as "IIED" for convenience.

Example: D threatens that if P, a garbage collector, does not pay over part of his garbage collection proceeds to D and his henchmen, D will severely beat P. Since D's conduct is extreme and outrageous, and since he has intended to cause P distress (which he has succeeded in doing), D is liable for IIED. [*State Rubbish Collectors Assoc. v. Siliznoff*]

B. Intent: "Intent" for IIED is a bit *broader* than for other intentional torts. There are three possible mental states on D's part that will qualify:

[a] D *desires* to cause P emotional distress;

[b] D knows with *substantial certainty* that P will suffer emotional distress; and

[c] D *recklessly disregards the high probability* that emotional distress will occur.

> **Example:** D commits suicide by slitting his throat in P's kitchen. D, or his estate, is liable for intentional infliction of mental distress because although D did not desire to cause distress to P, or even know that distress was substantially certain, he *recklessly disregarded the high risk* that distress would occur. [*Blakeley v. Shortal's Est.*]

C. "Extreme and outrageous": P must show that D's conduct was *extreme and outrageous*. D's conduct has to be *"beyond all possible bounds of decency."*

> **Example:** D, as a practical joke, tells P that her husband has been badly injured in an accident, and is lying in the hospital with broken legs. This conduct is sufficiently outrageous to qualify. [*Wilkinson v. Downton*]

1. **MBE Tip:** It's hard for the MBE examiners to concoct a fact pattern that clearly meets the "extreme and outrageous" standard. Therefore, sometimes they will test you on intentional infliction of emotional distress by merely requiring you to know that the conduct has to be extreme and outrageous to qualify.

> **Example:** D, a member of the paparazzi, follows P, a famous actress, in public places and repeatedly photographs her. D takes one such photo while P is sunbathing on a private beach with a married man; the photo is taken from 100 yards away while D is in a nearby public park and focusing through a telephoto lens. D then puts the photo on the Internet, causing great embarrassment to P. P sues for IIED.
>
> For this to be IIED, a jury would have to conclude that D's conduct was "extreme and outrageous" or "beyond all reasonable bounds of decency." If this fact pattern appeared on the MBE, the correct choice might merely say something like "P prevails *if* a jury finds that D's conduct was extreme and outrageous" rather than a choice embodying the conclusion of outrageousness, e.g., "P prevails *because* D's conduct was extreme and outrageous."

2. **Bill collectors:** A common fact pattern for IIED on the MBE is the conduct of *bill collectors*. That conduct can and often will be sufficiently extreme and outrageous to trigger IIED. And it's no defense to an otherwise proper IIED action that the plaintiff *really owed the money* that D was trying to collect.

> **Example:** D operates a collection agency. He is trying to collect a $1,000 bill for goods sold to P by Store. D goes to P's house and when Sis, P's sister, answers the door, D tells Sis he is there to collect a bill owed by P. Sis tells D that P has been unemployed for six months, and that she will pay the bill as soon as she can. D, in a loud voice, then demands to see P and says to Sis that if D does not receive payment immediately, he will file a criminal complaint charging her with fraud on creditors. P then comes to the door, and D in a loud voice that can be heard by neighbors across the street, repeats his demand for immediate payment and his threat to have P prosecuted.
>
> If P suffers severe emotional distress from D's conduct, she can recover for IIED against him, because D's conduct is extreme and outrageous. And that's true even if P *really does owe* the $1,000 to Store.

3. **Threats of physical harm:** One signal that conduct may be extreme and outrageous is that D has made a *threat of physical harm to P.* Even if D does not intend to make good on the threat, and even if the threat is not of imminent physical harm, the threat will often satisfy the extreme-and-outrageous requirement if it causes P extreme fear.

   Example: Boss fires Worker for chronic absenteeism. Worker telephones Boss and says, "You S.O.B., you fired me for no reason, so the next time I see you on the street — even if it's three years from now — don't be surprised if I shoot you in the head." Worker doesn't really intend to shoot Boss next time they meet, but Boss is very frightened, and subjectively believes that Worker may well shoot him as threatened.

   Worker's conduct — the threat — almost certainly meets the "extreme-and-outrageous" requirement. As long as Boss suffers actual severe distress (see below), Worker will therefore be liable for IIED.

   a. **Threat need not be of imminent harm:** Notice that where D makes a threat of physical harm, there is no requirement that the harm be *imminent*, as long as the threat is extreme and outrageous and induces the requisite severe distress. Therefore, on the MBE, when D makes a threat of harm to occur at some unspecified (and not imminent) future moment, IIED is a more likely choice than assault.

   Example: On the facts of the above example, Worker has committed IIED even though the threatened harm may not take place for years. But Worker has not committed assault, because only threats of *imminent* bodily contact will suffice for assault.

D. **Actual severe distress:** P must suffer *severe* emotional distress.

1. **Required element:** So no matter how extreme and outrageous D's conduct, P can't recover for IIED unless P suffered severe emotional distress (not just some level of distress).

   Example: Collector, a bill collector, attempts to collect a debt from Peggy on account of medical treatments furnished to Peggy by Doctor. Collector tells Peggy, in a loud voice that the neighbors hear, that if Peggy does not pay immediately, Collector will induce his friend the local District Attorney to charge Peggy with defrauding Doctor. Peggy is very worried about the legal risk. But the next day, her lawyer assures her that the D.A. is very unlikely to bring such charges even if Peggy doesn't pay the bill.

   Even if this conduct is found to be "extreme and outrageous" (which it probably is), Peggy can't recover against Collector for IIED unless she shows that she suffered severe emotional distress.

2. **Bodily harm not required:** But P is *not* required show that the distress resulted in *bodily harm — severe emotional distress is enough* by itself, assuming that D's conduct was directed at P. Rest. 2d, §46, Comm. k.

E. **Directed at third person:** If D intentionally or recklessly directs extreme and outrageous conduct at *someone other than P* (call this third person X), D will nonetheless be liable for IIED to P, if either of two scenarios occurs. (The scenarios differ as to whether P and X and close relatives). In both cases, P will have to be *physically present* (and known to D to be present) when the conduct occurs.

1. **P and X are close relatives:** First, let's talk about when P (the person who suffers the severe emotional distress) and X (the one at whom D's outrageous conduct is directed) are members of the *same immediate family.* P can recover for severe emotional distress, *even if it does not result in bodily harm,* as long as P was *present*, and known to D to be present.

2. **P and X are not close relatives:** Now, consider the situation in which P (the person suffering the emotional distress) and X (the one at whom the conduct is directed) are *not members of the same immediate family.* Here, P can recover only if P satisfies *two* conditions:

   - ❑ P was *present* at the time; *and*
   - ❑ The emotional distress suffered by P *led to bodily harm.*

   Example 1 (close relatives): In front of P, D pulls a gun and threatens to shoot X to death. P, who is X's wife, suffers great emotional distress from watching the episode. P can recover from D for IIED, even if P never suffered bodily harm from the distress.

   Example 2 (not close relatives): Same facts as Example 1, but now P and X are friends, not relatives. If P suffers great emotional distress without any bodily harm, she (probably) cannot recover from D for IIED. But if P's emotional distress leads to bodily harm (e.g., a miscarriage), she can recover.

F. **Suits by public figures:** When the plaintiff in an IIED suit is a *public official or public figure who is suing for a statement made by D*, a media defendant, there is also an additional requirement: the defendant must have published a *provably false statement*, and done so with *knowledge of the statement's falsity or with reckless disregard of its truth ("actual malice").* This principle (which applies the *NY Times v. Sullivan* actual-malice standard to IIED actions by public figures; see *infra*, p. 101) is required by the First Amendment, according to the U.S. Supreme Court. [*Hustler Magazine v. Falwell*]

   Example: P is a well-known activist for unpopular left-wing causes. Newspaper publishes a column by Writer saying, "P has all the morals of an alley cat, and would have sex with his mother." Writer hates P, and desires to cause him severe distress by publishing the column. P in fact suffers such distress. Unless a jury properly finds that P's statement contained a provably false statement of fact, published with knowledge of its falsity or reckless disregard of its truth, P cannot recover against either Writer or Newspaper for IIED. Since it's unlikely that this statement would be found to be purported fact rather than opinion or hyperbole, it's unlikely that P can recover.

CHAPTER 3

INTENTIONAL INTERFERENCE WITH PROPERTY

I. TRESPASS TO LAND

A. **Definition:** As generally used, *"trespass"* occurs when D does any of the following things:

   [1] D intentionally *enters P's land*, without permission;

   [2] D intentionally *remains* on P's land without the right to be there, even if she entered rightfully; or

   [3] D intentionally *puts an object on* (or refuses to *remove an object from*) P's land without permission.

B. **Intent:** The term "trespass" today refers only to *intentional* interference with P's interest in property. There is no strict liability or negligence liability for trespass.

   Example: D, a pilot, loses control of the aircraft and temporarily passes out. By the time D regains consciousness, the aircraft is 5 feet from the land surface. D lands it on P's property, because there is no time to do anything else. This is not trespass to land, because D did not voluntarily enter D's land.

1. **Negligence:** If D *negligently* enters P's land, this would typically be referred to as the tort of negligence, not trespass.

2. **Involuntary entry onto land of another:** On the MBE, you will often see a scenario in which D is a driver, pilot or boater who comes onto P's property as part of some sort of *emergency or involuntary reflex*. If D did *not voluntarily come onto P's property*, then there can be no trespass liability (and there is no negligence liability either, unless D behaved negligently either in putting herself in a risky position or failing to use due care to avoid the position in the first place).

   Example 1: P, while driving non-negligently, hits a patch of ice, tries to turn, and skids. The skid carries P onto D's property. Since P has not voluntarily (i.e., not intentionally) entered the property belonging to D, P has not committed trespass.

   Example 2: D knows that he is highly allergic to bee stings. One summer day, while D is driving with his windows open, a bee flies in. D, fearful of being stung, tries to swat away the bee. His violent swatting motion causes him to lose contact with the steering wheel. The car swerves, and enters P's property, where it makes a rut in P's soil. P sues D for trespass.

   Since D did not voluntarily (i.e., not intentionally) enter the property of another, D has not committed trespass. That's true even though D may have been negligent in driving with the window open on a hot day, given D's known severe allergy to bee stings. (That's because "trespass" requires an intent to enter another's land, not mere negligence in so entering.)

3. **No harm need be intended:** On the other hand, the defendant can have the requisite intent even though he does not intend any *harm* to the plaintiff's property interest — all that's required is an intent to enter land that belongs to another, not an intent to harm that land.

   Example: D, a pilot, realizes that his sole engine has just flamed out. D believes that he could probably cause the plane to glide for 5 miles so as to land in the Hudson River. However, D decides that it would be slightly safer to try to land in a wide open agricultural field (belonging to P) that's only 2 miles away. He does so, and in doing it damages P's crops. D has committed trespass, because he has intentionally entered land that belongs to another -- the fact that D did not desire to harm P's land is irrelevant. (D had the privilege of necessity, which would shield D if no harm were caused to P's land; but the privilege does not prevent D from having to pay for any actual damage. See *infra*, p. 28.)

4. **Effect of mistake:** If D has the intent to commit a physical contact with land that in fact belongs to P, D will have the requisite intent for trespass even if his decision to make the contact is the result of a *mistake*. Rest. 2d, §164. Thus D's mistake about *legal title* or *consent* won't block liability, even if the mistake is reasonable (assuming the mistake wasn't induced by anything P did or said).

   Example 1: D, an absentee owner, visits his property, which is a farm. He drives a tractor on what he thinks is his parcel, but unbeknownst to him (and without negligence on his part), he drives over what is really P's land. This is trespass, despite D's reasonable ignorance of the fact that the land he is entering belongs to someone other than D.

   Example 2: D is a crop duster. He gets a contract from X, the owner of Blackacre, to spray pesticide on Blackacre. D consults a generally-reliable map, and locates the coordinates that the map shows for Blackacre. D then sprays the indicated area. In fact, due to a mistake on the map (caused without negligence by the map company), what D is spraying is

Whiteacre, owned by P. P can recover from D for trespass. D intended to place an object (the pesticide spray) on land, and did so. The fact that D was reasonably ignorant of the boundaries (and thus reasonably believed he had permission to spray from the owner of the parcel) is irrelevant.

Example 3: D and P own adjacent parcels. D, relying on a reputable survey, builds a garage on what he thinks is entirely his own property. In fact, the garage extends 2 feet onto P's property. When P discovers these facts, she complains to D, who immediately has the portion of the garage on P's property removed. D has nonetheless committed trespass — once D intended to place an object (the garage) on particular land, and did so, the tort was complete even though D thought (reasonably) that the land was his own.

a. **Reasonableness irrelevant:** As noted, this rule about mistake being irrelevant applies even if the defendant's mistaken belief is entirely *reasonable*.

Example: In the above three examples about the tractor driver, the crop duster and the owner/builder of the garage, the reasonableness of each defendant's mistake about boundaries is irrelevant — once a person intentionally enters land, or intentionally puts an object on land, the tort of trespass is complete, even if the defendant was reasonably mistaken about attendant circumstances such as who owned the land or whether defendant had the permission of the true owner.

5. **Entry by holder of legal title:** If D enters without having the legal right to do so (or without having the right to do so for the particular purpose in question), D commits trespass even if D is the *holder of legal title to the premises.* So a *landlord* can easily commit trespass against her tenant.

Example: L leases an apartment to T. The lease gives L the right to enter the apartment for specified purposes (e.g., to make reasonably required repairs). L is romantically attracted to T, so he enters the apartment when he knows T is out, in hopes of finding out something about T's personal life. He uses his passkey, steps inside the foyer of the apartment, then has second thoughts and leaves without touching anything.

L has committed trespass even though he holds legal title to the premises, and even though he caused no physical damage. Once L set foot in the premises without a purpose allowed by the lease, the act of trespass was complete.

C. **Particles and gases:** If D knowingly causes *objects*, including *particles or gases*, to enter P's property, most courts consider this trespass.

Example: D's factory repeatedly spews pollutants onto P's land. This is a trespass. [*Martin v. Reynolds Metals Co.*]

1. **Light and sound don't qualify:** But there must be "particles," i.e., *tangible objects*, however small, that enter P's property, for trespass to occur. *Light and sound*, without any tangible particles, *won't qualify*. (Instead, in the light-and-sound scenario, the most likely tort is nuisance, described *infra*, p. 90.)

Example: Next door to P's house, D sets up a stone-crushing machine that emits an extremely unpleasant high-pitched sound. The machine runs all day. No smoke, dust, or other particles enter P's land, but anyone of normal hearing who is standing anywhere on P's property finds the noise from the machine unbearable.

Even if D knows with substantial certainty that the noise waves are continually entering P's property and causing P distress, D has not committed trespass. (P's best hope for recovery is an action based on nuisance.)

D. No harm need result: As long as the entry on P's land was intended by P, trespass occurs *whether or not any harm to the land results.*

Example: P and D are adjacent landowners. D, running out of space in his own backyard, takes some logs that he has cut, and puts them into D's backyard for one day, then removes them without harming P's property or inconveniencing P in any way. This is trespass — D has intentionally placed an object onto land belonging to another; the tort is complete when he does this.

II. TRESPASS TO CHATTELS

A. Definition: *"Trespass to chattels"* is defined as any *intentional interference* with a person's *use or possession* of a chattel. D only has to pay damages, not the full value of the property (as in conversion, below).

1. **Loss of possession:** If P *loses possession* of the chattel for any time, recovery is allowed even if the chattel is returned unharmed.

    Example: D takes P's car for a five-minute "joy ride," and returns it unharmed. D has committed trespass to chattels.

2. **Contact not causing dispossession:** Where D merely *makes contact* with the chattel, *without taking the chattel out of P's possession,* D is liable only where some *harm* to the chattel, or some interference with P's *use and enjoyment* of the chattel, occurs.

    Example: D, a child, climbs on top of P's large dog, and pulls its ears. No harm to the dog results. D has not committed a trespass to chattels, because D neither took the dog out of P's possession, nor harmed the dog or P's "use and enjoyment" of the dog. Rest. 2d, §218, Comm. e and Illustr. 2.

3. **Mistake as to ownership:** As with trespass, the required intent *does not encompass details about ownership.* So if D intends to take possession of an object, and does take possession of it, the fact that D *mistakenly believes the object is his own* is *no defense.* That's true even if the mistake is a *reasonable* one.

    Example: D enters a restaurant for lunch and hangs her coat on the coat rack. When she is leaving, she removes from the rack a coat which looks like hers, but which actually belongs to P. (At the time she took it, D believed it to be her coat.) When D has driven two miles from the restaurant, she realizes that the coat is not hers. D turns around and drives back to the restaurant, where she hands it to P, who has been angrily trying to figure out where her coat has gone.

    D committed trespass to chattels as soon as she took possession of P's coat. The fact that D honestly and/or reasonably thought the coat was her own does not negate the tort, or constitute an affirmative defense.

B. Measure of damages: D's liability for trespass to chattels is limited to the *loss of value* from D's interference. So D is not required to pay for the entire value of the chattel, in contrast to the situation where D commits conversion. Thus in the joy-riding example below (p. 22), if D caused $200 of damage to P's $20,000 car, and the court found that trespass to chattels rather than conversion was what occurred, D would be liable for $200 only, not $20,000.

III. CONVERSION

A. Definition: Conversion is an *intentional* interference with P's possession or ownership of property that is *so substantial* that D should be required to pay the property's *full value.*

Example: D steals P's car, then seriously (though not irreparably) damages it in a collision. D is liable for conversion, and will be required to pay P the full value of the car (though D gets to keep the car).

B. Intent: Conversion is an intentional tort, but all that is required is that D have intended to take possession of the property. Mistake as to ownership will generally not be a defense.

Example: D buys an old painting from an art dealer, and reasonably believes that the art dealer has good title. In fact, the painting was stolen from P years before. D keeps the painting in his house for 10 years. D is liable for conversion, notwithstanding his honest mistake about title.

C. Distinguished from trespass to chattels: Courts consider several factors in determining whether D's interference with P's possessory rights is severe enough to be conversion, as opposed to mere trespass to chattels. These factors include:

[1] the extent and duration of D's *dominion* over the property;

[2] D's *good or bad faith*;

[3] the degree of *harm* done to the property; and

[4] the *inconvenience* and *expense* caused to P.

Rest. 2d, §222A.

D. Different ways to commit: There are different ways in which conversion may be committed:

1. **Acquiring possession:** D can commit conversion by taking *possession* of the property from P.

   a. **Bona fide purchaser:** Most courts hold that a *bona fide purchaser* of *stolen goods* is a converter, even if there is no way he could have known that they were stolen.

2. **Transfer to third person:** D can also commit conversion by *transferring* a chattel to one who is not entitled to it.

   Example: D, a messenger service, delivers a package to the wrong person, X. X absconds with the goods. D has committed conversion, even though D did not end up with possession of the goods.

3. **Withholding goods:** D may commit conversion by *refusing to return* goods to their owner, if the refusal lasts for a substantial time.

   Example: D, a parking garage, refuses to give P back her car for a day. This is conversion.

4. **Destruction:** Conversion may occur if D *destroys* the goods, or fundamentally alters them.

E. Forced sale: If P is successful with her tort suit, a *forced sale* occurs: D is required to pay the *full value* of the goods (not just the amount of the use or damage, as in trespass to chattels), but gets to keep the goods.

Example: At a time when P's car is worth $20,000, D takes the car for a "joy ride," intending to return it 30 minutes later undamaged. D gets into a major accident, crumpling the hood and damaging the engine. The damage would cost $6,000 to fix and take three weeks, at which point the car would again be worth $20,000.

P can recover $20,000 (the value of the car before D took it) from D in a conversion action. After paying this amount, D will receive title to the car. The combination of D's complete bad faith, the significant damage to the car, and the long delay and resulting inconvenience to P while the car is fixed, makes it unfair for D merely to have to pay for the repairs, and instead entitles P to recover the full value of the chattel in a conversion action. (If P had been entitled to recover only for trespass to chattels, the measure of damages would have been limited to the $6,000 repair cost.)

CHAPTER 4

DEFENSES TO INTENTIONAL TORTS

I. CONSENT

A. Express consent: If P expressly *consents* to an intentional interference with his person or property, D will not be liable for that interference.

Example: P says to D, "Go ahead, hit me in the stomach — I'll show you how strong I am." If D does so, P's consent prevents P from suing for battery.

B. Implied consent: Existence of consent may also be *implied* from P's conduct, from custom, or from the circumstances.

1. Objective manifestation: It is the *objective manifestations* by P that count — if it reasonably seemed to one in D's position that P consented, consent exists regardless of P's subjective state of mind.

Example: D offers to vaccinate all passengers on their ship. P holds up her arm and receives the vaccination. Since it reasonably appeared to D that P consented, there will be consent regardless of P's actual state of mind. [*O'Brien v. Cunard*]

a. Sporting activities: On the MBE, be on the lookout for implied consent where the activity involves *sporting activities.* If P impliedly consented to some types of harmful or offensive contact during the activity, fellow-participant D won't be liable for contacts falling within the the scope of that implied consent, but *will* be liable for contacts going beyond the ones impliedly consented to.

Example: Recall the example involving recreational ice hockey from p. 12 *supra*: In a pick-up ice hockey game in a park, P and D are skirmishing for the puck near the side wall of the rink. D intentionally delivers a hard body check that throws P into the wall, and the collision between P and the wall badly injures P. P sues D for battery.

If the level of contact between P and D was within the level to which players in this pick-up game would be found to have impliedly consented (based on past practices, actual words, etc.), then consent would be a complete defense to P's claim. But if D intentionally delivered a body check (a body contact) that went beyond the level or type of contact D knew or should have known P was consenting to, then consent would not be a defense for D, and D will be liable for battery.

C. Exceeding scope: Even if P does consent to an invasion of her interests, D will not be privileged if he goes substantially *beyond the scope* of that consent.

Example: P visits D, a doctor, and consents to an operation on her right ear. While P is under anesthetic, D decides that P's left ear needs an operation as well, and does it. P's consent does not block an action for battery for the left-ear operation, since the operation went beyond the scope of P's consent. [*Mohr v. Williams*]

1. Emergency: However, in the surgery case, an *emergency* may justify extending the surgery beyond that consented to.

D. Consent to criminal acts: Where D's act against P is a *criminal act*, courts are split. The majority rule is that P's consent is *ineffective* if the act consented to is a crime.

Example: P and D agree to fight with each other. In most states, each may recover from the other, on the theory that consent to a crime — such as breach of peace — is ineffective.

II. SELF-DEFENSE

A. Privilege generally: A person is entitled to use *reasonable force* to prevent any threatened *harmful or offensive bodily contact*, and any threatened *confinement or imprisonment.*

B. Apparent necessity: Self-defense may be used not only where there is a real threat of harm, but also where D *reasonably believes* that there is one, even if the belief is mistaken.

C. Only for protection: The defense of self-defense applies only where D uses the force needed to *protect himself* against harm.

1. **Retaliation:** Thus D may not use any degree of force in *retaliation* for a tort already committed.

   Example: P hits D with a snowball. Ten minutes later, D hits P with a snowball, in retaliation. D has committed battery on P, because D's act was not done in true self-defense.

2. **Imminence:** D may not use force to avoid harm which is *not imminent*, unless it reasonably appears that there will not be a later chance to prevent the danger.

   Example: P says to D, "I will beat you up tomorrow." D cannot beat P up today, to prevent tomorrow's attack, unless it appears that there will be no way for D to defend tomorrow.

3. **Verbal provocation:** D may not use self-defense in response to *verbal provocation*, such as *taunting or insults*. In part that's because in tort law, self-defense is purely a forward-looking idea: D is entitled to prevent imminent future harm, not redress past harm, let alone redress purely verbal harm.

   Example: P calls D a liar and a cheat in front of D's friends. (Assume that D is not a liar and a cheat, and that P's words constitute slander for which D could recover.) P then says to D, "What're you gonna do about, you coward?" D hits P in the face. P can recover for battery, and D cannot successfully claim self-defense. That's because provocation does not justify self-defense in tort law; only the prevention of imminent bodily harm can justify it.

D. Degree of force: Only the *degree* of force necessary to prevent the threatened harm may be used. If D uses more force than necessary, he will be liable for damage caused by the excess.

1. **Deadly force:** Special rules limit the use of *deadly force*, i.e., force intended or likely to cause death or serious bodily injury.

   a. **Danger must be serious:** D may *not* use deadly force unless he himself is in danger of *death or serious bodily harm.*

      Example: P attacks D with his fists, in a way that does not threaten D with serious bodily harm. Even if there is no other way for D to prevent the attack, D may not use his gun to shoot P, even if the shot is intended only to injure P — D must submit to the attack rather than use deadly force.

E. Injury to third person: If the occasion calls for self-defense, and D does not use more force than reasonably justified, the fact that a *third person* rather than the attacker is injured by D's use of force *doesn't negate* D's self-defense defense.

Example: D, while being fired upon by X during a robbery, fires back. The bullet ricochets, hitting P, a bystander. If D's use of deadly force was reasonable in the circumstances to prevent D from being injured, D will be privileged even though the plaintiff is an innocent third party rather than the person (X) whose conduct gave rise to the need for D's use of force.

III. DEFENSE OF OTHERS

A. General rule: A person may use reasonable force to defend *another person* against attack. The same rules apply as in self-defense: the defender may only use reasonable force, and may not use deadly force to repel a non-deadly attack.

1. Reasonable mistake: The modern view is that if a person makes a *reasonable mistake about the need for force (including the degree of danger to the third person),* the defense-of-others defense is *not forfeited.* See Rest. 2d §72.

a. Unreasonable mistake: But all courts agree that D's belief in the need to use force in defense of another (and D's selection of the level of force to use) *must at least be reasonable.* So if D makes a *negligent mistake* about whether the third person (call her X) is in physical danger, or about whether D's proposed physical contact will help avoid the danger, D will not be able to use the defense-of-others defense.

Example: D, a good samaritan, sees P, a little old lady, who is slowly crossing the street. D believes that P is about to be struck by an SUV, so he pushes P out of the way, causing her to fall and break her hip. If D was negligent in believing that P was actually in danger, D will be liable to P for battery. But if D was reasonable in his belief that P would likely be hit by the SUV if she was not pushed out of the way, and reasonable in the amount of force he used, he will be able to use defense-of-others as a defense to a battery action by P. And that's true even if D was mistaken about the existence of the danger (e.g., because the driver of the SUV saw P and wouldn't have hit her).

IV. DEFENSE OF PROPERTY

A. General rule: A person may generally use reasonable force to *defend her property*, both land and chattels.

1. Warning required first: The owner must first make a *verbal demand* that the intruder stop, unless it reasonably appears that violence or harm will occur immediately, or that the request to stop will be useless.

Example: O posts "No-Trespassing" and "No Soliciting" signs around his property. Bill, a bill collector, reads the signs, then rings O's doorbell. When O answers, Bill steps inside the front door, and loudly demands that O pay a past-due bill to Bill's department-store client (which O validly owes). O gets angry, and without saying anything, in a rage hits Bill in the mouth.

This is battery, and O is not entitled to use the defense of defense of property. That's because O was required, before using force, to make a verbal demand or warning that the intruder leave, unless it reasonably appeared to O that such a request would be useless or dangerous. There was no such evidence here.

a. Allow time for intruder to obey: Furthermore, if the owner does make a request to leave, the owner must give the intruder *sufficient time to obey the request,* unless it's clear that the request will not be heeded.

Example: While O is walking around his rural property, he comes upon Neighbor, who is trespassing. O says, "Get off my property!" Neighbor pauses for two seconds without saying anything, at which point O hits him in the leg with a stick that O is carrying. This is battery, and the defense-of-property defense does not apply, because O was required to give Neighbor a reasonable time to obey the request to leave, unless it reasonably appeared to O (which it didn't) that Neighbor would not obey.

B. Mistake: The effect of a *reasonable mistake* by D varies:

1. Mistake as to danger: If D's mistake is about whether force is necessary, D is protected by a reasonable mistake.

Example: D uses non-deadly force to stop a burglar whom he reasonably believes to be armed. In fact, the burglar is not armed. D can rely on the defense of property.

2. Privilege: But if the owner's mistake is about whether the intruder has a *right* to be there, the owner's use of force will *not* be privileged.

Example: D reasonably believes that P is a burglar. In fact, P is a friend who has entered D's house to retrieve her purse, without wanting to bother D. Even non-deadly force by D will not be privileged.

C. Deadly force: The owner may use *deadly force* only where: (1) non-deadly force will not suffice; and (2) the owner reasonably believes that without deadly force, *death* or *serious bodily harm* will occur.

Example: D sees P trespassing in D's backyard. D asks P to leave, but P refuses. Even if there is no way to make P leave except by shooting at him, D may not do so, since P's conduct does not threaten D with death or serious bodily harm.

1. Burglary: But a homeowner is generally *allowed* to use deadly force against a *burglar*, provided that she reasonably believes that nothing short of this force will safely keep the burglar out.

D. Mechanical devices: An owner may use a *mechanical device* to protect her property only if she would be privileged to use a similar degree of force if she were present and acting herself.

1. Reasonable mistake: An owner's right to use a dangerous mechanical device in a particular case will be measured by whether deadly force could have been used against *that particular intruder*.

a. Owner's liability to trespasser: Even a trespasser who comes on the property with an intent to steal, but without posing a risk of serious bodily harm to any occupants who might have been there, will prevail as a battery plaintiff against an absent owner who causes serious bodily harm to the trespasser by means of an automatic device. In fact, because the absent owner who uses a dangerous device does not have the ability to ask the intruder to leave, the owner will almost never be able to use the defense-of-property defense. That's so because the owner has not complied with the above rule that deadly force may not be used unless it reasonably seems to the owner that a request that the intruder leave will be dangerous or fruitless.

Example: O, an absentee rural property owner, has suffered several recent thefts and acts of vandalism against the property. He therefore takes two actions: he posts large "No trespassing / Danger / Proceed at your own risk" signs around the perimeter; and he places a hard-to-see trip wire in the driveway, which is set to trigger a land mine if any object weighing more than forty pounds presses on it. Addict, a meth addict who intends to steal whatever loose items of value he can find, reads one of the signs, but walks up the driveway anyway, triggers the land mine, and gets his leg blown off. Assume that Addict did not intend to cause harm to any person he might encounter on the premises, and had never physically harmed anyone in his past illegal entries anywhere. Assume further that no one in O's position, had he been present and seen Addict, would have reasonably believed that Addict posed a serious risk of bodily harm. Lastly, assume that if Addict had encountered an occupant who asked him to leave, Addict would have done so.

If Addict sues O for battery, O will not be able to successfully claim defense of property. That's because O could not have used deadly force had O been physically present. (O would have been required to first ask Addict to leave, and Addict would have done so, our facts stipulate; therefore, deadly force would have been improper.)

V. RECAPTURE OF CHATTELS

A. Generally: A property owner has the general right to use reasonable force to *regain* possession of *chattels* taken from her by someone else.

1. **Fresh pursuit:** The privilege exists only if the property owner is in *"fresh pursuit"* to recover his property. That is, the owner must act without unreasonable delay.

   Example: *A* learns that *B* has stolen a stereo and is in possession of it. *A* may use reasonable force to reclaim the stereo if he acts immediately, but not if he waits, say, a week between learning that *B* has the property and attempting to regain it.

2. **Reasonable force:** The force used must be reasonable, and *deadly force* can never be used.

3. **Wrongful taking:** The privilege exists only if the property was taken *wrongfully* from the owner. If the owner parts willingly with possession, and an event then occurs which gives him the right to repossess, he generally will not be able to use force to regain it.

   Example: *O* rents a TV to *A*. *A* refuses to return the set on time. *O* may not use reasonable force to enter *A*'s home to repossess the set, because *A*'s original possession was not wrongful.

B. Merchant: Where a merchant reasonably believes that a person is stealing his property, many courts give the merchant a privilege to *temporarily detain* the person for investigation.

1. **Limited time:** The detention must be limited to a short time, generally 10 or 15 minutes or less, just long enough to determine whether the person has really shoplifted or not. Then, the police must be called (the merchant may not purport to arrest the suspect himself).

C. D's chattel on O's property without D's fault: There is a related privilege where D's chattel comes onto O's property *without D's fault.* Here, D is permitted to enter O's property at a reasonable time, and in a reasonable manner, to reclaim the chattel. However, D must normally ask permission first, unless the request would be futile or the delay in asking permission would subject the chattel to danger of serious harm.

1. **D must pay for damage:** However, when D uses this right of entry, D must *pay for any actual damage* caused by the entry. Rest. 2d, §198.

   Example: Trucker is driving a truckload of coconuts on a public road, when through no fault of her own, one of the tires on her truck blows out, causing the truck to go out of control. The truck overturns, spilling the coconuts onto the land of Owner, which is adjacent to the road. Trucker, who is unhurt, returns later with a small bulldozer. Trucker rings Owner's doorbell to ask permission to enter, but there is no answer. Trucker drives the bulldozer onto the edge of Owner's property, and uses it to scoop up the coconuts and carry them away. Because the ground is soft, the bulldozer damages some plantings belonging to Owner, which were not damaged by the original spill.

   Trucker will not be liable for the entry onto Owner's land or for the original spill, because neither was caused by any intentional tort or negligence on Owner's part. Nor will Trucker be liable for nominal damages for trespass for entering with the bulldozer, because Trucker had a qualified privilege to do so. But Trucker will be required to pay for any actual damage from the recapture operation (i.e., the use of the bulldozer), and must thus pay for the damage to the plantings.

VI. NECESSITY

A. General rule: Under the defense of *"necessity,"* D has a privilege to harm the property interest of P where this is *necessary* in order to prevent *great harm* to third persons or to the defendant herself.

B. Public necessity: If interference with the land or chattels of another is necessary to prevent a disaster *to the community* or to many people, the privilege is that of "*public necessity*." Here, no compensation has to be paid by the person doing the damage.

Example: Firefighters demolish D's house, in which a fire has just barely started, because that is the best way to stop the fire from spreading much further. The firefighters, and the town employing them, probably do not have to pay, because they are protected by the privilege of public necessity.

C. Private necessity: If a person prevents injury to *himself or his property*, or to the person or property of a *third person*, this is protected by the privilege of "*private* necessity," if there is no less-damaging way of preventing the harm.

Example: *A*, while sailing, is caught in very rough seas. To save his life, he may make the voluntary decision to moor at a dock owned by *B*, and when he does so will not be liable for trespass.

1. Actual damage: Where the privilege of private necessity exists, it will be a complete defense to a tort claim where P has suffered no actual substantial harm (as in the above example). But if *actual damage* occurs, P must *pay for the damage* she has caused.

Example: On the facts of the above example, suppose that as *A* was voluntarily mooring at *B*'s dock, *A*'s boat slammed into *B*'s dock and damaged it. *A* would have to pay for the actual damages caused, even though his exercise of the privilege of necessity prevented him from being liable for trespass.

a. Driving emergency: On the MBE, be especially on the lookout for scenarios in which a driver is confronted with a sudden emergency, and reacts by voluntarily entering P's property. Even though the doctrine of private necessity typically applies, P will have to pay for any damage caused.

Example: D, a driver, is driving down the street when a child cuts in front of his car. D voluntarily steers to the right to avoid the child, causing his car to jump the curb, enter P's property, and damage expensive landscaping. Even though the defense of necessity prevents D from having to pay nominal damages for trespass, D is required to pay for the actual damage he has caused.

2. Owner may not resist: The main purpose of the doctrine of private necessity is to prevent the person whose property might be injured from defeating the exercise of the privilege. So the property owner may not resist the entry, and must pay for any damages sustained by the person trying to enter under the privilege if the owner does resist.

Example: P moors his ship at D's dock, to avoid being shipwrecked by heavy seas. D, objecting to what he thinks is a trespass, unmoors the ship, causing the ship to be harmed and P to be injured. P may recover from D, because P's mooring was privileged by private necessity and D, therefore, acted wrongfully. [*Ploof v. Putnam*]

CHAPTER 5

NEGLIGENCE GENERALLY

I. COMPONENTS OF TORT OF NEGLIGENCE

A. Generally: The tort of "negligence" occurs when D's conduct imposes an *unreasonable risk* upon another, which results in injury to that other. The negligent tortfeasor's mental state is irrelevant.

B. Prima facie case: There are *five components* of a *prima facie case for negligence*:

[1] **Duty:** A legal *duty* requiring D to conduct herself according to a certain standard, so as to avoid unreasonable risk to others. (That standard is generally the *"reasonable care"* standard.)

[2] **Failure to conform to standard:** A failure by D to *conform her conduct to this reasonable-care standard.* This element can be thought of as *"carelessness"* or *"negligence."*

[3] **Cause-in-fact:** A showing that the failure by D to conform to the reasonable-care standard was the *"cause-in-fact"* of harm to the plaintiff (i.e., that the harm would not have occurred without D's deviation from reasonable care).

[4] **Proximate cause:** A sufficiently close *causal link* — i.e., a causal chain without unduly bizarre additional causal factors — between D's act of negligence and the harm suffered by P. This is *"proximate cause."*

[5] **Actual damage:** *Actual damage* suffered by P. (Compare this to most intentional torts, such as trespass, where P can recover nominal damages even without actual injury.)

1. **Meaning of "prima facie case":** What we mean by a *"prima facie" case* is that these are the elements that the plaintiff *must prove in her own case in chief, in order to avoid a directed verdict in favor of the defense.* That is, if at the close of plaintiff's evidence the trial judge believes that no reasonable jury could find, by a preponderance of the evidence, that each of these elements exists, the judge must *grant a directed verdict for the defendant*, and not let the jury decide the case or even make the defendant put on her own case. MBE negligence questions often revolve around this directed-verdict procedure, which is discussed more *infra*, p. 35.

II. UNREASONABLE RISK

A. Generally: P must show that D's conduct imposed an *unreasonable risk of harm* on P (or on a class of persons of whom P is a member).

1. **Not judged by results:** It is not enough for P to show that D's conduct resulted in a terrible injury. P must show that D's conduct, viewed *as of the time it occurred*, without benefit of hindsight, imposed an unreasonable risk of harm.

B. Balancing: In determining whether the risk of harm from D's conduct was so great as to be "unreasonable," courts use a *balancing test*: "Where an act is one which a reasonable [person] would recognize as involving a risk of harm to another, the risk is unreasonable and the act is negligent if the *risk* is of such magnitude as to *outweigh* what the law regards as the *utility* of the act or of the particular manner in which it is done." Rest. 2d, §291.

1. **MBE tip:** It's hard for the MBE examiners to give you a fact pattern where the cost/benefit analysis clearly makes D's conduct negligent, without tipping you off to the answer. Therefore, when the examiners give you a fact pattern that's somewhat ambiguous as to whether the risk/reward ratio made D's conduct negligent, they'll usually have to signal somehow that you

are to assume that the risks were high (or very likely to occur, i.e., foreseeable), or that the costs of preventing the harm were low.

Example: D is a garden store that sells pesticides. X, a terrorist, breaks into the store at night, steals 40 gallons of colorless, odorless pesticide, and dumps it in the local water supply, causing many to be sickened. One victim sues D for negligence. In a fact pattern like this, the examiners will have to give you information about the level of security imposed by D, or the magnitude of the risk of theft as known to D (or else give you assumptions about these items in the correct choice). Therefore, the correct choice might say something like "D is not liable unless it should have known of a high risk that someone might break into the store and steal pesticides."

C. **Warnings:** One of the ways the risks of conduct can be reduced is by giving *warnings* of danger. The fact that D gave a warning of dangers to P in particular, or the public in general, is thus a factor that will make it less likely that D will be found negligent when the danger that was warned of results in an accident.

1. **Failure to warn can itself be negligent:** If D *fails* to give a warning of a danger that he knows about, and the warning could have been easily given, the mere failure to warn can itself *constitute negligence.*

2. **Does not immunize D:** However, it's clear that even if D *does* give a warning, this *does not immunize D* from negligence liability — if D's activity is unreasonably dangerous (evaluated by balancing its benefits against its risks) despite D's warning to P, D will still be liable.

Example: Dave, while moving out of his second-floor apartment, throws an old television out the window, aiming for a dumpster on the ground below the window. Just before he throws the TV, he yells out "Look out below." Paula, a pedestrian, does not hear the warning because she is talking on her cellphone. Dave can be found negligent despite having given the warning — it is so dangerous to throw a heavy object out of an upstairs window, and so easy to discard the object by safer means, that the giving of the warning did not make the total benefits of Dave's conduct outweigh its dangers.

III. THE REASONABLE PERSON

A. **Objective standard:** The reasonableness of D's conduct is viewed under an *objective standard*: Would a *"reasonable person* of ordinary prudence," in D's position, do as D did? D does not escape liability merely because she intended to behave carefully or thought she was behaving carefully.

B. **Physical and mental characteristics:** The question is whether D behaved reasonably "under the circumstances." "The circumstances" generally include the *physical characteristics* of D himself.

1. **Physical disability:** Thus if D has a physical *disability*, the standard for negligence is what a reasonable person with that physical disability would have done.

Example: P is blind and is struck while crossing the street using a cane. If the issue is whether P was comparatively negligent, the issue will be whether a blind person would have crossed the street in that manner.

2. **Mental characteristics:** The ordinary reasonable person is *not* deemed to have the particular *mental* characteristics of D.

Example: If D is more stupid, or more careless, than an ordinary person, this will not be a defense.

3. **Intoxication:** Intoxication is no defense — even if D is drunk, she is held to the standard of conduct of a reasonable *sober* person.

4. **Children:** *Children* are *not* held to the level of care which would be exercised by a reasonable adult. A child must merely conform to the conduct of a "reasonably careful person of the *same age, intelligence, and experience.*" Rest. 3d (P.H.), §10(a).

   a. **Adult activity:** But where a child engages in a potentially *dangerous activity* normally pursued only by *adults*, she will be held to the standard of care that a *reasonable adult doing that activity* would exercise.

   Example: If D operates a motorboat, an activity that is potentially dangerous and normally pursued by adults, D must match the standard of care of a reasonable adult boater.

C. **Emergencies:** If D is confronted with an *emergency*, and is forced to act with little time for reflection, D must merely behave as a reasonable person would if confronted with the same emergency, not as a reasonable person would with plenty of time to think.

Example: D is a cab driver. A thief jumps into the cab, points a gun at D's head, and tells him to drive fast. D, in a panic, mistakenly puts the car in reverse and injures P. The issue is whether a cab driver confronted with a gun-pointing thief would or might have behaved as D did, not whether a cab driver in ordinary circumstances would have behaved that way.

D. **Anticipating conduct of others:** A reasonable person possesses at least limited ability to *anticipate the conduct of others.*

1. **Negligence:** D may be required to anticipate the possibility of *negligence* on the part of others.

   Example: It may be negligence for D to presume that all drivers near him will behave non-negligently, and that these others will not speed, signal properly, etc.

   a. **Parental supervision:** A *parent* has a duty to exercise reasonable care to *supervise the conduct of his or her minor child*, to prevent the child from intentionally harming others or posing an unreasonable risk of harm to others. Rest. 2d, §316.

      i. **Direct liability:** This principle does *not* make the parent *"vicariously liable"* (see *infra*, p. 71) for the child's torts. Instead, it constitutes *direct* negligence by the parent not to use reasonable care in controlling the child, where the parent has the ability to control the child, and knows or should have known of the risk being posed by the child's conduct.

      Example: As Mom is aware, Kid, her 10-year-old son, is skateboarding on the sidewalk in front of their house, in a way that poses great danger to pedestrian passersby. Mom knows that she could control Kid to prevent him from skateboarding in this manner, but she unreasonably decides that the risks posed by Kid are small enough to make it not worth Mom's while to intervene. Kid runs into P, a little old lady, who is badly injured.

      P can recover against Mom, for failing to use reasonable care to prevent Kid from dangerous skateboarding, given that Mom knew or should have known that she had the ability to control Kid and knew or should have known that Kid's behavior was risky to pedestrians.

2. **Criminal or intentionally tortious acts:** Normally the reasonable person (and, hence, D) is entitled to presume that third persons will *not* commit *crimes* or *intentional torts.*

a. **Special relationship:** But if D has a *special relationship* with either P or a third person, or special knowledge of the situation, then it may be negligence for D not to anticipate a crime or intentional tort.

i. **Premises liability:** For example, operators of *businesses open to the public* have an obligation to use reasonable care to *protect people on the premises* from foreseeable harm from *intentional torts and crimes by third persons on the premises*, including other *customers*. Rest. 2d, §318.

Example: Potter and Fitch are customers sitting at the bar in a tavern operated by Dexter. Fitch starts shouting at Potter, who ignores him. Dexter, who is acting as bartender, does not intervene as Fitch becomes more and more verbally abusive. Finally, Fitch suddenly punches Potter in the face.

If Potter can show that one in Dexter's position as tavern-operator/bartender should reasonably have realized that there was a substantial risk that Fitch would progress from being verbally abusive to physically abusive of Potter, Potter will be able to recover against Dexter for negligence. That's because one who occupies premises and permits another to be on the premises has a duty to take reasonable precautions to prevent that person from harming others on the premises.

E. **MBE tip:** Always look for some *specific evidence* in your fact pattern suggesting (or at least permitting the inference) that defendant *behaved negligently*, in a way that caused the accident. The MBE examiners like to give you fact patterns in which a horrible accident occurs, and you're left with the feeling that P ought to be able to recover, but there's actually no hard evidence that D failed to use reasonable care. So when that happens, don't be afraid to conclude that D was not negligent, and P therefore can't recover.

1. **Left in care of defendant:** For instance, your fact pattern may involve a child or object *left in D's care*, after which some injury occurs to the child or object. By itself, that sequence is not enough for negligence liability; there's got to be some specific evidence that D behaved in a negligent way (i.e., in a way that didn't manifest reasonable care in the circumstances).

Example: P, a bright 5-year-old, is delivered by his father to a nursery school, operated by D, on the second floor of a building. While the teacher is dealing with a different child's sudden and unforeseeable illness, P opens the window, climbs out, falls, and is badly injured. If these are the only facts stipulated in the MBE fact pattern, you should conclude that D cannot be liable for negligence, and that the judge should not permit the case to go to the jury. That's because nothing suggests, or even permits the reasonable inference, that anyone working for D has behaved negligently. (For more about the judge's role in keeping a case from the jury, see *infra*, p. 35.)

2. **Failure to supervise customers or others:** Similarly, on the MBE the element of negligence may be missing in a fact pattern in which P alleges that D *failed to anticipate the negligence of some third person*, X (not an employee of D), who ends up injuring P. Injuries on *premises* owned by D, where the injury is caused by a *customer*, are examples — unless D had some particular reason to anticipate that the customer posed a substantial risk to P, D will not be liable.

Example: D owns a grocery store with its own parking lot. P parks in the lot, and is about to enter the store to shop. X, an elderly man with poor vision, who has just finished shopping at the store, pulls out of his parking spot and hits P after failing to notice him. In the absence of some evidence that D knew or should have known of the danger to pedestrians posed by X (or some evidence that the design or other features of the parking lot contributed to the accident), D will not be liable to P. That's because there's no evidence of D's failure to use due care.

IV. VIOLATION OF STATUTE

A. "Negligence *per se*" doctrine, generally: Courts apply the *"negligence per se"* doctrine: when a safety statute has a sufficiently close application to the facts of the case at hand, an unexcused *violation* of that statute by D is "negligence *per se*," and thus *conclusively establishes that D was negligent.*

1. Restatement standard: The Third Restatement articulates the doctrine this way: "An actor is *negligent* if, *without excuse,* the actor *violates a statute that is designed to protect against the type of accident the actor's conduct causes*, and the accident *victim* is *within the class of persons the statute is designed to protect.*" Rest. 3d (P.H.), §14.

Example: D drives at 65 m.p.h. in a 55 m.p.h. zone. While so driving, he strikes and injures P, a pedestrian. Because the 55 m.p.h. limit is a safety measure designed to protect against accidents, and because pedestrians are among those the statute aims to protect, the fact that D has violated the statute without excuse conclusively establishes that D was negligent — D will not be permitted to argue that it was in fact safe to drive at 65 m.p.h.

2. Ordinances and regulations: In virtually all states, the negligence *per se* doctrine applies to the violation of a *statute*. Where the violation is of an *ordinance* or administrative *regulation*, courts are split about whether the doctrine should apply, but most courts still apply it. You should assume on the MBE that violation of an ordinance or administrative regulation will trigger negligence per se.

B. Statute must apply to facts: The negligence *per se* doctrine will apply only where P shows that the statute was intended to guard against the *kind of injury or risk* in question.

1. Protection against particular type of risk: This means that the statute must have been intended to protect against the *particular type of risk or accident* that P seeks to recover for.

a. MBE Tip: The MBE examiners love to test you on this element — they give you a clear statutory violation, and an accident, but the accident comes about because of a risk that is not one of the risks that the statute was designed to prevent. So keep in mind that negligence per se won't apply in this situation, and plaintiff will have to show some other proof of negligence by the defendant.

Example: A statute requires that when animals are transported, each breed must be kept in a separate pen. The statute was enacted to prevent the spread of disease. D, a ship operator, violates the statute by herding P's sheep together with other animals. Because there are no pens, the sheep are washed overboard during a storm. P cannot use the negligence *per se* doctrine, because the statute was intended to protect only against spread of disease, not against washing overboard. [*Gorris v. Scott*]

2. Class of persons protected: Also, P must be a member of the *class of persons* whom the statute was *designed to protect.*

Example: A statute requires all factory elevators to be provided with a certain safety device. The legislative history shows that the purpose was only to protect injuries to employees. P, a business visitor, is injured when the elevator falls due to lack of the device. P cannot use the negligence *per se* doctrine, because he was not a member of the class of persons whom the statute was designed to protect.

C. Excuse of violation: The court is always free to find that the statutory violation was *excused*, as long as the statute itself does not show that no excuses are permitted.

1. **Typical reasons:** Some typical reasons for finding D's violation to be excused are:

[a] D was reasonably *unaware* of the *"factual circumstances"* that made the statute applicable.

Example: A statute prohibits any contractor from doing excavation within 10 feet of a high-voltage power line. D, a contractor, excavates within 6 feet of such a line. However, D reasonably fails to realize that the line is present because it is obscured by heavy foliage. D knocks down the line, injuring P, a bystander.

Because D neither knew nor should have known of "the factual circumstances" that made the statute applicable to his particular excavation session, the negligence per se doctrine will not apply to his conduct.

[b] D made a reasonable and diligent *attempt* to comply.

[c] The violation was due to the *confusing way* the requirements of the statute were *presented to the public.*

Example: A road sign on Main St. says "No Left Turn." The sign is placed just before two roads turn off of Main St., Maple and Oak. A reasonable driver could be confused about whether the sign means that left turns are prohibited onto Maple, Oak, or both. D, reasonably believing that the sign applies to Maple but not to Oak, turns left onto Oak, and collides with P. D would not be subject to liability under negligence per se, because the confusing nature of the sign would excuse his non-compliance.

[d] Compliance would have involved a *greater risk of harm.*

[e] The violation was due to the fact that D was *incapacitated.*

Example: A local ordinance makes it an offense to drive through a stop sign without stopping. After a collision between cars driven by P and D, in which D dies, P sues D's estate for damages. P produces uncontested evidence that D drove through a stop sign, and that that action proximately caused the collision, while P drove properly. D's estate produces undisputed evidence that (1) D had no previously known heart condition; (2) D was driving properly until moments before the accident; (3) D suffered a fatal heart attack a few seconds before arriving at the stop sign; and (4) the heart attack prevented D from pressing the brake when the car got to the stop sign.

P will not recover. The only evidence of negligence in the case is D's violation of the stop sign ordinance. But this violation will be excused due to D's incapacity, making negligence per se inapplicable. Therefore, there is no evidence of D's negligence, entitling D's estate to a directed verdict.

D. Causation still required: Even if negligence per se applies, it doesn't eliminate the need to show *causation.* And, indeed, if P relies on negligence per se as the sole source of negligence by D, then P will have to show that the *statutory violation* was the *cause-in-fact* (p. 39) and *proximate cause* (p. 41) of the accident. The MBE examiners like to give you fact patterns in which the accident or harm *would have happened anyway,* even if the defendant had obeyed the statute. In such a scenario, P will lose, because if the accident would have happened anyway even had the statute been followed, the required "but-for" causation is lacking.

Example: A local ordinance requires every hotel room to have a smoke detector that is operational, and that is connected to the front desk of the hotel. P is staying in Room 101. Late at night, a fire starts in Room 104, down the hall. A smoke detector in Room 104 works properly and gives notice to the front desk. However, the smoke detector in Room 101, although it emits a high-pitched beep, is not connected to the front desk as required. P wakes up from the sound, but the fire travels so fast that P is overcome with smoke and dies of asphyxiation before he can leave the room. The front desk clerk summons the fire department as soon as the signal comes from Room 104, and all hotel employees make all reasonable efforts to evacuate all guests.

On these facts, P's estate will not be able to rely on the Room 101 detector's failure to be connected to the front desk as required by statute. That's because the lack of a connection did not make any factual difference — P would have died in the fire in exactly the same way if the detector had been connected. So the statutory violation was not the "cause-in-fact" of P's death or P's injuries prior to death.

E. **Compliance not dispositive:** The fact that D has *fully complied* with all applicable safety statutes does not by itself establish that he was *not* negligent — the finder of fact is always free to conclude that a reasonable person would take precautions beyond those required by statute.

V. PROCEDURE IN JURY TRIALS

A. **Burden of proof:** In a negligence case (as in almost all tort cases) P bears the "burden of proof." This is actually two distinct burdens:

1. **Burden of production:** First, P must *come forward* with some evidence of each element of the prima facie case (e.g., that P was negligent, that P suffered an injury, that D's negligence proximately caused the injury, etc.). This burden is known as the *"burden of production."* This burden shifts from P to D, and perhaps back again during the trial.

2. **Burden of persuasion:** Second, P bears the *"burden of persuasion."* This means that as the case goes to the jury, P must convince the jury that it is *more probable than not* that each element of her prima facie case is satisfied.

B. **Function of judge and jury:** MBE questions often require you to know something about the division of labor between the judge and the jury in a tort case.

1. **Judge decides law:** The judge decides all questions of *law*. Most importantly, the judge decides *whether reasonable people could differ* as to what the material facts of the case are; if they could not, he will *direct a verdict.*

Example: Car accident case, in which Ped claims that Drive drove his car negligently, and struck Ped, a pedestrian who was crossing in a crosswalk. At the close of the evidence, Drive moves for a directed verdict. If the trial judge does not believe that a reasonable jury could find, by a preponderance of the evidence, that Drive behaved negligently and that that negligence proximately caused the accident, the judge will direct a verdict for Drive and will not let the case go to the jury.

a. **MBE tip:** MBE Torts questions often give you directed-verdict-motion fact patterns. That is, the examiners give you a set of facts that the plaintiff proves in a negligence case, and then ask you whether plaintiff can survive a defense motion for directed verdict, i.e., whether plaintiff can "get to the jury." The answer will often be *"no,"* that if all that P proves is what's recited, P has failed to come up with evidence that would allow a reasonable jury to find each element of a prima facie case for negligence (with proof of negligent behavior — i.e., lack of reasonable care — being the most commonly missing element).

i. **Circumstantial evidence:** Fact patterns like this on the MBE often make use of *circumstantial evidence.* That's especially likely in *slip-and-fall* cases. The examiners tell you how much D (the premises owner) knew or should have known, and you have to decide whether that's enough to permit a reasonable jury to infer that D was negligent.

Example 1 (not enough to go to the jury): P slips on a banana peel in D's grocery store, and sues D for negligence. P testifies only that she slipped on the peel, and that when she looked at the peel, it was clean, except for the mark of P's heel on it. There is no other evidence about whether or when D knew of the fallen peel.

On these facts, D should be entitled to a directed verdict. There is evidence that the peel was on the floor, but no evidence (even circumstantial) about whether it fell long enough before the accident that D knew or should have known about it and cleaned it up. Therefore, there was no evidence that permitted a reasonable jury to infer that D was negligent in a way that contributed to the fall.

Example 2 (enough to go to the jury): Same basic facts as Example 1. Now, however, assume that there is one additional piece of testimony by P: "After I fell, when I looked at the banana peel, I saw that it was dirty, and squashed apart from where my heel imprint was."

This would be enough extra evidence that the court will likely deny D's motion for a directed verdict. If P's testimony is believed, the peel probably got dirty and squashed by being on the floor for a substantial time pre-accident. Therefore, a reasonable jury could infer that the peel was on the floor for long enough that it was negligence for D's personnel not to spot it (or be told about it by other shoppers) and clean it up.

ii. **Summary:** The point of the above two examples is that you have to examine the stipulated evidence closely, and make all reasonable inferences from circumstantial evidence, in order to decide the outer limits of what a reasonable jury could (not would) do — if a reasonable jury could not find by a preponderance of the evidence that each element of a prima facie case for negligence (duty, negligence, cause-in-fact, proximate cause, and damages) was satisfied, then you should conclude that the judge ought to direct a verdict for D rather than letting the case go to the jury.

2. **Jury decides facts:** The jury is the finder of the *facts*. In a negligence case (assuming that the judge does not direct a full or partial verdict), the jury decides: (a) what really happened; and (2) whether D breached his duty to P in a way that proximately caused P's injuries. This means that it is the jury that usually decides whether D's conduct satisfied the "reasonable person" standard.

VI. *RES IPSA LOQUITUR*

A. **Generally:** The doctrine of *res ipsa loquitur* ("the thing speaks for itself") allows P to point to the fact of the accident, and to create an *inference* that, even without a precise showing of how D behaved, D was probably negligent.

Example: A barrel of flour falls on P's head as he walks below a window on the street. At trial, P shows that the barrel fell out of a window of D's shop, and that barrels do not fall out of windows without some negligence. By use of the *res ipsa loquitur* doctrine, P has presented enough evidence to justify a verdict for him, so unless D comes up with rebuttal evidence that the barrel did not come from his shop or was not dropped by negligence, D will lose. [*Byrne v. Boadle*]

B. **Requirements for:** On the MBE, there are only two requirements for application of *res ipsa* that you should worry about — if they're present, you should apply the doctrine:

[1] the event must be of a kind which *ordinarily does not occur in the absence of negligence*; and

[2] *other causes*, including the conduct of the plaintiff and third persons, must be sufficiently *eliminated* by the evidence.

Rest. 2d, §328D.

C. P's failure to exclude other causes: On the MBE, if *res ipsa* doesn't apply, the most likely reason is requirement [2] above: plaintiff fails to satisfactorily *eliminate the conduct of third persons* (whether negligent or not) as the alternative causes of the accident instead of defendant's negligence.

1. Object falling from window in multi-tenant building: For instance, the examiners may give you a scenario in which P is a pedestrian who is injured when hit by an *object that falls from a building owned by D*, but in which *other people are tenants*. Since the object may have been dropped by a tenant (for whose conduct D as owner is not vicariously liable), *res ipsa* won't apply.

Example: P is a pedestrian, who is hit and injured by a table lamp that has fallen from some window in a 10-story office building owned by D. Most offices are rented by a variety of commercial tenants. (D uses just two of the offices himself.) Neither side produces evidence of which window the lamp fell from. There is no other evidence in the case bearing on how the accident occurred.

Res ipsa will not apply, because P has not sufficiently excluded alternative explanations that don't involve D's negligence (e.g., negligence of a tenant). Furthermore, D will be entitled to a directed verdict, because without *res ipsa* there is no evidence permitting a reasonable jury to infer or conclude that D's negligence was a but-for or proximate cause of the accident.

D. Typical contexts: Here are a couple of contexts in which the *res ipsa* issue is most likely to arise on the MBE:

1. Airplane accidents: A commercial *airplane* accident in which the plane *crashes into an obstruction* like a mountain, often furnishes a good illustration of *res ipsa*.

a. ***Res ipsa* applies:** Today, airplanes don't usually fly into obstructions without someone's negligence, at least in clear weather. And typically, the influence of factors other than the airline won't be pointed to by the evidence. Therefore, the estate of a dead passenger will normally be deemed to have established negligence merely by showing that the plane crashed into an obstruction in good weather.

i. Rebuttal: But the airline is always free to try to *rebut* the evidence, such as by showing that an unforeseeable explosion caused the airplane to veer off course into the obstruction. See the discussion of rebuttal evidence *infra*, p. 39.

2. Car accidents: MBE fact patterns often involve attempts to apply *res ipsa* to *car accidents*. The analysis varies sharply with whether there are multiple vehicles involved or just one.

a. Multiple vehicles: *Res ipsa* usually does *not* apply to car crashes involving *multiple vehicles*. In most multi-vehicle crashes, it generally cannot be said that that type of accident does not happen without someone's negligence. Furthermore, even if someone's negligence were probable, usually the negligence of persons other than the defendant (e.g., the plaintiff) cannot be sufficiently eliminated by the evidence.

i. MBE Tip: Therefore, if you have a multi-car-accident fact pattern on the MBE, you should hesitate long and hard before picking a choice that turns on *res ipsa* (or on the concept that a reasonable jury could "infer" that D was negligent).

b. Single-car accident: On the other hand, if the accident is a *single-vehicle one* (e.g., between a driver and a pedestrian, or between a driver and some fixed obstruction), then *res ipsa* will often *apply*, since such accidents usually involve driver negligence. In such a single-vehicle fact pattern, if defendant (typically the driver) cannot come up with affirmative evidence of his non-negligence, or of some other cause, the plaintiff will not only win, but may be entitled to a directed verdict.

Example: P, a pedestrian, is struck in broad daylight by a car driven by D, while P is crossing at a crosswalk with the green light in her favor. These are the only facts proven by either side in P's suit against D. P will be entitled to a directed verdict. That's because *res ipsa* applies; pedestrians don't normally get hit by motorists while walking in a crosswalk with the light in their favor on a clear day, unless the driver has been negligent. Since *res ipsa* means that P has met her burden of producing some evidence of D's negligence, and since there is no countervailing evidence of D's non-negligence or some other cause, no reasonable jury could find for D. That's enough to entitle P to a directed verdict from the judge. (Even if P might have also been negligent for not spotting D's approaching car, on the MBE you are to assume comparative negligence, in which case P's negligence would not negate D's liability, and would merely reduce P's damages; see *infra*, p. 66.)

i. **Rebuttal evidence:** But D is always free to come up with evidence *rebutting* the *res ipsa* inference of negligence, and in MBE single-vehicle accident cases D will often succeed in doing so. For instance, D may be able to show that he had an unforeseeable *heart attack* just before the accident, which is a non-negligence explanation that, if believed, would remove the *res ipsa* inference. See the example *infra*, p. 39, for an illustration.

E. **Effect of *res ipsa* on burden of production:** Usually, the *effect* of *res ipsa* is to permit an inference that D was negligent, even though there is no direct evidence of negligence. *Res ipsa* thus allows a particular kind of circumstantial evidence. When *res ipsa* is used, P has *met his burden of production*, and is thus entitled to go to the jury.

1. **Often tested on MBE:** This procedural aspect of *res ipsa* — its use to meet P's burden of production — is often tested on the MBE. The examiners will tell you that P proves certain facts at trial (which, you must recognize, establish P's entitlement to *res ipsa*), and that there is no other evidence in the case about how the accident occurred. D then moves for a directed verdict, and you have to decide the motion. Typically, the answer will be that D's motion *fails* — P gets to go to the jury — because P's evidence shows his entitlement to *res ipsa*, and D has not rebutted the doctrine's applicability. Therefore, P has met his burden of production on the issue of whether D's negligence caused the accident.

Example: P brings his car into D's service station to have one tire replaced. D replaces that tire, and P drives off. One mile away, the wheel containing the new tire falls off, causing P's car to hit a car at the side of the road. P sues D in negligence, and in his case in chief proves no facts other than those recited here. D moves for a directed verdict.

D's motion will be denied (and the case will go to the jury), because P has met the requirements for *res ipsa*: in the absence of negligence a wheel on which a tire has just been changed doesn't simply fall off, and there is nothing in these facts to suggest that P's conduct, or that of any third party, caused the falling off. Therefore, by proving just these facts, P has brought forward enough evidence to entitle a reasonable jury to infer that D must have been negligent in the way he changed the tire. D has done nothing to rebut this inference. Consequently, P has satisfied his prima facie case, and is entitled to go to the jury.

a. ***Res ipsa* not mentioned:** Usually, even when *res ipsa* is the secret to an MBE question, the doctrine will *not be explicitly mentioned* anywhere in the question — you'll have to know that the doctrine is operating "behind the scenes" by letting P get to the jury. For instance, in an MBE question built around the fact pattern in the above example, the right answer might be something like "Motion [for directed verdict] denied, because a reasonable jury could infer that D behaved negligently" — *res ipsa* wouldn't be mentioned, and it would be up to you to notice that the *reason* this is the correct choice is that *res ipsa* gives the jury the right to infer that D was, more likely than not, negligent and the cause of the accident.

F. Rebuttal evidence: D is entitled to *rebut* P's *res-ipsa*-based evidence.

1. General evidence of due care: If D's rebuttal is merely in the form of evidence showing that he was *in fact careful*, this will rarely be enough to give D a directed verdict — the case will still go to the jury, on the theory that a reasonable jury could find that the *res ipsa* inference of negligence is more powerful than D's evidence of due care.

2. Rebuttal shows some other explanation: But if the rebuttal comes in the form of *direct evidence of some alternative explanation* for the accident, showing that it was not due to D's negligence, then the rebuttal, if uncontested, may be so powerful that it *wipes out the res ipsa inference entirely*, and perhaps even entitles D to a directed verdict.

Example: A single-vehicle collision occurs between Driver and Ped (a pedestrian), who is crossing the street at a cross-walk with the light in his favor. These facts alone would justify *res ipsa* in a suit by Ped against Driver (since that sort of accident usually doesn't happen in the absence of negligence). But if Driver supplies uncontested evidence that he suffered a heart attack just before the collision, preventing him from hitting the brakes, this would mean that *res ipsa* should not be applied because alternative explanations not involving Driver's negligence have not been sufficiently ruled out. If Ped did not furnish any other direct proof of Driver's negligence (e.g., that Driver knew of his predilection to heart attacks and drove anyway), then there would be no evidence of Driver's negligence in the case at all, and Driver would be entitled to a directed verdict.

a. Frequent on MBE: In fact, in many MBE fact patterns in which plaintiff initially qualifies for *res ipsa* by showing that the type of accident in question usually doesn't happen without negligence, D *successfully rebuts* the doctrine's applicability. D does this either by showing his own affirmative lack of fault, or showing the affirmative fault of some third person. (The above example illustrates rebuttal by an affirmative demonstration of D's own lack of fault.) Sometimes, D's rebuttal is so convincing and uncontested that D is entitled to a direct verdict. Other times, D's rebuttal merely stops P from getting a directed verdict.

CHAPTER 6

ACTUAL AND PROXIMATE CAUSE

I. CAUSATION IN FACT

A. Generally: P must show that D's conduct was the *"cause-in-fact"* of P's injury.

B. "But-for" test: The vast majority of the time, the way P shows "cause-in-fact" is to show that D's conduct was a *"but-for"* cause of P's injuries — *had D not acted negligently, P's injuries would not have resulted.*

Example: P takes her prescription for a medication to D, her local pharmacy. D mistakenly fills the prescription by giving P pills containing 30 mg of the active ingredient rather than the 20 mg called for by the prescription. After taking the pills, P suffers serious heart arrhythmia, and sues D for this harm. P can recover only if she proves that had D provided the correct, 20 mg, pills, P would not have suffered the arrhythmia. In other words, for P to recover, the trier of fact must be satisfied that the wrong pills were the but-for cause of P's arrhythmia.

1. **Medical or other crisis intervention:** On the MBE, the lack of but-for causation will often cause the plaintiff to lose where the defendant was a provider of *medical services*, or was responsible for supplying some other sort of *crisis intervention.* If the medical services, medical device or drug, rescue attempt, or other intervention *wouldn't have changed the outcome of the crisis,* then the person who failed to intervene properly can't have been the cause-in-fact or but-for cause of the harm to the plaintiff. The above Example is one illustration.

2. **Applies to negligence per se cases:** The requirement that defendant's negligence be a cause-in-fact or but-for cause of the harm *applies* in *negligence per se cases*, just as in garden-variety negligence cases. So if defendant's *compliance* with the statute or ordinance *wouldn't have prevented the accident or harm from occurring*, the lack of compliance can't have been a but-for cause of the harm, and negligence per se will drop out of the case.

   Example: D, a bus company, is required by federal regulations to have a portable cardiac defibrillator on board at all times. P suffers a fatal cardiac arrest while on board a bus operated by D that was not equipped with a defibrillator. Evidence at trial shows that for the type of cardiac arrest that P suffered, a defibrillator would not have prevented or slowed down the fatal course of the attack. The fact that D committed negligence per se by not having the defibrillator aboard is irrelevant, because the violation was not the (or a) cause-in-fact of D's death.

3. **Applies to failure-to-warn product liability cases:** The requirement of causation in fact also applies in *product liability cases,* especially ones brought on a *failure-to-warn* theory. That is, if what makes a productive defectively dangerous is a lack of adequate warnings or instructions (see *infra*, p. 85), then if the accident *would have happened the same way* even had the warnings/instructions been supplied, the lack of them couldn't have been the cause-in-fact of the injuries.

   Example: P cuts his left hand using a power saw (made by D) with his right hand only. Reasonable instructions would have warned against one-handed operation. P sues D on a failure-to-warn strict products liability theory. If D can show that P would certainly have disregarded such instructions or warnings had they been provided (e.g., because he disregarded such warnings contained on other power saws he used), D will win. That's because the failure-to-warn/instruct was not a cause-in-fact of P's harm — the harm would have occurred the same way had the warnings been given. (See *infra*, p. 86, for more about this.)

4. **Joint tortfeasors:** There can be *multiple* but-for causes of an event. D1 cannot defend on the grounds that D2 was a but-for cause of P's injuries — as long as D1 was also a but-for cause, D1 is viewed as the cause-in-fact. (For more about this, see "Both combine to cause harm," *infra*, p. 41.)

5. **Must be tied to D's negligence:** Keep in mind that D's *negligence*, not merely D's *conduct*, must be a cause-in-fact (as well as a proximate cause) of the harm to P. So always check to make sure that: (1) D was negligent; and (2) without that negligence, the harm to P wouldn't have occurred.

   a. **Rescue scenarios:** For instance, in scenarios in which P is injured trying to *rescue* D, it's not enough for liability that D's "conduct" was the cause-in-fact of P's injuries, in the sense that D's conduct put him in a position to need rescuing. Instead, D's negligence — his failure to use reasonable care — must be what triggered the need for him to be rescued, and thus led to P's injuries.

      Example: D is a "heli-skier," who is dropped by helicopter into freshly fallen snow. D gets stranded, and sends out an emergency beacon. P, a member of the ski patrol, is badly injured while he and his colleagues are trying to ski to D's location to rescue him. In a suit by P against D, it won't be enough for P to show just that D's conduct (of getting stranded) was the cause-in-fact and proximate cause of P's injuries. Rather, P will have to show that D behaved negligently (in putting himself in the position of needing rescue), and that the need for rescue would not have occurred but for that negligence.

C. **Multiple fault:** Where two or more defendants are tortfeasors implicated in a single harm to P, the analysis depends on whether it's clear that only one actually inflicted the damage.

1. **Only one at fault:** Where P can show that each of two (or more) defendants was at fault, but *only one could have caused the injury*, the *burden shifts* to each defendant to show that the other caused the harm. If the defendants don't show which one was at fault, then both are jointly and severally liable.

   Example: P, D1 and D2 go hunting together. D1 and D2 simultaneously fire negligently, and P is struck by one of the shots. It is not known who fired the fatal shot. The court will put the burden on each of the Ds to show that it was the other shot which hit P — if neither D can make this showing, both will be liable. [*Summers v. Tice*]

2. **Both combine to cause harm:** If two defendants are at fault, and their conduct *combines to cause the harm* to the plaintiff, then they will *both be liable* (jointly and severally). That's true even if *neither's conduct would have been enough by itself* to be a cause-in-fact of the harm. In this situation, both actions are said to be *"substantial factors"* in bringing about the harm, and an act will be a cause-in-fact if it was a substantial factor (even if some other tortious act was also a substantial factor). Rest. 2d, §§431, 432(2), 433B, Comm. c.

   a. **Multiple polluters:** This principle is most likely to apply on the MBE where there are two *water polluters* whose pollution combines to harm P, but neither's pollution would have been enough to harm P by itself. *Both are liable* in this multiple-polluter scenario.

   Example: D1 and D2 both negligently cause pollutants to be dumped from their riverside factories into the river. The pollution causes P's sheep, that graze near the riverbank, to become sick. Neither pollution would have been enough by itself to sicken the sheep. Both D1 and D2 are liable, because each defendant's negligent conduct was a substantial factor, and thus a cause-in-fact, of P's harm (and a proximate cause as well).

II. PROXIMATE CAUSE GENERALLY

A. **General:** Even after P has shown that D was the cause-in-fact of P's injuries, P must still show that D was the *"proximate cause"* of those injuries. The proximate cause requirement is a *policy determination* that a defendant, even one who has behaved negligently, should not automatically be liable for *all* of the consequences, no matter how *improbable* or *far-reaching*, of his act. Today, the proximate cause requirement usually means that D will *not be liable* for the consequences that are highly *unforeseeable*.

   Example: D, driving carelessly, collides with a car driven by X. Unbeknownst to D, X's car contains dynamite, which explodes. Ten blocks away, a nurse who is carrying P, an infant, is startled by the explosion, and drops P. P will not be able to recover against D, because the episode is so far-fetched — it was so unforeseeable that the injury would occur from D's negligence — that courts will hold that D's careless driving was not the "proximate cause" of P's injuries.

1. **Multiple proximate causes:** Just as an occurrence can have many "causes in fact," so it may well have *more than one proximate cause.*

   Example: Each of two drivers drives negligently, and P, a pedestrian, is injured. Each driver is probably a proximate cause of the accident.

   a. **MBE Tip:** On the MBE, be sure to remember this principle that a single harm may have multiple proximate causes (and multiple causes in fact). The examiners like to present you with two possible tortfeasors (call them D1 and D2) and then give you a choice that implicitly assumes that if D2 is liable, D1 can't be (e.g., "D1 will avoid liability, because D2 was the proximate cause of P's injuries"). Don't be fooled — if D1's tortious conduct was a substantial factor in P's injuries, the fact that D2 may also be liable *won't block D1 from being liable* as well. (See the principle of joint-and-several liability, *infra*, p. 47.)

III. PROXIMATE CAUSE — FORESEEABILITY

A. The foreseeability rule generally: Most courts hold that D is liable, as a general rule, only for those consequences of his negligence which were *reasonably foreseeable* at the time she acted.

Example: D's ship spills oil into a bay. Some of the oil adheres to P's dock. The oil is then set afire by some molten metal dropped by P's worker on the dock, which ignites a cotton rag floating on the water. P's whole dock then burns. *Held*, D is not liable, because the burning of P's dock was not the foreseeable consequence of D's oil spill, and thus the oil spill was not the proximate cause of the damage. This is true even though the burning may have been the "direct" result of D's negligence. [*Wagon Mound No. 1*]

1. Third Restatement: The Third Restatement formulates the idea this way: a defendant is "*not liable* for harm *different from the harms whose risk made the [defendant's] conduct tortious.*" Rest. 3d (P.H.), §29. The Restatement would presumably agree with the result in the above example: what made D's oil spill tortious was that it was a nuisance (and perhaps a trespass) that risked junking up the wharf with a foreign substance. The risk of a fire from the spill was *not* one of the risks that made the spill tortious, so D isn't liable for it.

B. Unforeseeable plaintiff: The general rule that D is liable only for foreseeable consequences is also usually applied to the *"unforeseeable plaintiff"* problem. That is, if D's conduct is negligent as to X (in the sense that it imposes an unreasonable risk of harm upon X), but not negligent as to P (i.e., does not impose an unreasonable risk of harm upon P), P will not be able to recover if through some fluke he is injured.

Example: X, trying to board D's train, is pushed by D's employee. X drops a package, which (unknown to anybody) contains fireworks, which explode when they fall. The shock of the explosion makes some scales at the other end of the platform fall down, hitting P.

Held, P may not recover against D. D's employee may have been negligent towards X (by pushing him), but the employee's conduct did not involve any foreseeable risk of harm to P, who was standing far away. Since D's conduct did not involve an unreasonable risk of harm to P, and the damage to her was not foreseeable, the fact that the conduct was unjustifiably risky to X is irrelevant. D's conduct was not the "proximate cause" of the harm to P. [*Palsgraf v. Long Island R.R. Co.*]

C. Extensive consequences from physical injuries: A key *exception* to the general rule that D is liable only for foreseeable consequences is: once P suffers any foreseeable impact or injury, even if relatively minor, D is liable for *any additional unforeseen physical consequences* to P.

1. Egg-shell skull: Thus if P, unbeknownst to D, has a very *thin skull* (a skull of "egg-shell thinness"), and D negligently inflicts a minor impact on this skull, D will be liable if, because of the hidden skull defect, P dies. The defendant *"takes his plaintiff as he finds him."*

a. Worsening of pre-existing disability: This rule means that if P has a *pre-existing physical disability* or condition that is *aggravated* by D's conduct, P can recover for the worsening of the condition, even though a person of ordinary physical condition wouldn't have suffered any injury.

Example: P has a chronically bad back due to a long-ago auto accident. D, driving negligently, collides with a car carrying P. A person with an "ordinary" back would have suffered only minor back pain from the incident. But P's back condition is worsened, causing her enormous pain and missed work.

P may recover for the full worsening of her condition, due to the "egg-shell skull" or "defendant takes the plaintiff as he finds him" principle.

D. The "extraordinary in hindsight" rule: Many courts articulate the foreseeability rule as an *"extraordinary in hindsight"* rule. D's conduct will not be the proximate cause of P's harm if, "after the event and the *looking back* from the harm to [D's] negligent conduct, it appears to the court *highly extraordinary* that it should have brought about the harm." Rest. 2d, §435.

E. How tested on the MBE: It's hard for the MBE examiners to give you a fact pattern where the harm is clearly unforeseeable, and proximate cause is lacking. Therefore, when the examiners want to test you on the requirement of foreseeability, they'll generally give you an ambiguous situation and just ask to you notice that lack-of-foreseeability is a *good argument* for D to make.

Example: If the railroad-fireworks-explosion scenario of *Palsgraf, supra*, p. 42, were an MBE question, the examiners probably wouldn't ask to figure out that P would lose. Instead, the examiners would likely ask you something like, "What's the best argument D can make for non-liability?", and the answer would be something like, "D's employee's duty not to push persons on the platform did not encompass the risk of injury to P, standing elsewhere on the platform, from falling scales."

IV. PROXIMATE CAUSE — INTERVENING CAUSES

A. Definition of "intervening cause": Most proximate cause issues arise where P's injury is precipitated by an *"intervening cause."* An intervening cause is a force which takes effect *after* D's negligence, and which contributes to that negligence in producing P's injury.

1. **Superseding cause:** Some, but not all, intervening causes are sufficient to prevent D's negligence from being held to be the proximate cause of the injury. Intervening causes that are sufficient to prevent D from being negligent are called *"superseding"* causes, since they supersede or cancel D's liability.

B. Foreseeability rule: Generally courts use a *foreseeability* rule to determine whether a particular intervening cause is superseding.

1. **Test:** Thus if D should have *foreseen* the possibility that the intervening cause (or one like it) might occur, *or* if the *kind of harm* suffered by P was foreseeable (even if the intervening cause was not itself foreseeable), D's conduct will nonetheless be the proximate cause. But if *neither* the intervening cause nor the kind of harm was foreseeable, the intervening cause will be a superseding one, relieving D of liability.

2. **Tested on the MBE:** When proximate cause is tested on the MBE, it will usually be in the context of whether an intervening cause interrupted the chain of causation. Often, the examiners don't expect you to make the determination that the intervening event was or wasn't foreseeable — they just expect you to *recognize* that *if* the intervening event was reasonably foreseeable as a source of harm, then it won't be superseding.

Example: D's car (driven negligently by him) and X's car collide in a fender-bender. X gets his car fixed, but the mechanic fails to notice a small gas leak in the engine caused by the collision. X gets the supposedly-fixed car back, and collides with Y. Due to the preexisting gas leak, X's car catches fire, injuring P, a pedestrian who is standing nearby. P sues D for having started the whole causal chain.

If this were an MBE fact pattern, the correct answer would likely be something like, "P can recover if the later injury to P was a proximate consequence of D's negligent driving." In other words, you probably won't be required to say whether D's negligence was or wasn't a proximate cause (or whether P's injury was reasonably foreseeable) — you'll merely be required to see that proximate cause/foreseeability is the central issue.

C. Foreseeable intervening causes: Often the risk of a particular kind of intervening cause is the *very risk* (or one of the risks) which made D's conduct negligent in the first place. Where this is the case, the intervening cause will almost *never* relieve D of liability.

Example: D leaves his car keys in the ignition, and the car unlocked, while going into a store to do an errand. X comes along, steals the car, and while driving fast to get out of the neighborhood, runs over P. If the court believes that the risk of theft is one of the things that makes leaving one's keys in the ignition negligent, the court will almost certainly conclude that X's intervening act was not superseding.

1. Vehicle defects: MBE fact patterns often involve defects in *vehicles*. In such scenarios, accidents that result from the defect will usually be found to be sufficiently foreseeable consequences of the defect that the accident will be found *not superseding.* Thus design defects in things like *brakes, steering wheels, or ignitions* will likely be a proximate cause of a resulting accident to the vehicle, even if some other events had to "cooperate" to bring about the accident.

Example: CarCo makes a car with a defectively-designed ignition, which causes the car to stall a lot. While P is driving on the highway, the car stalls suddenly, and comes to a dead stop. X, driving behind, slams into the rear of the car, injuring P. Since one of the things that makes a defective car ignition dangerous is the risk of a stall on a busy road, X's conduct in driving into the back of P's car won't be superseding.

2. "Second collision" scenarios: MBE questions also often involve an initial automobile accident that is caused by the negligence of a driver D, followed by a *"second collision"* in which a person (P) who stopped in response to the first accident is injured in a collision with someone else (call him X). As long as it was reasonably foreseeable that D's negligence, if it led to an accident, might also lead to a second collision, the second collision *won't be deemed superseding,* and P will be able to recover from D.

Example: D drives negligently fast on a 2-lane road at night, and slams into a retaining wall at the side of the road. This causes D to block the road. P drives up behind D, and has to stop because she can't get by. X, driving carefully coming around a bend behind them, rear-ends P and injures her.

As long as it was reasonably foreseeable to one in D's position (which it probably was) that D's negligence might cause an accident that would or might trigger a second accident, D's negligence will be found to be the proximate cause of P's injuries. In that case, P will be able to recover from D.

3. Foreseeable negligence by third persons: The *negligence of third persons* may similarly be an intervening force that is sufficiently foreseeable that it will not relieve D of liability.

Example 1: In the above defective-ignition example involving CarCo (p. 44), even if X was speeding, this fact won't likely prevent CarCo's negligent starter design from being a proximate cause of the accident.

Example 2: D is a tavern owner, who serves too much liquor to X, knowing that X arrived alone by car. D also does not object when X gets out his car keys and leaves. If X drunkenly runs over P, a court will probably hold that X's conduct in negligently (drunkenly) driving, although intervening, was sufficiently foreseeable that it should not absolve D of liability.

4. **Criminally or intentionally tortious conduct by third person:** A third person's *criminal conduct*, or *intentionally tortious act*, may also be so foreseeable that it will not be superseding. But in general, the court is somewhat more likely to find the act superseding if it is criminal or intentionally tortious than where it is merely negligent.

   a. **Poor security by D:** On the MBE, the foreseeability of the third-party crime or tort as a consequence of the defendant's *failure to provide security* will be a *jury question.* Thus D's failure to provide additional security, leading to the third person's crime or intentional tort, will usually *not* be superseding, at least as *a matter of law.* So the defendant usually won't be entitled to a directed verdict on account of the third party's intentional tort or crime (but *will* be entitled not to have a directed verdict given for the plaintiff either).

      Example: D, a gun dealer, stores its guns in a glass case that has a single low-cost lock on it. D also locks the premises at night, with an inexpensive lock. X breaks in one night, steals a revolver, and uses it to shoot P to death in a holdup. At trial, P's estate shows that D knew that robberies of gun dealers occasionally occurred in the neighborhood, but D shows that such robberies were rare, and that other local gun dealers did not use more security than D used. D claims that X's crimes are superseding, negating any negligence that D might otherwise have for low security. Both parties move for a directed verdict.

      A court is likely to conclude that the case should go to the jury. In other words, the issue of whether a break-in, theft of a gun and subsequent use of that gun to injure a bystander was a reasonably foreseeable consequence of the level of security chosen by D is probably one on which a reasonable jury could go either way. If so, the court will not grant either party a directed verdict.

      i. **Correct choice has an "if" in it:** It's pretty hard for the MBE examiners to concoct a situation in which D's failure to provide security either clearly is or clearly isn't a lack of reasonable care. Therefore, in failure-to-provide-security scenarios on the MBE, the correct answer will often be that D is liable "*if*" D unreasonably failed to provide adequate security. In other words, you won't need to decide whether the failure was reasonable or unreasonable, you'll merely have to know that *if* the failure was unreasonable, the third party's intentional crime or tort won't be a supervening act that lets the person who failed to supply security off the hook.

         Example: P stays at D's hotel. A never-identified criminal enters the hotel, picks the lock on P's room, and rapes P in the room. P sues D for negligence; D defends on the grounds that the criminal's act was supervening. The correct answer is likely to be something like "D is liable *if* the crime would probably not have occurred had D provided reasonable security precautions."

D. **Responses to defendant's actions:** Where the third party's intervention is a *"normal" response* to the defendant's act, that response will generally *not* be considered superseding. This is true even if the response was not all that foreseeable.

1. **Escape:** For instance, if in response to the danger created by D, P or someone else attempts to *escape* that danger, the attempted escape will not be a superseding cause so long as it was not completely irrational or bizarre.

   Example: D, driving negligently, sideswipes P's car on the highway. P panics, thrusts the wheel to the right, and slams into a railing. Even though most drivers in P's position might not have reacted in such an extreme or unhelpful manner, P's response is not sufficiently bizarre to constitute a superseding cause.

2. **Rescue:** Similarly, if D's negligence creates a danger which causes some third person to attempt a *rescue*, this rescue will normally not be an intervening cause, unless it is performed

in a *grossly careless* manner. D may be liable to the *person being rescued* (even if part or all of the rescuee's injuries are directly due to the rescuer's ordinary negligence), or *to the rescuer.*

a. **Firefighters' rule:** But if the rescuer is a firefighter, police officer, or other public employee paid to assume particular risks, most states apply the so-called *"firefighters' rule,"* also known as the *"professional risk takers rule."* Under this rule, a professional risk taker may not recover for injuries caused by another's negligence, where "the negligently created risk was the very reason for [the plaintiff's] presence on the scene." Dobbs, §286. Despite the term "firefighters' rule," the rule extends to *police officers* as well, when they are called to premises to perform law-enforcement duties.

Example: D negligently invites guests to his house, whom he has reason to know often get into fights. Two guests get into a fight, and D calls the police. P, a police officer, responds, and suffers a broken jaw while breaking up the fight.

Under the common-law firefighters' rule, still in force in most jurisdictions, P will not be able to recover against D. That's because the rule says that a professional risk-taker such as a police officer may not recover in negligence against one who created the peril, if that peril was the very reason for the risk-taker's presence on the scene, and the peril is one of the special risks inherent in the plaintiff's job. The facts here meet these requirements for application of the rule.

i. **Beyond premises liability:** Originally, the firefighters' rule applied only to premises liability. But those courts that apply it today generally extend it to cover professional rescue efforts that take place *outside of D's (or anyone's) premises.* And they extend it to non-rescue situations, such as *chasing suspects.*

Example: D is speeding. P, a police officer, chases him at high speed, and is injured in a collision. If the jurisdiction follows the modern version of the firefighters' rule, P will not be permitted to recover against D for creating the peril, because police officers are deemed to have voluntarily accepted the risk of injury from high-speed chases. Dobbs, §285, p. 770.

ii. **Normal risks:** Even among courts that apply the firefighters' rule, the doctrine is generally limited to *risks* that are *inherent in, and special to,* that particular occupation. Dobbs, §286.

Example: While driving on the job, P, a police officer, is injured in a collision in ordinary traffic with a car driven negligently by D. Even if the jurisdiction applies the firefighters' rule, P can recover against D, because the rule doesn't apply to the collision here. That's because the risk of a collision in ordinary traffic is not one of the special risks inherent in police work.

3. **Aggravation of injury by medical treatment:** If D negligently injures P, who then undergoes *medical treatment*, D will be liable for anything that happens to P as the result of negligence in the medical treatment, infection, etc.

Examples: P is injured by D's negligence. P is then further injured when the ambulance carrying her gets into a collision, or when, due to the treating surgeon's negligence, P's condition is worsened rather than improved. D is responsible for these further injuries.

a. **Gross mistreatment:** But some results of attempted medical treatment are so *gross* and unusual that they are regarded as superseding.

Example: While P is hospitalized due to injuries negligently inflicted by D, a nurse kills P by giving him an injection of morphine which she knows may be fatal, because she wants to spare him from suffering. D is not liable for P's death because the nurse's conduct is so bizarre as to be superseding.

E. Dependent vs. independent intervention: Courts sometimes distinguish between *"dependent"* intervening causes and *"independent"* ones.

1. **Dependent:** A dependent intervening cause is one which occurs only in *response* to D's negligence.

2. **Independent:** An independent intervention is one which would have occurred *even had D not been negligent* (but which combined with D's negligence to produce the harm).

3. **Classification not dispositive:** Dependent intervening events are probably somewhat more foreseeable on average, and thus somewhat less likely to be superseding, than independent ones. But the foreseeability rule applies to *both sorts of events*. Therefore, a dependent cause can be superseding (e.g., a grossly negligent rescue attempt), and an independent intervention can be non-superseding.

F. Third person's failure to discover: A third person's *failure* to *discover and prevent* a danger will almost never be superseding.

> **Example:** In 2002, Manu manufactures a power saw that it sells to Factory. The saw contains a hidden design defect that makes the saw blade likely to snap off, potentially injuring the user. In 2004, Manu discovers the problem as the result of consumer complaints. Manu then promptly writes a letter to Factory (addressed to Factory's president) describing the problem and offering to fix it for free. The president negligently throws the letter away, instead of reading it or telling anyone on the shop floor about the danger. In 2007, User, a Factory employee, uses the saw and is injured when the blade breaks.
>
> A third person's failure to discover a danger will virtually never, by itself, constitute a superseding cause relieving the original tortfeasor of liability. Therefore, the negligence of Factory's president in discarding the letter will not prevent Manu's defective design from being a proximate cause of User's injury, so that negligence won't block User from recovering against Manu in strict product liability.

1. **Third person does discover:** Even if the third person *does* discover a danger caused by the defendant, the third person's *failure to warn* the plaintiff about that danger usually *won't be superseding.*

> **Example:** Same facts as above example. Now, however, Factory's president reads the recall letter, then due to press of other business fails to mention it to User or to get the saw fixed. It's unlikely that this third-party failure to warn will be deemed superseding. So Manu's defective design will still likely be considered a proximate cause of User's injuries. (A different result — an interruption of the causal chain — might occur if Manu then called up Factory, or otherwise did everything reasonably in its power to fix the saw, and Factory's president simply refused to allow the saw to be fixed or replaced by Manu for free.)

CHAPTER 7

JOINT TORTFEASORS

I. JOINT LIABILITY

A. Joint-and-several liability generally: If more than one person is a proximate cause of P's harm, and the harm is *indivisible*, under the traditional approach *each defendant* is liable for the *entire* *harm*. The liability is said to be *"joint and several."*

1. **MBE Tip:** The instructions to the MBE tell you to assume that joint-and-several liability applies unless you are instructed otherwise on the particular question (which will rarely happen). So you'll definitely need to master the joint-and-several-liability principle for the MBE, even though many states today have backed away from the rule in many instances.

2. **P can recover entire loss from either D:** The principle of joint-and-several liability means that plaintiff can *recover the entire loss from any defendant,* no matter *how small* that defendant's share of the total responsibility.

   Example: P, a pedestrian, is injured when a car negligently driven by D1 collides with a car negligently driven by D2. A jury applying comparative negligence (applicable by default on the MBE; see *infra*, p. 66) concludes that P wasn't at fault at all, D1 was 70% at fault and D2 30% at fault. P suffers $100,000 in damages.

   P may collect all $100,000 from D1 (or all $100,000 from D2). If either D ends up having to pay P more than that D's share of the total liability, that D can recover the overage from the other D in a contribution action (see *infra*, p. 50).

3. **Meshing with P's comparative negligence.** Often on MBE problems, P will have some responsibility (under the default comparative-negligence rule that you are to assume applies on the MBE), and the remaining responsibility will be split among two or more Ds. When this happens, P's share of fault is in effect *deducted "off the top,"* and the Ds are jointly and severally liable for the rest.

   Example: In a three-car accident, a car driven by P collides with ones driven by D1 and D2. P has $100,000 in damages. The jury determines that P was 30% at fault, D1 50% and D2 20%. Under comparative-negligence principles, P's recovery will be reduced by $30,000. Of the remaining $70,000, P may collect it all from D1, all from D2, or in any proportions. If D1 pays more than his 5/7's share of the $70,000, or D2 pays more than his 2/7's share of the $70,000, the overpaying defendant may collect the overage in contribution from the other defendant.

B. **Indivisible versus divisible harms:** Even where the traditional rule of joint-and-several liability is in force, it applies only where P's harm is *"indivisible,"* i.e., *not capable of being apportioned* between or among the defendants. If there is a rational basis for apportionment — that is, for saying that some of the harm is the result of D1's act and the remainder is the result of D2's act — then *each will be responsible only for that directly-attributable harm.*

1. **Rules on apportionment:** Here is a summary of the rules on when harms will or won't be capable of being apportioned:

   a. **Action in concert:** If the two defendants can be said to have acted *in concert*, each will be liable for injuries directly caused by the other. In other words, apportionment does not take place.

      Example: D1 and D2 drag race. D1's car swerves and hits P. D2, even though his car was not part of the collision, is liable for the entire injuries caused by D1's collision, because D1 and D2 acted in concert.

   b. **Successive injuries:** Courts often are able to apportion the total harm if individual harms occurred in *successive incidents*, separated by substantial periods of time.

      Example: D1, owner of a factory, pollutes P's property from 1970-1990. D1 sells to D2, who pollutes P's property from 1991-2007. The court will apportion the damage — neither defendant will have to pay for damage done by the other.

i. **Consequence of non-apportionability:** In any scenario in which P is harmed in successive incidents involving multiple Ds, courts will usually place the *burden of allocating the damages* on the *Ds*, not on P. In other words, if no one proves how much of P's damages from the two successive torts are reasonably allocated to D1 and how much to D2, the court will typically make the Ds jointly and severally liable, so that the tortfeasors, not the innocent plaintiff, bear the "burden of unallocability."

Example 1: P suffers upper-back injuries in a collision with D1. Six months later, P suffers lower-back injuries in a collision with D2. At P's trial of claims against D1 and D2 jointly, P is unable to produce evidence allocating her extreme and ongoing back pain between the upper-back injuries and the lower-back ones. Neither D1 nor D2 produces allocation-of-harm evidence.

A court will likely hold that D1 and D2 are jointly and severally liable, because if damages cannot be allocated, the tortfeasor defendants, not the innocent plaintiff, should bear the financial consequence of that impossibility.

Example 2: D1 and D2 both pollute a stream, poisoning P's livestock, and damaging P by $100,000. Neither D (nor P) offers proof allocating the damages as between D1 and D2. A court will likely hold D1 and D2 jointly and severally liable, on the theory that the uncertainty about how damages should be allocated between the two should hurt them, not P.

ii. **Greater liability for first tortfeasor:** Where the successive harms are apportionable, and both were tortiously caused, often the consequence is that the *first* tortfeasor will be liable for *both* harms, but the *second* tortfeasor will be liable *only for the second harm.* This successive-harm scenario is often tested on the MBE.

Example: P suffers a left-knee injury when her car is hit by a car negligently driven by D1. Three months later, while P is wearing high heels and going down stairs in a building owned by D2, P's left heel catches in a small hole in the stairs. Had D2 not negligently failed to maintain the stairs, the hole would have been filled and the heel would not have caught. When the heel catches, P's left knee buckles, causing P to fall and injure her head. The fall would not have occurred without both the prior injury to P's knee and the negligently-caused hole in the stairs.

D1 will be liable for *both* the initial injury to P's left knee, and for the head injury. That's true because D1's original negligence was a proximate cause, and cause-in-fact (but-for cause), of both injuries. D2, however, will be liable *only* for the head injury, and as to that head injury will have joint-and-several liability with D1. (Since the head injury is a single harm that cannot be even theoretically divided between D1's fault and D2's fault, the two Ds will be jointly and severally liable for it — see paragraph (c) immediately below).

c. **Indivisible harms:** Some harms are theoretically *indivisible.* When this is this case, each co-defendant is jointly and severally liable for the entire harm.

i. **Death or single injury:** Thus the plaintiff's *death* or any *single personal injury* (e.g., a broken arm) is *not divisible.*

Example: On the facts of the above example, D1 and D2 are both jointly and severally liable for P's head injury. That's true because each D was a proximate and a but-for cause of the injury, and as a single injury it cannot be apportioned.

ii. **Fires:** Similarly, if P's property is *burned* or otherwise destroyed, this will be an indivisible result.

Example: D1 and D2 each negligently contribute to the starting of a fire, which then destroys P's house. There will be no apportionment, so D1 and D2 will each be liable for P's full damages in a state applying traditional joint-and-several liability.

C. **One satisfaction only:** Even if D1 and D2 are jointly and severally liable, P is only entitled to a *single satisfaction* of her claim.

Example: P suffers harm of $1 million, for which the court holds D1 and D2 jointly and severally liable. If P recovers the full $1 million from D1, she may not recover anything from D2.

II. CONTRIBUTION

A. **Contribution generally:** If two Ds are jointly and severally liable, and one D pays more than his *pro rata share*, he may usually obtain partial *reimbursement* from the other D. This is called *"contribution."*

Example: A court holds that D1 and D2 are jointly and severally liable to P for $1 million, and that D1 and D2 were equally at fault. P collects the full $1 million from D1. In most instances, D1 may recover $500,000 contribution from D2, so that they will end up having each paid the same amount.

1. **Amount:** Under *comparative negligence* (which you are to assume applies on the MBE), the duty of contribution is usually *proportional to fault*, with the plaintiff's award reduced by his percentage of fault "off the top."

Example: A jury finds that P was 20% at fault, D1 60% and D2 20%. P's damages are $1 million. The jurisdiction follows pure comparative negligence and joint-and-several liability. P can recover her entire $800,000 net award from D1. D1 can then recover the amount by which he overpaid ($200,000) from D2 in contribution.

B. **Limits on doctrine:** Most states *limit* contribution as follows:

1. **No intentional torts:** Usually an *intentional* tortfeasor may *not* get contribution from her co-tortfeasors (even if they, too, behaved intentionally).

2. **Contribution defendant must have liability:** The contribution defendant (that is, the co-tortfeasor who is being sued for contribution) must *in fact be liable* to the original plaintiff.

Example: Husband drives a car in which Wife is a passenger. The car collides with a car driven by D. The jury finds that Husband and D were both negligent. Wife recovers the full jury verdict from D. If intra-family immunity (see *infra*, p. 71) applies and would prevent Wife from recovering directly from Husband, then D may not recover contribution from Husband either, since Husband has no underlying liability to the original plaintiff (Wife).

III. INDEMNITY

A. **Definition:** Sometimes the court will not merely order two joint-and-severally-liable defendants to split the cost (contribution), but will instead completely *shift* the responsibility from one D to the other. This is the doctrine of *"indemnity"* — a 100% shifting of liability, as opposed to the sharing involved in contribution.

B. **Some contexts:** Here are two important contexts in which indemnity is often applied:

1. **Vicarious liability:** If D1 is only *vicariously liable* for D2's conduct, D2 will be required to indemnify D1.

 Example: Employee injures P. P recovers against Employer on a theory of respondeat superior (*infra*, p. 71). Employer will be entitled to indemnity from Employee; that is, Employee will be required to pay to Employer the full amount of any judgment that Employer has paid.

2. **Retailer versus manufacturer:** A *retailer* who is held *strictly liable* for selling a d*efective injury-causing* product will get indemnity from others further up the distribution chain, including the *manufacturer*.

 a. **Higher up the chain:** In fact, more generally, anyone in the distribution chain who is held strictly liable can probably get indemnity from *anyone higher up in the chain*, especially where the higher-up person is more at fault.

 Example 1: A dangerously defective product causes injury to P. P sues (in strict product liability) the wholesaler who sold it to the retailer who sold it to P. If the wholesaler has to pay P, the wholesaler can get full indemnity from the manufacturer.

 Example 2: Manu, a manufacturer of a product whose defective design made it dangerous, is required to pay a strict product liability judgment to P, who was injured by the product. Manu licensed the design for the product from Des, an industrial designer. Manu made the product exactly according to Des' full set of specifications. Manu did not know, or have reason to know, of the product's defective design or dangerousness. Des will be required to fully indemnify Manu for the judgment.

 Example 3: EngineCo sells an engine to Pilot for her private plane, and installs it. Due to a defect in the engine, the plane crashes into Paul's building. Paul recovers against Pilot's estate under strict liability for ground damage from airplanes (see *infra*, p. 75). Pilot's estate is entitled to full indemnity from EngineCo for the judgment it had to pay, even if EngineCo acted without fault in selling and installing the engine.

3. **Negligent vs. intentional tortfeasor:** If one tortfeasor is merely negligent, and the other commits an intentional tort, the intentional tortfeasor will be required to indemnify the negligent one. This can happen, for instance, if D1's negligence consists of not preventing D2 from committing an intentional tort where D1 had an obligation to use reasonable care to prevent such a tort.

 Example: D1 negligently entrusts his car to his friend D2, knowing that D2 is unstable and often violent. D2 takes the car and purposely runs over P, D2's former girlfriend. P's estate recovers in negligence from D1 for entrusting the car to D2. D1 will be entitled to full indemnity from D2 for the judgment, since D2 was an intentional tortfeasor and D1 was merely negligent.

CHAPTER 8

DUTY

I. DUTY GENERALLY

A. **Concept:** Generally, a person owes everyone else with whom he comes in contact a general *"duty of care."* Normally, you don't have to worry about this duty — it is the same in all instances, the duty to behave with the care that would be shown by a reasonable person. But there are several situations in which courts hold that the defendant owes plaintiff *less* than this regular duty. The most important of these situations are:

[1] D generally has *no duty* to take *affirmative action* to help P;

[2] D generally has *no duty* to avoid causing unintended *emotional distress* to P (unless there is also physical danger to or impact upon P); and

[3] D has *no duty* to avoid causing *pure economic loss* to P in the absence of more tangible types of harm to P such as physical injury.

We consider each of these situations below.

II. FAILURE TO ACT

A. No general duty to act: A person generally cannot be liable in tort solely on the grounds that she has *failed to act.*

1. Duty to protect or give aid: This means that if D sees that P is in danger, and fails to render assistance (even though D could do so easily and safely), as a general rule D is *not liable for refusing to assist.*

Example: D, passing by, sees P drowning in a pond. D could easily pull P to safety without risk to D, but instead, D walks on by. D is not liable to P.

B. Exceptions: But there are a number of commonly-recognized *exceptions* to the "no duty to act" rule:

1. Special relationship: A duty to give assistance may arise out of a *"special relationship"* between D and P. (This is distinct from any special relationship between D and a third person who poses harm to P, as to which see *infra*, p. 53.) Here is a list (from the Third Restatement) of relationships between P and D that impose such a duty of care:

[a] the relationship of "a *common carrier* with its *passengers*";

[b] "an *innkeeper* with its *guests*";

[c] "a *business* or other possessor of land that *holds its premises open to the public* with those who are *lawfully on the premises*";

Example: Without any negligence by D, a store where P is shopping, P gets his finger stuck in an escalator that is part of the store. If D does not give P assistance after discovering P's plight, D will be liable for any injuries occurring after that discovery that could have been prevented by reasonable assistance.

[d] "an *employer* with its *employees*";

[e] "a *school* with its *students*";

[f] "a *landlord* with its *tenants*"; and

[g] "a *custodian* with *those in its custody*, if the custodian is required by law to take custody or voluntarily takes custody of the other and the custodian has a *superior ability to protect* the other."

Example: A prison has a duty of care to a prisoner. Therefore, the prison has a duty to use reasonable care to protect an inmate from being attacked by another inmate.

2. **Defendant involved in injury:** If the danger or injury to P is *due to D's own conduct*, or to an instrument under D's control, D has the duty of assistance. This is true today even if D acted without fault.

   Example: A car carefully driven by D strikes P, a pedestrian. Even though D has driven completely non-negligently, and the accident is due to P's carelessness in crossing the street, D has a duty to stop and give reasonable assistance to P, and will be liable for any additional injuries suffered by P if D doesn't do so.

3. **Defendant and victim as co-venturers:** Where the victim and the defendant are engaged in a *common pursuit*, so that they may be said to be *co-venturers*, some courts have imposed on the defendant a duty of warning and assistance. For instance, if two friends went on a jog together, or on a camping trip, their joint pursuit might be enough to give rise to a duty on each to aid the other.

4. **Assumption of duty:** Once D *voluntarily begins* to render assistance to P (even if D was under no legal obligation to do so), D must *proceed with reasonable care.*

   a. **Preventing assistance by others:** D is especially likely to be found liable if she begins to render assistance, and this has the effect of *dissuading others* from helping P.

      Example: If D stops by the roadside to help P, an injured pedestrian, and other passers-by decline to help because they think the problem is taken care of, D may not then abandon the attempt to help P.

   b. **Mere promise:** Traditionally, a mere *promise* by D to help P (without actual commencement of assistance) was *not* enough to make D liable for not following through. But most modern courts would make D liable even in this situation, if P has a reliance interest.

      Example: D promises P that while P is away on a two-week trip, D will visit P's apartment every day and feed P's dog. D then forgets to do this, and the dog is seriously injured. Today, most courts (and the Third Restatement) would say that D is liable to P, because once he made the promise to render the assistance, he was required to fulfill the promise with reasonable care.

5. **Duty to control others:** If D has a duty to *control third persons*, D can be negligent for failing to exercise that control.

   a. **Special relationship:** A duty to control a third person may arise either because of a *special relationship between D and P*, or because of a *special relationship between D and the third person.*

      i. **Business open to public:** For instance, many courts now hold that any *business* open to the public must protect its patrons from wrongdoing by third parties who are on the premises.

         Example: D, a storekeeper, fails to take action when X, an obviously deranged man, comes into the store wielding a knife. (Assume that D, because of his martial arts background, could have restrained X with minimal risk to D.) X stabs P, a patron. D is liable for failing to take reasonable measures to restrain X to prevent the harm to P.

      ii. **Medical professional:** Similarly, where D is a *medical* or social-work *professional* who learns that her *patient X poses a specific danger to P*, many courts recognize a duty on D's part to warn P.

         Example: D, a psychiatrist who is treating X, learns that X plans to kill P. D could easily give P a warning of what X plans to do. D says nothing, and X kills P. A court would likely hold that D and X had a special relationship, and that that relationship imposed on D a duty to take reasonable precautions (e.g., the giving of a warning) to any person to whom he knew that X posed a danger. If the court so concluded, it would allow P's estate to recover in negligence against D. [*Tarasoff v. Regents of California*]

[1] **Danger only to patient:** On the other hand, if the medical professional only has reason to believe that the patient is dangerous to *herself* (e.g., is suicidal), then the professional has no duty to warn others (e.g., the patient's family) of that danger. And that's true even if the patient commits suicide and a close family member suffers great emotional distress as a consequence.

Example: D, a psychiatrist, is treating V, a young man of college age. V has signed a consent form relieving D of any restriction on communicating with V's mother in regards to V's emotional condition, but the form does not impose any duty on D in this respect beyond what exists at common law. Based on statements V makes in treatment, D suspects (reasonably) that V is planning to commit suicide. But because D is pre-occupied, she does not notify V's mother P of D's suspicions. V commits suicide. P suffers extreme emotional distress as the result of her son's death. P sues D for negligent infliction of emotional distress.

A court would be unlikely to hold that D had a duty to warn P of V's precarious mental state. Although D and V had a special relationship, the fact that V posed a danger only to himself would be likely to cause the court to conclude that D had no duty to anyone else regarding V's mental state.

III. EMOTIONAL DISTRESS

A. **Accompanied by physical impact:** If D causes an actual *physical impact* to P's person, D is liable not only for the physical consequences of that act but also for all of the *emotional* or mental *suffering* which flows naturally from it. Such mental-suffering or emotional-distress damages are called "parasitic" — they attach to the physical injury.

B. **Emotional distress without physical impact:** But where there has been *no physical impact* on (or threat of physical impact to) P, courts *limit* P's right to recover for emotional distress. (We are assuming the action is for negligence, not intentional infliction of emotional distress, as to which see *supra*, p. 15.)

1. **No bodily harm:** Where P not only doesn't suffer a physical impact or a threat of physical impact, but doesn't suffer any *bodily harm from* the emotional distress, courts *deny recovery* as a general rule.

Example: D narrowly misses running over P. Neither P nor anyone else is hurt. P has no physical symptoms, but is distraught for weeks. Few if any courts will allow P to recover for her emotional distress. Therefore, on the MBE you should assume that P cannot recover.

a. **Exceptions:** But many courts recognize an exception to this no-recovery rule in special circumstances.

i. **Negligent handling of corpse:** The most important exception recognized by most courts is where D *negligently handles a corpse* belonging to P's close relative; here, P may recover for pure emotional distress, even if P has not suffered bodily harm from the distress.

Example: P hires D, a funeral home, to handle the burial of P's late husband X. Due to negligence, D buries X in the grave set up for Y (an unrelated person) and vice versa. P learns of the mix-up and suffers severe emotional distress but no bodily harm. P can recover for this pure emotional distress, because of the exception recognized by most courts for negligent handling of corpses.

b. **The "at risk" plaintiff:** If P, by virtue of his exposure to a certain substance, suffers an *increased likelihood* of a particular disease, most courts say P may not recover for the purely emotional harm of being at risk.

Example: D releases toxic chemicals into the public water supply. This exposure does not cause any discernible bodily harm to P, who drinks the local water. The exposure does, however, mean that actuarially speaking, P has a greatly increased risk of throat cancer. Most courts will not allow P to recover for distress at being extra vulnerable to cancer.

i. **Strict product liability:** We're talking mainly about negligence cases in this chapter. But as in cases brought on a *strict product liability* theory, most courts similarly don't allow P to recover for the pure emotional harm of being at increased risk.

ii. **Where P suffers bodily harm:** But this rule against recovery assumes that P has suffered no physical harm. If P has suffered *some bodily harm* by exposure to a dangerous substance, then P can also recover — as a "tacked on" element of damage — damages for emotional distress at the increased risk of a more serious (and different) bodily harm, like *cancer.*

Example: P is exposed to asbestos produced and sold by D. From this exposure, he gets a mild case of asbestosis, an abnormal inflammation of the lungs that is not itself cancerous but that is considered a disease. The asbestos exposure also makes it much more likely that P will get lung cancer than if he hadn't had the exposure. But P has not so far suffered any symptoms of lung cancer.

Because P has already suffered some bodily harm (asbestosis) due to D's product, he can also recover for the emotional distress of knowing he is at increased risk of a different sort of bodily harm or disease, cancer.

c. **Intentional torts:** Remember that the general rule of "no liability for pure emotional distress" applies only to *negligent* conduct by D (or the sale of a defective product by D) — if D's wrongful conduct is *intentional* or *willful*, P may recover for purely emotional harm with no physical symptoms, by use of the tort of intentional infliction of emotional distress (IIED).

i. **Third party:** That's true even if D's intentionally tortious conduct is directed only at X, and P, a close relative who is present, suffers emotional distress as a result. See *supra*, p. 17.

Example: In front of P, D pulls a gun and threatens to shoot X to death. P, who is X's wife, suffers great emotional distress from watching the episode. P can recover from D for IIED, even if P never suffered bodily harm from the distress.

2. **Physical injury without impact:** Where D's negligent act (1) physically *endangers* P, (2) does not result in physical *impact* on P, and (3) causes P to suffer emotional distress that has *in turn caused serious bodily harm* to P, nearly all courts *allow* recovery.

Example: D, driving negligently, narrowly avoids running over P. P is so frightened that she suffers a miscarriage. P may recover for emotional distress for the miscarriage.

3. **Fear for others' safety:** If P suffers purely emotional distress (without physical impact) from D's negligence, and P suffers severe emotional distress due to fear or grief about harm to *another person* from the event, you must analyze whether P was in the "zone of danger."

a. **Zone of danger:** If P *was* in the *"zone of danger"* (i.e., *physically endangered* but not struck), nearly all courts *allow* him to recover for emotional distress due to injuries, at least where the injuries are to a *close relative*. So on the MBE, you should answer that P can recover for negligently-inflicted emotional distress where P was in the zone of danger, and a close relative of P was injured.

Example: D, driving negligently, narrowly avoids running over P, and in fact strikes P's child S. Most courts will allow P to recover for her emotional distress at seeing S injured. And that's true even if P suffers no bodily harm from the distress. Therefore, on the MBE you should answer that P can recover.

i. **D must be negligent:** But make sure that D *was in fact negligent* — if D wasn't negligent, then it's irrelevant that P was in the zone of danger, or feared for the safety of a close relative who was injured or also put in danger. The MBE examiners like to try to trick you with scenarios in which D was not negligent, but caused P, who was in the zone of danger, emotional distress at the plight of a relative; P cannot recover in this scenario.

Example: Same facts as above example, except that D was not negligent when D's car narrowly missed P and struck P's child S. P can't recover, even though she was in the zone of danger, because D did not violate any duty to P or S.

b. **Abandonment of zone requirement:** Some states — but only a *minority* — have *abandoned* the "zone of danger" requirement. In these courts, so long as P *observes* the danger or injury to X, P may recover. (Some require that X, the third person, be a close relative. Others require bodily harm from the distress.) But on the MBE, you should assume that the jurisdiction does *not* allow recovery here unless the question tells you that the jurisdiction has abandoned the zone of danger requirement.

Example: P is watching on the sidewalk (and in no danger of being struck) when D negligently runs over P's son, S. In a court which has abandoned the "zone of danger" requirement, such as California, P will be able to recover for his emotional distress at seeing his son injured, even though P himself was never in physical danger. [*Dillon v. Legg*] But on the MBE, you should assume that P cannot recover unless the question specifies that the state has abandoned the zone of danger requirement.

i. **MBE Tip:** Since the MBE examiners know that states are split on whether P can recover for pure emotional distress from the threat of injury to another, they may ask you simply to *identify* that this is an issue, without your being required to say how the issue will be decided.

Example: P, looking through her living room window, sees a speeding car driven by D hit a neighbor's child, who is riding a bicycle. P suffers a miscarriage. The correct answer to a fact pattern like this likely to be something like, "P's recovery will depend on whether the jurisdiction allows a person to recover damages from distress caused solely by witnessing another's peril or injury."

ii. **Where injured person is a stranger:** Where P suffers emotional harm by watching an injury to a *stranger*, you can be quite confident on the MBE that P *cannot recover* unless she was in the zone of danger. See Rest. 2d, §313(2). That's because, even in the minority of courts that have abandoned the zone-of-danger requirement, most require that the plaintiff be a *close relative* of the person who actually suffers the impact.

Example: P, standing on the sidewalk, sees a car driven negligently by D strike X, a pedestrian who is a stranger to P, in the middle of a crosswalk. P, horrified, rushes out into the street and tries unsuccessfully to administer CPR to X's motionless body, then watches an ambulance take the body away. P suffers nightmares and severe headaches in the ensuing months. P sues D for negligence.

On the MBE, you should answer that P cannot recover, because P was neither in the zone of danger (i.e., never believed he was about to be hit himself) nor was related to X. Even in the minority of courts abandoning the zone-of-danger requirement in some instances, most require that the plaintiff be a close relative of the person who is actually injured.

IV. PURE ECONOMIC LOSS

A. Traditional rule: Where D negligently causes physical injury or property damage to X, but only *pure economic loss* to P, the traditional rule is that P may *not* recover anything.

Example 1: A ship owned by D negligently damages a dock owned by X. P, owner of a different ship, is required to dock elsewhere and suffers extra labor and docking costs, but no physical injury. Under the traditional view, P may not recover these expenses from D, even though D was a tortfeasor vis-á-vis X. [*Barber Lines v. M/V Donau Maru*])

Example 2: D negligently causes a fire to X's factory one weekend, when no one is present. P, a worker at the factory, is laid off, and cannot get a new job for four months. Under the traditional rule, P will not be able to recover from D for his financial loss from joblessness, because he suffered only economic harm. That's true even though D would be liable in negligence to X.

1. **Rationale:** The rationale for this restrictive rule is the fear of *open-ended liability*.

B. Possible exceptions: But some courts today recognize some case-by-case exceptions to the general no-liability rule. A court is most likely to allow recovery where the following factors are all present: (1) the injury to P was relatively *foreseeable*; (2) relatively *few plaintiffs* would be permitted to sue if liability were found for pure economic loss; and (3) D's conduct is relatively *blameworthy*.

Example: D, a railroad, negligently causes a fire. P, an airline with nearby operations, is forced to close for 12 hours and loses business. *Held*, P may maintain its suit, because it was part of an "identifiable class" who D knew or had reason to know was likely to suffer such damages from its conduct. [*People Express Airlines v. Consolidated Rail Corp.*]

1. **MBE Tip:** On the MBE, you should assume that there will be no liability for pure economic damage to P unless all of the three above factors are present (which they will generally not be).
2. **Distinguish from property damage:** But don't ignore the distinction between pure "economic" loss (generally not covered) and loss due to interference with P's *tangible property*. *Property damage can* be recovered for in a negligence action, even if the damage is subtle, and is not accompanied by direct physical impact.

Example: D negligently starts a fire in his backyard, during the wintertime in a cold climate. The heat from the fire causes an ice sculpture next door, in P's backyard, to melt, hours before P is due to hold a large party. This damage is damage to property, not pure economic loss, so P can recover for it from D.

CHAPTER 9

OWNERS AND OCCUPIERS OF LAND

I. OUTSIDE THE PREMISES

A. Effect outside: There are special rules lowering a *landowner's* standard of care in some scenarios. However, these rules do not apply to conduct by the landowner that has effects *outside* of his property. Therefore, the general *"reasonable care"* standard usually applies to such effects.

1. Natural hazards: However, if a hazardous condition exists *naturally* on the land, the property owner generally has *no duty* to remove it or guard against it, even if it poses an unreasonable danger to persons outside the property. But in an urban or other thickly-settled area, courts are less likely to apply this traditional rule.

> **Example:** O allows a tree to grow in such a way that it may hit a tall truck passing on the roadway. Traditionally, O may not be held liable to the driver of the truck. But in an urban or suburban context, O might be liable.

2. Artificial hazards: Where the hazardous condition is *artificially* created, the owner has a general duty to prevent an unreasonable risk of harm to persons outside the premises.

> **Example:** D, a homeowner, negligently fails to maintain the roof of her house, so that there are many loose slates, some of which risk falling onto the public sidewalk below. P, while walking on the sidewalk, is injured by a falling slate. Since the condition (loose slates) is an artificial one, and since the accident was brought about by D's failure to use due care to avoid the risk, P can recover from D in negligence even though D is a landowner.

3. Must be unreasonable risk, as known to D: Whether the condition is natural or artificial, don't lose sight of the fact that there is *no strict liability* on the part of the owner for damage done to persons or property outside the premises. In other words, P must always *prove negligence,* which will generally mean that P must show that D *knew or should have known* of the danger. So if a reasonable person in the owner/defendant's position would not have recognized the danger, then even if the hazard is from an artificial condition the owner will not be liable when the condition produces an injury off the premises. The MBE examiners like to test this point, because it's somewhat counter-intuitive.

> **Example:** D plants a small oak tree in his side yard. 20 years later, the tree has grown large enough that a branch extends over the property of D's next-door neighbor P. The tree has become infested with insects that have damaged its strength, but a reasonable person in D's position would not have recognized the infestation or its consequence. One day the branch falls off due to weakness from the infestation, and lands on P's head as she works in her yard.
>
> D will not be liable to P. A property owner does not have strict liability for a condition on his premises that causes damage off the premises, even if the condition is an artificial one (which the one here would probably be considered to be, since D planted the tree). Since we are told that an owner in D's position wouldn't have known of the infestation, D had no reason to trim the branch or otherwise take an action that would have avoided the accident.

II. TRESPASSERS

A. General rule: As a general rule, the landowner owes *no duty to a trespasser* to make her land *safe*, to *warn* the trespasser of dangers on it, to avoid carrying on dangerous activities on it, or to protect the trespasser in any other way.

Example: P trespasses on D railroad's track. His foot gets caught, and he is run over by a train whose engineer doesn't see P. Even if the reason that P caught his foot was that D negligently maintained the roadbed, P cannot recover because D owed him no duty before discovering his presence. [*Sheehan v. St. Paul Ry. Co.*]

1. **Invitee who goes beyond scope of invitation:** Keep in mind that a person who starts out being an invitee (one who is on the premises for a business purpose; see *infra*, p. 61) or a licensee (one who has the owner's consent but not a business purpose; see *infra*, p. 60) can become a trespasser by *failing to stay within the scope of the area* in which the premises owner has invited him.

   a. **"Employees only" or "Keep out":** Thus a customer or patron who goes into an area of business premises marked "private" or "employees only" or "keep out" will be a trespasser once she does so, and the owner will no longer owe the customer any duty of reasonable care if the owner is not aware of the customer's presence or peril.

   Example: P is a customer of D, a department store. P sees a door marked, "Men's Room," which bears a sign "Employees only. Customers, please use bathroom on main floor." P enters anyway, and slips on a wet floor. A court will probably hold that although P started by being an invitee, P became a trespasser when he entered the bathroom. In that event, D will be found to have not owed P any duty of care to keep the floor non-slippery.

B. **Exceptions:** There are three main *exceptions* to the general rule that there is no duty of care to trespassers:

1. **Constant trespass on a limited area:** First, if the owner has reason to know that a *limited portion* of her land is *frequently used* by various trespassers, she must use reasonable care to make the premises safe or at least warn of dangers. This is the *"constant trespass on a limited area"* exception.

   Example: If trespassers have worn a path across a railroad, the railroad must use reasonable care, such as whistles, when traversing that crossing.

2. **Discovered trespassers:** Second, once the owner has *knowledge* that a particular person is trespassing, the owner *is* then under a duty to exercise reasonable care for the trespasser's safety. This *"discovered trespasser"* exception is *frequently tested* on the MBE.

   Example 1: A railroad's engineer must use reasonable care in stopping the train once he sees P trespassing on the tracks.

   Example 2: P is a customer at a department store operated by D. When P is about to take an escalator marked, "Not for the public," D's employee Emp spots what P is doing, and says nothing even though Emp knows that the escalator is under repair and possibility dangerous. P is injured by the mechanism under repair.

   A premises owner has the duty to warn a discovered trespasser of a peril known to the owner. Therefore, even if P is viewed as being a trespasser when he went beyond the scope of Store's invitation by going on the escalator, once D's employee Emp discovered P's pending peril, D and Emp had a duty to warn P and assist him.

3. **Children:** Finally, a landowner owes a duty of reasonable care to a trespassing *child* if all the following elements are present:

   [1] the owner *knows* that the area is one where children are *likely to trespass*;

   [2] the owner has reason to know that the condition poses an *unreasonable risk* of serious injury or death to trespassing children;

[3] the injured child either *does not discover the condition* or *does not realize the danger*, due to his youth;

[4] the *benefit* to the owner of maintaining the condition in its dangerous form is *slight* weighed against the *risk* to the children; and

[5] the owner *fails to use reasonable care* to eliminate the danger.

Note: Traditionally, some or all of these elements are summarized by saying that O is liable for maintaining an *"attractive nuisance."*

Example: O knows that children often swim in a swimming pool on O's land. One part of the pool is unexpectedly deep. It would not cost very much for O to install fencing. P, a child trespasser, walks on the bottom of the pool, panics after suddenly reaching the deep part, and drowns. O is probably liable to P on these facts.

a. **Not usually the answer on the MBE:** On the MBE, hesitate long and hard before assuming that D is liable to a trespassing child on an attractive-nuisance theory. It's more likely that the attractive-nuisance doctrine *doesn't* quite apply for some reason. *Most likely* is that the danger is *obvious* to one in the child's position, so that in fact she *did not fail to discover* the danger (and instead ignored it).

Example: D owns a vacant lot which contains a pond. D knows children often try to skate on the pond in winter. Therefore, D posts a large sign saying, "No skating on pond. Pond may not be frozen even though it appears to be." P, a bright 9-year-old, enters the property in winter, reads and understands the sign, knows the pond might not be entirely frozen, but decides to take the risk by skating. These facts mean that the requirement that the injured child not have discovered or realized the danger is not satisfied. Therefore, P will not be able to recover from D on an attractive-nuisance (or any other) theory, even if D did not use reasonable care in, say, fencing off the pond.

b. **Natural conditions:** The court is less likely to find liability to a child trespasser where the condition is a *natural* one than where it is artificial.

c. **No duty of inspection:** The child trespasser rules do not generally impose any *duty of inspection* upon O.

III. LICENSEES

A. **Definition of "licensee":** A *licensee* is a person who has the owner's *consent* to be on the property, but who does *not have a business purpose* for being there, or anything else entitling him to be on the land apart from the owner's consent.

B. **Duty to licensee:** The owner does *not* owe a licensee any duty to *inspect for unknown dangers*. On the other hand, if the owner *knows* of a dangerous condition, she must *warn* the licensee of that danger.

Example: Rear steps leading from O's house to her backyard contain a rotten wood plank. If O knows of the rotten condition, she must warn P, a licensee, if P cannot reasonably be expected to spot the danger himself. But O need not inspect the steps to make sure they are safe, even if a reasonably careful owner would do so.

C. **Social guests:** The main class of persons who qualify as licensees are *"social guests."*

Example: Even if P is invited to O's house for dinner, P is a "licensee," not an "invitee." Therefore, O must warn P of any danger actually known to O. But O need not inspect the property to make sure that dangers not already known to O are removed (even if it's negligence on O's part not to discover such dangers).

IV. INVITEES

A. **Duty to invitee:** The owner *does* owe an *invitee* a duty of *reasonable inspection to find hidden dangers*. Also, the owner must use reasonable care to take *affirmative action* to remedy a dangerous condition.

B. **Definition of "invitee":** The class of invitees today includes: (1) persons who are invited by O onto the land to conduct *business* with O; and (2) those who are invited as members of the *public* for purposes for which the land is held *open to the public*.

1. **Meaning of "open to the public":** The *"open to the public"* branch of invitees covers those who come onto the property for the purposes for which it is held open, even if these people will *not confer any economic benefit on the owner.*

   Example: P, a door-to-door sales representative, pays an unsolicited sales call on D, a storekeeper. D in fact never buys from such unsolicited callers. However, since P reasonably understood that the premises were held open to salespeople, P is an invitee.

2. **Scope of invitation:** If the visitor's use of the premises goes *beyond* the business purpose or beyond the part of the premises held open to the public, that person will change from an invitee to a licensee (if the additional use is with the owner's consent) or to a trespasser (if the additional use is not with the owner's consent).

   Example: P visits O's store to buy cigarettes. O then allows P to use a private bathroom in the back of the store not held open to the public. Even though P was an invitee when he first came into the store, he became a licensee when he went into the private bathroom with O's consent. [*Whelan v. Van Natta*]

C. **Duty of due care:** The owner owes an invitee the duty of *reasonable care.*

1. **Consequences:** This duty of reasonable care typically means the following for an owner of premises:

   a. **Duty to inspect:** The owner has a duty to *inspect* her premises for hidden dangers. O must use *reasonable care* in doing this inspecting. This is true even as to dangers that existed before O moved onto the premises.

   b. **Warning:** The giving of a *warning* will often, but not always, suffice. If O should realize that a warning will not remove the danger, then the condition must actually be remedied.

   c. **Control over third persons:** Reasonable care by O may require that she exercise *control over third persons* on her premises such as by providing *security* to prevent third persons' crimes or torts.

2. **How tested on MBE:** When the MBE examiners test you on duty to invitees, usually they *won't* require you to figure out whether D actually behaved with due care. Instead, they'll typically require you just to *identify that P is indeed an invitee*, and that because that is so, D is liable if D didn't use reasonable care to make the premises safe for that invitee.

   Example: P accompanies her father to an office building owned by D, at which the father's lawyer, L, is located. P is just along to provide transportation. While in the lobby, P trips on a recently waxed marble floor.

   If this were an MBE question, you'd be required to know that: (1) P is an invitee (she's on the premises for the general purposes for which they're held open to the public, and the fact that her father, not P, was the client of the building's tenant L would not matter); and (2) *if* D failed to use reasonable care to keep the lobby from being slippery, D will be liable. You probably *won't* have to make the determination whether D in fact failed to use reasonable care (i.e., was negligent).

a. **Obvious lack of negligence by D:** Sometimes on the MBE, it will be pretty clear that the owner has *not failed to use reasonable care* in protecting an invitee. For instance, where a customer or other *third person* for whom the owner is not vicariously liable suddenly and without warning behaves tortiously, the owner won't be liable to an invitee unless there was some way the owner should have anticipated this type of tortious conduct and counteracted it.

Example: X is an apparently-healthy and careful shopper who parks in the parking lot of D's grocery store and shops. X then leaves the store, backs up her car in the lot, and negligently strikes Ped, a pedestrian who is about to shop at the store. On these facts, D could not have premises liability — it was not a failure of due care for D not to have prevented the accident, since nothing gave D notice of the danger posed by X.

b. **Effect of warning:** MBE questions sometimes ask you whether a landowner's *warning* of a peril negates the owner's liability to an invitee if that peril comes to pass. The general answer is *"no"* — a duty to warn about a danger, and a duty to take affirmative steps to prevent the danger from causing harm, can, and often will, *co-exist* as independent forms of the duty to use reasonable care to protect invitees.

i. **Torts by third persons:** This principle is sometimes tested by scenarios in which a third person commits a tort against P while on D's premises. Recall (*supra*, p. 61) that one of the ways a premises owner can fail to render due care to protect an invitee is by failing to provide reasonable security against the torts of third persons that the owner should anticipate. Generally, this duty to protect is *not negated* by the fact that the owner has warned its invitees against the kind of third-party tort in question.

Example: D runs a convenience store that is open 24 hours per day, in an area of town where there are frequent muggings. D posts a sign in the lot, "Warning, there are often thieves in the parking lot; walk here at your own risk." P, a customer, is mugged in the lot at night. The fact that D gave this warning doesn't negate D's obligation to supply a higher level of security (e.g., better lights or a guard) if it would have been reasonable for an owner or operator in D's position to supply that greater security.

D. **Firefighters and other public-safety personnel:** Under the common-law *"firefighters' rule," firefighters, police officers* and other *public-safety officials* who come onto private property in the performance of their duties are treated as *mere licensees*, so that the owner does not owe them a duty to inspect the premises or to make the premises reasonably safe. The most common application of the common-law doctrine is that a firefighter who is injured while fighting a blaze cannot recover from the owner of the premises, *even if the owner's negligence caused the fire*. Most states continue to apply the rule to this core fire- or police-emergency scenario.

For more about the firefighters' rule, see *supra*, p. 46.

V. LIABILITY OF LESSORS AND LESSEES

A. **Lessee:** A *tenant* is treated *as if she were the owner* — all the rules of owner liability above apply to her.

B. **Lessors:** In general, a *lessor* is *not* liable in tort once she transfers possession to the lessee. However, there are a number of exceptions to this general rule:

1. **Known to lessor, unknown to lessee:** The lessor will be liable to the lessee (and to the lessee's invitees and licensees) for any dangers existing at the start of the lease, which the lessor *knows or should know about*, and which the lessee has no reason to know about. (This usually does not impose on the lessor a duty to *inspect* the premises at the start of the lease.)

2. **Open to public:** If the lessor has reason to believe that the lessee will hold the premises *open to the public*, the lessor has an affirmative duty to *inspect* the premises to find and repair dangers before the lease starts.

3. **Common areas:** The lessor has a general duty to use reasonable care to make *common areas* (e.g., the lobby or stairwells of an apartment building) safe.

4. **Lessor contracts to repair:** If the lessor *contracts*, as part of the lease, to keep the premises in good repair, most courts hold that the landlord's breach of this covenant to repair gives a tort claim to anyone injured. However, P must show that D failed to use reasonable care in performing — it is not enough to show that D breached the contract.

5. **Negligent repairs:** The landlord may incur liability even without a contractual repair obligation if she *begins* to make repairs, and either performs them unreasonably, or fails to finish them. This is clearly true where the landlord worsens the danger by performing the repair negligently. Courts are split about what happens where the landlord starts the repair, then abandons it, without worsening the danger.

VI. VENDORS

A. **Vendor's liability:** Generally, a *seller* of land is released from tort liability to persons on the property once he has turned over the property to the buyer. But there are exceptions. All these exceptions involve *artificial conditions* that exist on the day of the sale, as to which the seller *knew or should have known* of the danger. The exceptions can apply to a person injured either on the property or outside it. We consider the on-the-property and outside-the-property scenarios separately.

1. **Danger to one on the property:** First, let's assume that the accident happens to one *on the property* (e.g., a tenant of the new buyer). You only have to worry about an exception (i.e., post-closing liability of seller to persons on the property) if the seller *knew or should have known* of the condition and its dangerousness. If that condition is satisfied, then the duration of the seller's post-closing liability varies depending on whether the seller actively *concealed* the danger:

   a. **Seller actively conceals:** If the seller *actively concealed* the condition, her liability persists after sale until the buyer *actually discovers* the condition and has a reasonable opportunity to correct it (whether the buyer takes the opportunity or not). So here, there's no cutoff if the buyer negligently fails to discover (or fix) the problem.

   Example: S sells a house to B on April 1. Prior to the sale date, S is aware of a rotten step in the back, and puts wood-colored putty over the rot rather than fix it. Assume that B should have immediately, after closing, inspected the step and would have discovered the rot had she done such an inspection. However, B never inspects or fixes the step. On Nov. 1, B rents to T. T falls through the step. S will be liable, because: (1) he actively concealed the condition; and therefore (2) his liability for negligence to persons on the land persisted until B actually learned of the danger (not merely "should have learned"), which had not happened by the time of the accident.

   b. **Seller doesn't conceal:** If the seller *didn't actively conceal* the condition, the seller's liability continues only until the buyer "has had *reasonable opportunity to discover*" the condition and correct it. In other words here, the seller's liability is *cut off* as soon as the buyer *should have* discovered and fixed the problem, even if the buyer negligently failed to actually discover it.

Example: Same basic facts as above example. Now, however, assume that S knew of the danger but didn't putty it over or actively try to prevent B from learning of it (e.g., S didn't give B false assurances of the step's safe condition). For any accident after the date on which B should have learned (but didn't) of the condition prior to T's accident, S won't be liable to T.

As to both concealment and non-concealment, see Rest. 2d, §353.

2. **Danger to one outside the property:** Essentially the same rules apply to a seller's post-closing liability to one *outside the property*, except that the seller has longer liability not only for active concealment but for having *created* the artificial condition. Rest. 2d, §373. Thus:

   a. **Seller conceals or creates:** If the seller *actively concealed* the condition, *or originally created* the condition, her liability persists after sale until the buyer actually discovers the condition and has a reasonable opportunity to correct it (whether the buyer takes the opportunity or not). So here, there's no cut-off if the buyer negligently fails to discover (or fix) the problem.

   Example: In 2007, S puts a new roof on his house. S should have known that several slates were dangerously loose, and risked falling on passersby on the public sidewalk running next to and near the house. S sells the property to B on Feb. 1, 2008. S makes no mention to B of the roof's condition, and doesn't attempt to conceal the existence of the loose slates. B never inspects or discovers the loose slates, though it is negligence for B not to inspect and thus discover the problem. On Sept. 1, 2008, a slate falls off and injures P, a passerby on the sidewalk.

   S is liable to P, because: (1) S created the hazardous condition; and (2) S therefore had liability until B actually discovered the condition and had an opportunity to fix it (even though it was negligent of B not to have discovered it prior to P's accident). B would also be liable to P in this situation, for having failed to use reasonable care to discover and fix dangers to persons outside the property.

   b. **Seller doesn't conceal or create:** If the seller *neither* actively concealed the condition nor created it, the seller's liability continues only until the buyer "has had *reasonable opportunity to discover*" the condition and correct it. In other words, here the seller's liability is cut off as soon as the buyer should have discovered and fixed the problem, even if the buyer negligently failed to even discover it.

As to liability to one outside the property, see Rest. 2d, §373.

CHAPTER 10

DAMAGES

I. PERSONAL INJURY DAMAGES GENERALLY

A. **Actual injury required:** In any action based on negligence, the existence of *actual injury* is required. Unlike intentional tort actions, *nominal* damages may *not* be awarded.

1. **Physical injury required:** Furthermore, P must usually show that he suffered some kind of *physical* harm.

   Example: In a negligence action, P may generally not recover where he sustained only emotional distress, with no physical impact and no physical symptoms (though there are exceptions, such as where P witnesses harm to a close relative). See *supra*, p. 54.

2. **Elements of damages:** But once physical harm has been proven, a *variety of damages* may be recovered by P. These include:

   a. **Direct loss:** The value of any direct loss of bodily functions.

      Example: $500,000 compensation for the loss of a leg.

   b. **Economic loss:** Out-of-pocket *economic losses* stemming from the injury.

      Examples: Medical expenses, lost earnings, household attendant.

   c. **Pain and suffering:** *Pain and suffering* damages.

   d. **Hedonistic damages:** Damages for loss of the ability to *enjoy* one's previous life.

      Example: Compensation for loss of the ability to walk, even if loss of that ability has no economic consequences.

B. **Future damages:** P brings only *one action* for a particular accident, and recovers in that action not only for past damages, but also for likely *future* damages.

   1. **Present value:** When P is recovering future damages, courts generally instruct the jury to award P only the *"present value"* of these losses.

C. **Mitigation:** P has a *"duty to mitigate."* That is, P cannot recover for any harm which, by exercise of reasonable care, he could have *avoided.* In particular, P cannot recover for any harm which would have been avoided had P promptly sought *adequate medical care.*

II. PUNITIVE DAMAGES

A. **Punitive damages generally:** Punitive damages can be awarded to penalize a defendant whose conduct is particularly *outrageous.*

   1. **Negligence cases:** In cases of negligence (as opposed to intentional torts), punitive damages are usually awarded *only* where D's conduct was *"reckless"* or *"willful and wanton."* You will rarely see an MBE negligence fact pattern where punitive damages are appropriate.

      a. **Product liability suits:** Punitive damages are also frequently awarded in *product liability suits*, if P shows that D knew its product was defective, or recklessly disregarded the risk of a defect.

CHAPTER 11

DEFENSES IN NEGLIGENCE ACTIONS

I. CONTRIBUTORY NEGLIGENCE

A. **General rule:** Courts used to apply the doctrine of *contributory negligence.* The doctrine provided that a plaintiff who was negligent, and whose negligence contributed proximately to his injuries, was *totally barred from recovery.*

   Example: P, while crossing the street, fails to pay attention. D, travelling at a high rate of speed while drunk, hits and kills P. Had P behaved carefully, he would have been able to get out of the way. Even though D's negligence is much greater than P's, P would be totally barred from recovery because of his contributory negligence, if the doctrine applied.

1. **Not applicable on the MBE:** Nearly all states have *abolished* contributory negligence in favor of comparative negligence (see *infra*, p. 66.) The instructions to the MBE tell you to assume that comparative negligence, rather than contributory negligence, is in force unless the question specifies otherwise. The question will very rarely so specify. So *don't apply contributory negligence* (including "*contributory negligence per se,*" where P violates a statute such as a safety statute) unless the question tells you to do so.

II. COMPARATIVE NEGLIGENCE

A. **Definition:** A *"comparative-negligence"* system rejects the all-or-nothing approach of contributory negligence. It instead attempts to divide liability between P and D in proportion to their *relative degrees of fault.* P is not barred from recovery by his negligence or other fault, but his recovery is *reduced by a proportion* equal to the ratio between his own negligence and the total negligence contributing to the accident.

Example: P suffers damages of $100,000. A jury finds that P was 30% negligent and D was 70% negligent. P will recover, under a comparative-negligence system, $70,000 — $100,000 minus 30% of $100,000.

1. **Commonly adopted:** Nearly all states (46) have adopted some form of comparative negligence.

2. **Default rule on MBE:** The MBE instructions tell you to *assume that comparative negligence is in force* unless the particular question specifies otherwise. The question will rarely specify otherwise, so *always assume that comparative negligence applies.*

B. **"Pure" comparative negligence:** In a *"pure"* comparative-negligence system, P may recover *no matter how high P's percentage of fault is* relative to the fault of P and all Ds together.

Example: Car accident involving P's car, D1's car and D2's car. Only P sustains damages, equal to $1 million. A jury finds that P was 60% responsible, D1 30% and D2 10%. In a pure comparative-negligence jurisdiction that also applies traditional joint-and-several liability (*supra*, p. 47), P may recover $400,000 from D1 or $400,000 from D2. In other words, the fact that P's proportion of fault was greater than 50% doesn't matter.

1. **MBE:** The instructions to the MBE tell you to assume that *"pure"* comparative negligence is in force. Therefore, on the above example, on the MBE you'd say that P can recover even though she bore more than 50% of the overall responsibility or fault.

C. **Multiple parties:** On the MBE, principles of comparative negligence will often interact with the fact that there are multiple defendants.

1. **All parties before court:** If all defendants are *joined in the same lawsuit*, the solution is simple: only the negligence due directly to P is deducted from his recovery.

Example: P sues D1 and D2, each of whom is capable of satisfying any judgment. The trier of fact determines that counting all negligence by all parties, P is 20% negligent, D1 is 50% negligent, and D2 is 30% negligent. P has $1 million in damages. P will recover 80% of his damages, or $800,000, which the court will allocate 5/8's to D1 and 3/8's to D2.

2. **Not all parties before court:** If *not all* defendants are before the court, the issue is whether the defendant(s) before the court, who is/are found to be only partly responsible for P's loss, must pay for the whole loss aside from that caused by P's own fault.

a. **MBE approach:** On the MBE, you should as noted assume that joint-and-several liability applies, unless the question specifies otherwise (which it usually won't). If the default joint-and-several-liability assumption applies, any defendant who is before the court (i.e., against whom there has been a judgment) will be responsible for paying the *entire judgment* to P (but may then seek contribution or indemnity from the absent defendant(s) in a separate action).

Example: P's accident is caused by the negligence of both D and X. P sues D, but can't find or sue X. The jury finds that P was 20% responsible; D 30% responsible; and X 50% responsible. P's damages total $1 million. Under traditional "joint-and-several liability" rules, generally applicable on the MBE, P would be able to collect this full $800,000 from D. D would then have to sue X in a separate contribution action for 5/8s of the $800,000.

D. MBE questions on whether P "prevails": In an MBE question in which P behaves negligently, the question may ask you whether P *"prevails."* Even if P's recovery will be reduced on account of comparative negligence, you should answer "yes" if P would recover *anything at all.* In other words, a plaintiff whose recovery is reduced by comparative fault but not eliminated should be deemed to have "prevailed."

E. Seat belt defense: The *"seat belt defense"* is increasingly *accepted* in comparative-negligence jurisdictions. In this defense, D argues that P's injuries from a car accident could have been reduced or entirely avoided had P worn a seat belt. In a court accepting this defense, P's damages will be reduced to reflect the portion of damages that would have been avoided had P worn a belt.

F. Imputed comparative negligence: Occasionally, the comparative fault of one person (call her *A*) may by *imputed to another* (*B*), so as to reduce *B*'s recovery.

1. **"Both ways" rule:** But under the so-called *"both ways" rule,* this imputation will happen *only* if *B* would be vicariously liable (see *infra*, p. 71) for *A*'s torts. As the Third Restatement puts it, "The negligence of another person is *imputed* to a plaintiff *whenever the negligence of the other person would have been imputed had the plaintiff been a defendant[.]*" Rest. 3d (Apport.), §5.

   a. **Employer/employee:** This means that if suit is brought by an *employer* for damages arising out of an accident involving the employer's *employee*, any contributory fault by the employee will reduce the plaintiff employer's recovery.

   Example: Company hires Worker to drive a delivery truck for Company's business. (Assume that Company is not negligent in selecting or training Worker for this role.) Worker has a collision with a car driven by Dave, which damages Company's truck. Company sues Dave for the damage to the truck. If Worker was negligent in driving the truck, this negligence will be imputed to Company under the "both ways" rule. That's because, if Company were the defendant in a suit by Dave, Company would have been vicariously liable for Worker's negligence under the respondeat superior doctrine. (See Rest. 3d (Apport.), §5, Illustr. 1, reaching this conclusion on exactly these facts.) Therefore, in a comparative-negligence jurisdiction, Company's recovery will be reduced by the percentage of fault attributable to Worker.

   b. **Not attributed from parent to child:** On the MBE, the "both ways" rule may apply to a situation in which a *child is the plaintiff*, the child's parent has contributed to the accident (e.g., by a *failure to supervise*) and some third party has also been negligent. At least where intra-family immunity has been abolished (as the question will probably stipulate; see *infra*, p. 71), the both-ways rule means that any fault attributable to the child's parents *won't reduce the child's recovery against the third person.*

   Example 1: Kid, riding in a car driven by his father Dad, is injured when the car collides with a car driven negligently by Drive. Kid suffers $10,000 of injuries. Kid was not properly seat-belted. If he had been, he would have had only $5,000 of injuries. Dad's failure to fasten the seat belt violated a statute designed to prevent or minimize just this sort of injury. Kid sues Drive.

Kid can recover all $10,000 of damage from Drive. The recovery won't be reduced by Dad's negligence per se in failing to fasten Kid's seat belt. That's because: (1) Dad's fault won't be attributed to Kid (that's the prevailing rule today); and (2) therefore Dad and Drive are each tortfeasors, and are jointly and severally liable. If Drive has to pay for more than his percentage of fault (computed by taking as the numerator Drive's fault and the denominator Drive's plus Dad's fault), Drive will be able to get contribution from Dad.

Example 2: Kid is injured in a playground accident, due in part to Guard's failure to supervise rough playing between Kid and Ted, another child. The accident was also due in part to a negligent failure of supervision by Dad, Kid's father, who was also present. Kid has suffered $10,000 in damages, and sues Guard for this sum.

Kid can collect the entire $10,000 from Guard, without reduction for any percentage of fault due to Dad. That's because: (1) Dad would not be vicariously liable for Kid's negligence if Kid were a defendant in an action brought by Ted (since parents are not vicariously liable for their children's torts; see *supra*, p. 31); (2) consequently, under the "both ways" rule, Dad's fault won't be attributed to Kid, and can't reduce Kid's recovery against either Guard or Dad; and (3) therefore, Dad and Guard are jointly and severally liable, and Guard can be required to pay the whole amount. (Guard could then seek contribution from Dad.)

III. ASSUMPTION OF RISK

A. Definition: A plaintiff is said to have *assumed the risk* of certain harm if she has *voluntarily consented* to take her chances that harm will occur. Where such an assumption is shown, the plaintiff is, at common law, completely barred from recovery.

B. Express assumption: If P *explicitly* agrees with D, in advance of any harm, that P will not hold D liable for certain harm, P is said to have *"expressly"* assumed the risk of that harm. An express assumption of risk (also called a *"contractual limitation of liability")* is generally *enforceable*, in which case it will completely bar P from recovery.

Example: P wants to go bungee jumping at D's amusement park. P signs a release given to him by D in which P agrees to "assume all risk of injury" that may result from the bungee jumping. Assuming that none of the exceptions to express-assumption-of-risk (see below) applies, if P is injured he will not be able to sue D, because he has expressly assumed the risk.

1. Exceptions: There are three important *exceptions* to the general enforceability of express agreements to assume risk:

- ❑ first, when the party protected by the clause (typically the defendant) either *intentionally causes* the harm, or else brings about the harm by acting in a *reckless or grossly negligent* way;
- ❑ second, when the *bargaining power* of the party protected by the clause is *grossly greater* than that of the other party, typically a status the court finds to exist only when the good or service being offered is *"essential"* (e.g., the services of public carriers or public utilities);
- ❑ finally, where the court concludes that there is some *overriding public interest* which demands that the court refuse to enforce the exculpatory clause. (Typically, this category overlaps with the above "unequal bargaining power because the good or service is essential" category.)

[*Seigneur v. National Fitness Institute, Inc.*]

a. **Private companies:** Where a good or service is offered by a relatively *unregulated private company,* and there are a *number of competitors* offering the plaintiff substantially the same good or service, the court will typically find that an exculpatory clause in the contract should be *enforced* to bar claims for negligence. That's because in this situation, generally none of the three exceptions discussed above will be found applicable.

Example: P signs a contract with D (the operator of a chain of fitness clubs), in which P agrees that D "shall not be liable to me for any injuries to my person or property[.]" P is injured while working out, and sues. *Held,* for D: None of the above exceptions to the enforceability of express assumptions of risk applies, so P is deemed to have assumed the risk of injury. [*Seigneur v. National Fitness Institute, Inc.*]

C. **Implied assumption of risk:** Even if P never makes an actual agreement with D whereby P assumes the risk, P may be held to have assumed certain risks *by her conduct.* Here, the assumption of risk is said to be *"implied."*

1. **Merely reduces recovery:** In a comparative-negligence jurisdiction (which is the default on the MBE), implied assumption of risk, if it's found to exist at all, will *merely reduce, not eliminate,* P's recovery.

2. **Other requirements:** Furthermore, for P to be found to have impliedly assumed a risk (so that P's recovery will be reduced), D must show that P: (1) *knew of the risk in question*; and (2) *voluntarily consented* to bear that risk herself. We consider each of these requirements below.

Example: D owns a baseball team. D posts big signs at the gates warning of the danger of foul balls. P has attended many games, and in each game buys a seat right behind home plate, a place where she and all other fans know many foul balls are hit. If P is hit by a foul ball, her recovery will almost certainly be reduced by her implied assumption of the risk of being so hit. That's because she knew of the risk in question, and voluntarily consented to bear it (by selecting a seat that posed the risk rather than one that was further away and thus posed much less of a risk). But if D was found to be negligent in not screening the area from foul balls (and it's not clear whether D would be so found, considering that many fans like unscreened areas because they think a chance to catch a foul ball is worth the risk of being hit), then P would still be able to recover a reduced amount compared with a no-assumption-of-risk scenario.

3. **Knowledge of risk:** The requirement that P be shown to have *known* about the risk is *strictly construed.*

a. **Risk that was actually known:** For instance, the risk must be one which was *actually* known to P, not merely one which *"ought to have been"* known to her.

i. **Particular risk:** Furthermore, P must have actually known of the *particular type of risk that eventuated,* not some other vaguely-similar risk. So, for instance, in the case of an argument by D that P voluntarily assumed the risk of an absent safety precaution, D must show that P actually knew that the precaution was missing, as well as knew of the specific risk that eventuated.

Example 1: P, a young woman, agrees to go for a pleasure drive with D, a 21-year-old man. D asks P whether she wants him to drive fast on a "roller coaster" road. She says yes. P does not realize that D is a very inexperienced driver, even as compared with other 21-year-old drivers. D drives at 89 mph, and loses control as the car goes over a bump, resulting in a crash into a side guardrail that a more experienced driver would probably not have had even at high speed. The crash causes P to become a quadriplegic.

P's recovery will probably not be reduced at all by virtue of her consent. That is, P will not be found to have impliedly assumed the risk of such a crash. By her consent, P may have implicitly assumed certain risks, such as the risk of hitting her head against the roof of the car during a bump. But she did not know of, or consent to, the specific risk of D's being an inexperienced driver who might lose control under circumstances in which another driver would not. Cf. Rest. 2d, §496C, Illustr. 7.

Example 2: P eats at D, an ethnic restaurant that warns on the menu that certain dishes are "extremely spicy — may cause upset stomach." P knowingly orders a chicken item that has been marked this way on the menu. P later suffers severe gastrointestinal symptoms, and sues D for negligence. P shows evidence that P's illness was due to bacterial contamination in all chicken served by D that night.

P will not be deemed to have impliedly assumed the risk of gastrointestinal symptoms here — P may have assumed the risk of upset stomach from spicy foods, but not upset stomach from bacterial contamination.

4. **Voluntary assumption:** The requirement that P consented *voluntarily* is also strictly construed in implied-assumption scenarios.

   a. **Duress:** For instance, there is no assumption of the risk if D's conduct left P with *no reasonable choice* but to encounter a known danger.

   Example: P rents a room in a boarding house from D. P has to use a common bathroom at the end of a hallway. After the lease starts, a hole in the floor leading to the bathroom develops, and D negligently fails to fix it. P knows about the hole, but nonetheless steps in it while going to the bathroom. P will not be barred from recovery by an implied assumption of risk, because D's conduct left P with no reasonable alternative but to walk down the hallway to get to the bathroom.

   b. **Public accommodation:** Where the accident takes place in a place of *public accommodation* (e.g., a *store*), the court is unlikely to conclude that P impliedly assumed the risk of a negligently-caused accident — there are a limited number of stores or other places of accommodation, so even if P was aware of the risk, this choice is unlikely to have been truly voluntary.

   Example: Store, a convenience store, has a parking lot where muggings have often occurred. Store places a sign on the lot saying, "Use this lot at your own risk. Muggings often occur in this lot." P reads the sign, but parks anyway, and is assaulted by X on the way to the inside of Store. P sues Store for negligence. If Store could easily have provided better security, it's very unlikely that P's recovery will be reduced by virtue of implied assumption of risk — P's consent to the risk of being assaulted wasn't truly voluntary, since P had limited places in which to shop.

   c. **Choice not created by D:** Where it is *not D's fault* that P has no reasonable choice except to expose herself to the risk, the defense *will* apply.

   Example: P is injured and needs immediate medical help. He asks D — who had nothing to do with the injury — to drive him to the hospital, knowing that D's car has bad brakes. P assumes the risk of injury due to an accident caused by the bad brakes, because P's dilemma is not the result of D's wrongdoing.

5. **MBE tip:** Implied assumption of risk (i.e., knowing assumption of the risk by P, without an express contractual limitation-of-liability agreement) will *almost never supply the correct answer* on the MBE. The doctrine is far more likely to be an incorrect "distractor" choice.

IV. IMMUNITIES

A. Intra-family immunity: The common law recognizes two *immunities* in the family relationship: between *spouses*, and between *parent and child.*

1. **Husband and wife:** At common law, inter-spousal immunity prevented suits by one spouse against the other for personal injury. But most courts have abolished this immunity.

    Examples: If W is injured while a passenger in a car driven negligently by H, W cannot sue H. If H intentionally strikes W, at common law W could not sue for battery.

2. **Parent and child:** At common law, there is an immunity that bars suit by a *child against his parents* or vice versa. Again, many (though not most) states have abolished this immunity, and others have limited it.

3. **MBE Tip:** On the MBE, if the possibility of a suit between spouses or between parent and child would be relevant to the outcome of the question, the examiners will usually tell you that intra-family immunities have been *abolished.* If so, then in the MBE fact pattern one spouse may sue the other, and a child may (via a guardian) sue a parent. Also, a parent's comparative negligence will not be attributed to the child if the child is suing a third person who, together with the parent, caused the child's injury; see *supra*, p. 67.

B. Governmental immunity: At common law, there is *"sovereign immunity,"* preventing anyone from suing the *government.*

1. **MBE tip:** On the MBE, you will rarely have to worry about sovereign immunity.

CHAPTER 12

VICARIOUS LIABILITY

I. EMPLOYER-EMPLOYEE RELATIONSHIP

A. ***Respondeat superior* doctrine:** If an employee commits a tort during the *"scope of his employment,"* his employer will be *liable* (jointly with the employee). This is the rule of *"respondeat superior."*

1. **Applies to all torts:** The doctrine applies to *all* torts, including intentional ones and those in which strict liability exists, provided that the tort occurred during the scope of the employee's employment.

B. Who is an "employee": *Respondeat superior* is applied to all cases involving *"employees,"* but *not* to most cases involving *"independent contractors."* You must therefore distinguish between these two.

1. **Distinction:** The main idea is that an employee is one who works *subject to the close control* of the person who has hired him. An independent contractor, by contrast, although hired to produce a certain result, is not subject to the close control of the person doing the hiring.

    a. **Physical details:** The "control" required to make a person an employee rather than an independent contractor is usually held to be control over the *physical details* of the work, not just the general manner in which the work is turned out.

    Example: An individual "newspaper carrier" is likely to be an independent contractor, not an employee, because the newspaper usually controls only the general terms of employment — such as the time by which the deliveries must take place — not the physical details, such as whether the work should be done by bike or automobile.

C. Scope of employment: *Respondeat superior* applies only if the employee was acting *"within the scope of his employment"* when the tort occurred. The tort is within the scope of employment if the tortfeasor was acting with an *intent to further his employer's business purpose*, even if the means he chose were indirect, unwise or even forbidden.

1. **Forbidden acts:** Even if the act done was *expressly forbidden* by the employer, it will be "within the scope of employment" if done in furtherance of the employment.

   Example: D, a gun dealer, expressly orders his clerk never to load a gun while showing it to a customer. The clerk ignores this rule and loads the gun, the gun goes off and the customer is hurt. D will be liable because the loading, though forbidden, was done in furtherance of the employer's business purposes, i.e., sale of guns.

2. **Intentional torts:** The fact that the tort is an *intentional* one does not relieve the employer of liability.

   Example: X is a bill collector for D. X commits assault, battery and false imprisonment on P in attempting to collect a debt. D will be liable.

   a. **Personal motives:** But if the employee acts solely from *personal motives*, the employer will generally not be liable.

   Example: Nurse, an employee of D hospital, has always hated P because of a prior fight. While P is in the hospital, Nurse kills P. D will not be liable, because Nurse has acted from personal motives, not in an attempt to further D's business.

D. Torts by non-employees (e.g., guests and customers): The MBE examiners will sometimes try to trap you into thinking that a tort by a *customer* of the defendant triggers vicarious liability on the defendant's part. Don't be fooled. Vicarious liability occurs only when there is an employment relationship (or, occasionally, an independent contractor relationship; see p. 72) between the defendant and the tortfeasor. So a defendant can't be vicariously liable for the torts of a customer, or of some *non-employee* on the defendant's premises. (The defendant may be liable for not having adequate security, or for having negligently allowed the tortfeasor to come on the premises, but that's direct liability, not vicarious liability.)

Example: While P is shopping at a department store owned by StoreCo, P is assaulted by X, a person who purports to be a customer. StoreCo won't be vicariously liable for X's tort; only if StoreCo is found to have been directly negligent (e.g., by not having adequate security) will StoreCo be liable to P.

II. INDEPENDENT CONTRACTORS

A. No general liability: One who hires an *independent contractor* is *not* generally liable for the torts of that person.

B. Exceptions: However, there are two important *exceptions* to the rule that an employer is not liable for the torts of her independent contractor:

1. **Employer's own liability:** First, if the employer is *herself* negligent in her own dealings with the independent contractor, this can give rise to employer liability.

   Example: D knows that the work to be done is hazardous if not done with special precautions. She chooses a contractor, X, who she should know will probably not do the work safely. X, performing the work negligently, injures P. D is liable for the consequences, because of her own negligence in selecting X.

2. **Non-delegable duty:** Second, there are some duties of care that are deemed so important that the delegator is liable for negligence by an independent contractor the delegator hires, even if the delegator used all due care in selecting that particular contractor. These are called "*non-delegable duties*." Here are some types of non-delegable duties:

   [1] The work is likely to involve a "*peculiar risk of physical harm* to others unless special precautions are taken." Rest. 2d, §416.

   Example 1: O owns a parcel of land in a city, and hires Contractor, a reputable contractor with a good safety record, to build a building on it. Contractor fails to put netting around the building as a reasonable contractor would do. A piece of construction material falls off, injuring a passerby on the city sidewalk below. Because of the peculiar danger from falling construction materials, O will be vicariously liable for Contractor's failure to use reasonable care in putting up the netting.

   Example 2: A driver cannot delegate the duty to keep her brakes in good working order, because of the peculiar risk of harm to third persons if the work is not carefully done.

   [2] The work is done in a *"public place,"* such as a road, sidewalk, park, etc. Rest. 2d, §§417; 418.

   Example: City hires Contractor to repair a public street. Contractor digs a hole in the street, and fails to use reasonable care in putting up a barrier around the hole. P drives his car into the hole at night. City will be liable for Contractor's negligence.

   [3] The person hiring the contractor is a *landowner*, who owes the plaintiff a duty to use reasonable care to keep the premises safe. (Here, the owner has the same duty as if she did the work herself or via an employee, instead of via an independent contractor.) Rest. 2d, §§422, 425

   Example: Store, a department store, hires Contractor to renovate its premises, while the store remains open. Contractor negligently renovates a display cabinet. The cabinet falls on the head of Cust, a customer. Store will be vicariously liable for Contractor's negligence, since Store had a duty to Cust to keep the premises reasonably safe (see *supra*, p. 52), and this duty was non-delegable on account of Store's status as a landowner.

CHAPTER 13

STRICT LIABILITY

I. STRICT LIABILITY GENERALLY

A. **Generally:** Apart from the special situation of defective products (see *infra*, p. 80), there are two contexts in which D can have "*strict liability*" — that is, liability regardless of D's intent and regardless of whether D was negligent. We examine those contexts here. They are:

- strict liability for keeping *wild or other dangerous animals*; and
- strict liability for carrying out *abnormally dangerous* (or "*ultrahazardous*") *activities*.

II. WILD OR DANGEROUS ANIMALS

A. **Trespassing animals:** In most states, the owner of livestock or other animals is liable for property damage caused by them if they *trespass* on another's land. This liability is "strict" — even though the owner exercises utmost care to prevent the animals from escaping, he is liable if they do escape and trespass. And this liability is true even if the animal is not wild or dangerous to humans (e.g., cattle or horses).

B. Non-trespass liability: A person is also strictly liable for non-trespass damage done by any *"dangerous animal"* he keeps.

1. Wild animals: A person who keeps a *"wild"* animal is strictly liable for all damage done by it, as long as the damage results from a *"dangerous propensity"* that is *typical of the species in question.*

Example: D keeps a lion cub, which has never shown any violent tendencies. One day, the cub runs out on the street and attacks P. Even if D used all possible care to prevent the cub from escaping, he is liable for P's injuries, because lions are wild animals, and the damage resulted from a dangerous propensity typical of lions, that they can attack without warning.

a. Fear of humans is factor: If you have to decide on the MBE whether a wild animal's "dangerous propensities" caused the damage in question, the fact that the *average person fears animals of that species* is part of what makes the animal dangerous. So don't assume that a defanged, declawed, or generally-docile animal that is part of a wild species hasn't caused the damage, if the damage stems from the *plaintiff's panic* over the animal's presence.

Example: D keeps a very tame bear in his backyard. Without negligence by D, the bear escapes, and walks into P's backyard 1/2 mile away. P, who is barbecuing, is so frightened by the bear that he suffers a fatal heart attack. The bear would not have attacked or otherwise harmed P. D is nonetheless strictly liable for P's death, because humans' fear of unrestrained bears is part of what makes bears a dangerous species.

b. Injury from factor that is not part of species' dangerousness: On the other hand, if the accident or injury occurs on account of a factor that is *unrelated* to the "*dangerous propensities*" that are typical of the species in question, then there will *not* be strict liability.

Example: D is a retired animal trainer who keeps a small tame bear that previously appeared with him as part of D's circus act. The bear is old, slow-moving, almost blind, and the size of a small dog. D keeps the bear in the fenced yard alongside his house. P is a thirteen-year-old girl who delivers newspapers to D. One day, P comes to D's home to collect for the past week's deliveries. Since she knows the bear, P opens the gate and calls the animal so that she can pet him. The bear bounds toward the place from which the sound has come, but because he is almost blind, he bumps into P. P falls to the ground, fracturing her ankle.

P will not be able to recover against D in strict liability. Strict liability is imposed on the keeper of a wild animal, but only for harm which proximately results from a dangerous propensity that is characteristic of wild animals of that particular class. Rest. 2d, §507(2). Bears are dangerous because they bite or attack. The risk that they may clumsily knock someone over is not one which makes them more dangerous than a dog or other domestic animal, so strict liability does not apply in this scenario.

2. Domestic animals: Injuries caused by a *"domestic"* animal such as a cat, dog, cow, pig, etc., do *not* give rise to strict liability unless the owner *knows* or has *reason to know* of the particular animal's dangerous characteristics.

Example: D keeps a dog in the backyard. The dog escapes, and bites P, the mail carrier, in the street in front of D's house. If the dog has never attempted to bite anyone before, D is not subject to strict liability, since dogs are a domesticated rather than wild species. But if D knew or had reason to know that the dog sometimes attacks people, he would be strictly liable.

III. ABNORMALLY DANGEROUS ACTIVITIES

A. General rule: A person is *strictly liable* for any damage which occurs while he is conducting an *"abnormally dangerous"* activity (sometimes called an *"ultrahazardous"* activity).

1. **Six factors:** There are *six factors* that make it more likely that an activity is "abnormally dangerous":

   [1] there is a *high degree of risk* of some harm to others;

   [2] the harm that results is likely to be *serious*;

   [3] the risk *cannot be eliminated* by the exercise of reasonable care;

   [4] the activity is *not common*;

   [5] the activity is not *appropriate* for the place where it is carried on; and

   [6] the danger outweighs the activity's *value* to the *community*.

   Example: D, a construction contractor, carries out blasting operations with dynamite, to excavate a foundation. D uses utmost care. However, a piece of rock is thrown out of the site during an explosion, striking P, a pedestrian, on the street. Blasting is an abnormally dangerous activity, in part because it cannot be conducted with guaranteed safety. Therefore, D will be strictly liable for the injury to P.

B. Examples: Here are some types of activities that are generally held to be abnormally dangerous:

[a] Nuclear reactor: Operation of a *nuclear reactor*;

[b] Explosives: The use or storage of *explosives* (see above example);

[c] Crop dusting: The conducting of *crop dusting* or spraying with pesticides.

1. **MBE Tip:** On the MBE, the ultrahazardous activities you're most likely to see are operation of a *nuclear power plant* and the manufacture or use of *explosives*.

2. **Airplane accidents:** On the other hand, there usually is *not* strict liability in suits by passengers for *airplane accidents*. Therefore, in a suit by the estate of a passenger against the airline, the plaintiff must show negligence.

   a. **Ground damage:** But most courts *do* impose strict liability for *ground damage* from airplane accidents. That's true for both objects that fall from aircraft, and for damage done by a crashing aircraft itself. Both the owner and the operator of the aircraft are strictly liable. Rest. 2d, §520A. (But if the owner or operator are held strictly liable, they may be entitled to indemnity from someone higher up in the distribution channel — such as the plane manufacturer — if the accident was due to a defective product; see *supra*, p. 51.) This is a variety of strict liability for ultrahazardous activities.

   Example: D operates an aircraft that crashes into P's building, causing property damage. P can recover from D (or his estate), even if D operated the aircraft without negligence.

3. **Construction activities:** Similarly, *construction activities* will generally *not* be ultrahazardous, even if they are somewhat dangerous.

   Example 1: Building an office tower in the downtown part of a densely populated city, using a crane to add each new story, is probably not ultrahazardous. That's because such activities are common in cities, the risk can be almost completely reduced by using careful precautions, and the activity is appropriate for a downtown commercial area. So if a crane falls on P, P (or his estate) will have to prove negligence.

Example 2: Builder builds a house using glues customarily found in construction, that can be toxic unless fully vented. P, a worker for a subcontractor, is overcome by glue used by Builder, and suffers brain damage. The use of the glue is probably not ultrahazardous, since the glue is commonly used and appropriate for the task in question. Therefore, P will probably have to prove negligence by Builder.

4. **No strict liability for common carrier:** Although a *common carrier* has a special relationship with its passengers, placing upon the carrier the obligation to make reasonable efforts to protect them (see *supra*, p. 52), the common carrier is *not strictly liable* for harm to passengers. In other words, the common carrier merely has to act non-negligently. MBE examiners sometimes try to fool you into thinking that a common carrier is strictly liable for bodily harm to passengers, especially bodily harm imposed by other passengers — this is not true.

C. **Limited to scope of risk:** There is strict liability only for damage that results from the *kind of risk* that made the activity abnormally dangerous. This is the aspect of strict-liability-for-abnormally-dangerous-activities that is most often tested on the MBE.

Example 1: D operates a truck carrying dynamite. The truck strikes and kills P. P must show negligence. Transporting dynamite may be ultrahazardous, but P's death has not resulted from the kind of risk that made this activity abnormally dangerous.

Example 2: D owns a dynamite factory. A special chemical, PET, is sprayed by D's workers on the dynamite during the manufacturing process. Each day for several weeks, some of the PET is vented out from a smokestack in the factory, and is breathed by P, who lives next door to the factory. PET is usually odorless and non-harmful to humans. However, because P is unusually sensitive, she becomes repeatedly nauseated by the exposure to the chemical, though she suffers no other harm. She brings a strict liability action against D for her nausea.

P will lose. While manufacturing dynamite is an abnormally dangerous activity that will trigger strict liability if the dynamite *explodes*, what caused the harm to P here was not an explosion. That is, the harm to P did not stem from the kind of risk (explosions) that makes dynamite-manufacture ultra hazardous. Therefore, P cannot recover. (Even if P sues on a nuisance theory, she will have to show either negligence, intent to make a harmful contact, or strict liability; see *infra*, p. 91. Since we're told that the claim is based on strict liability, we know that it must fail because of the harm-must-result-from-the-kind-of-risk-that-made-the-activity-abnormally-dangerous rule.)

1. **Abnormally sensitive activity by plaintiff:** A related rule is that D will not be liable for his abnormally dangerous activities if the harm would not have occurred except for the fact that P conducts an *"abnormally sensitive"* activity.

Example: D's blasting operations frighten female mink owned by P; the mink kill their young in reaction to their fright. D is not strictly liable, because P was conducting an abnormally sensitive activity. [*Foster v. Preston Mill Co.*]

D. **Requirement that D "carry out" the activity:** On an MBE abnormally-dangerous-activity question, be sure that the defendant is actually the one *"carrying out"* the activity. The examiners will sometimes give you a fact pattern in which *A* is actually carrying out the activity, but *B* has some relation to the activity sufficiently tangential that it's not fair to regard *B* as "engaging" in the activity. In that event, *B* won't be strictly liable, only liable for negligence.

Example: Des, an industrial designer, designs a plant for manufacturing explosives, under a commission from Explosives, a manufacturer of explosives. Explosives then builds the factory and begins to operate it. Some of the explosives explode at the plant, injuring Neighbor. If Des did his design work without negligence, Neighbor can't recover against him. Strict liability for abnormally dangerous activities will not apply to Des, because he was not "carrying out" the activity of making explosives, only Explosives was doing that.

1. **Use of independent contractor:** On the other hand, a person who *hires an independent contractor* to perform a task that is abnormally dangerous has strict liability, just as the contractor does. In other words, just as an employer has vicarious liability for torts by the employee committed within the scope of the employment (see *supra*, p. 71), so a person who engages an independent contractor has a special form of *vicarious liability* for the contractor's strict liability for ultrahazardous activities. Rest. 2d, §427A.

   Example: O, a landowner, hires DemoCo, a reputable demolition and blasting contractor, to excavate a foundation on O's land by what O knows will be the use of dynamite. DemoCo uses all care in doing the blasting. However, due to the peculiarities of local geology, the blast waves propagate through the ground and cause cracks to appear in the foundation of P's nearby house. O is strictly liable to P for this damage from the ultrahazardous activity of blasting, just as DemoCo would be. Cf. Rest. 2d, §427A, Illustr. 2.

E. **Contributory fault no defense:** Ordinary *contributory fault* by P will usually *not* bar her from strict liability recovery.

1. **Unreasonable assumption of risk:** But *assumption of risk is* a defense to strict liability. Thus if P *knowingly and voluntarily* subjects herself to the danger, this will be a defense, whether P acted reasonably or unreasonably in doing so.

   Example: P, an independent contractor, agrees to transport dynamite for D, in a truck owned by P. P understands that dynamite can sometimes explode spontaneously. If such an accident occurs and injures P, P cannot recover from D in strict liability, because P has assumed the risk; this is true whether P acted reasonably or unreasonably.

CHAPTER 14

PRODUCT LIABILITY

I. INTRODUCTION

A. **Three theories:** "Product liability" refers to the liability of a seller of a tangible item which, because of a defect, causes injury to its purchaser, user, or, sometimes, bystander. Usually the injury is a personal injury. The liability can be based upon any of three theories:

1. *Negligence;*
2. *Warranty;*
3. *"Strict tort liability."*

II. NEGLIGENCE

A. **Negligence and privity:** Ordinary negligence principles apply to a case in which personal injury has been caused by a carelessly manufactured product.

   Example: D, a car manufacturer, carelessly fails to inspect brakes on a car that it makes. P buys the car directly from D, and crashes when the brakes don't work. P can recover from D under ordinary negligence principles.

1. **Privity:** All states have now *rejected* any *privity* requirement — i.e., any requirement that P show that he contracted *directly* with D — where a negligently manufactured product has caused personal injuries. Therefore, *one who negligently manufactures a product is liable for*

any personal injuries proximately caused by his negligence, even to one who never bought the product.

Example: D manufactures a car, and negligently fails to make the brakes work properly. D sells the car to a dealer, X, who resells to P. While P is driving, the car crashes due to the defective brakes. P may sue D on a negligence theory, even though P never contracted directly with D.

a. **Bystander:** Even where P is a *bystander* (as opposed to a purchaser or other user of the product), P can recover in negligence if he can show that he was a "foreseeable plaintiff."

Example: A car negligently manufactured by Manu and driven by Owner fails to stop due to defective brakes, and smashes into P, a pedestrian. P can sue Manu on a negligence theory.

B. **Classes of defendants:** Several different classes of people are frequently defendants in negligence-based product liability actions:

1. **Manufacturers:** The manufacturer is the person in the distribution chain most likely to have been negligent. He may be negligent because he: (1) carelessly *designed* the product; (2) carelessly *manufactured* it; (3) carelessly performed (or failed to perform) reasonable *inspections* and tests of finished products; (4) failed to package and ship the product in a reasonably safe way; or (5) did not take reasonable care to obtain quality *components* from a reliable source.

2. **Retailers:** A *retailer* who sells a defective product may be, but usually is *not*, liable in negligence. The mere fact that D has sold a negligently manufactured or designed product is *not by itself* enough to show that she failed to use due care. The retailer ordinarily has *no duty to inspect* the goods. Thus suit against the retailer is now normally brought on a warranty or strict liability theory, not negligence.

   a. **MBE Tip:** On the MBE, you will sometimes be given a scenario involving a defective product, but you will be told that the plaintiff sues the retailer *"based solely on negligence."* It's up to you to spot this kind of "negligence only" provision, and to select a choice that makes it clear that the retailer cannot be liable unless it acted without due care. So selling a product that is defective (even a product whose defect came about due to the manufacturer's negligence) will not result in negligence liability on the part of the retailer.

      i. **Consequence:** Typically, a negligence-only suit means that the retailer will be liable only if it either (1) failed to use care in selecting that particular item to sell (or selecting that particular manufacturer); (2) failed to notice an obvious defect; (3) failed to respond to reports of dangers based on previous sales of the item; or (4) failed to inspect the goods prior to sale, under circumstances such that a reasonably careful retailer would have inspected the goods and found the defect.

3. **Other suppliers:** *Bailors* of tangible property (e.g., rental car companies), *sellers* and *lessors* of *real estate*, and suppliers of product-related *services* (e.g., hospitals performing blood transfusions) may all be sued on a negligence theory.

III. WARRANTY

A. **General:** A buyer of goods which are not as they are contracted to be may bring an action for *breach of warranty*. The law of warranty is mainly embodied in the *Uniform Commercial Code* (UCC), in effect in every state except Louisiana. There are two sorts of warranties, *"express"* ones and *"implied"* ones.

B. Express warranties: A seller may make an *express* warranty, i.e., *expressly represent* that her goods have certain qualities. If the goods turn out not to have these qualities, the purchaser may sue for this breach of warranty.

Example: D, a car dealer, promises that a particular car has "shatterproof glass." While P is driving the car, a pebble hits the windshield, shatters the glass, and damages P's eyes. P can sue D for breach of the express warranty that the glass would be shatterproof. [*Baxter v. Ford Motor Co.*]

1. **UCC:** UCC §2-313 gives a number of ways that an express warranty may arise: (1) a statement of *fact* or promise about the goods; (2) a *description* of the goods (e.g., "shatterproof glass"); and (3) the use of a *sample or model*.

Example: D manufactures ColorSafe, a washing-machine detergent that according to the label "Will not cause the dye in your clothes to run." P buys a bottle of the product and washes her expensive antique red silk blouse. The dye runs on account of the detergent.

P can recover from D for a breach of express warranty. By its "no-run" label, D was expressly warranting that the dye in users' clothes wouldn't run, and P will therefore recover as long as P can show that the loss wouldn't have occurred (i.e., the dye wouldn't have run) if the statement on the label had been true. P can recover for pure property damage (damage to the blouse's value), even though the property damage is not accompanied by any bodily harm to P.

C. Implied warranty: The existence of a warranty as to the quality of goods can also be *implied* from the fact that the seller has offered the goods for sale.

1. **Warranty of merchantability:** The UCC imposes several implied warranties *as a matter of law*. Most important is the warranty of *merchantability*. Section 2-314(1) provides that *"a warranty that goods shall be merchantable is implied in a contract for their sale if the seller is a merchant with respect to goods of that kind."*

a. **Meaning of "merchantable":** To be *merchantable*, the goods must be "fit for the *ordinary purposes for which such goods are used.*"

Example: A car which, because of manufacturing defects, has a steering wheel that does not work, is not "merchantable," since it is not fit for the ordinary purpose — driving — for which cars are used. Therefore, if such a car made by Manufacturer and driven by Owner hits Pedestrian, Pedestrian may recover from Manufacturer for his injuries on a breach-of-implied-warranty theory.

i. **Significance of warning labels:** In determining what the "ordinary purposes" are for which the goods are used, any *warning labels* will play a role — if the manufacturer specifies that the goods are not suitable for purpose X, then an implied warranty claim based on the goods' unsuitability for purpose X will probably fail (at least if there's no evidence that consumers regularly use the goods for X).

Example: A ladder comes with a large bold-print label on the top step, saying, "Top step not intended or suitable for standing on." P stands on the top step, and the ladder collapses. P will be unlikely to recover for breach of the implied warranty of merchantability, because the warning makes it clear that the ladder was not designed for someone to stand on the top step. (P will probably not recover in strict product liability for a defectively dangerous design, for the same reason.)

b. **Seller must be a merchant:** The UCC implied warranty of merchantability arises only if the seller is a *"merchant with respect to goods of that kind."* Thus the seller must be *in business* and must regularly sell the *kind of goods* in question.

Examples: A consumer who is reselling her car does not make any implied warranty of merchantability. Nor does a business person who is selling a piece of equipment used in that person's business rather than held in inventory.

2. **Fitness for particular purposes:** A second UCC implied warranty is that the goods are *"fit for a particular purpose."* Under §2-315, this warranty arises where: (1) the seller knows that the buyer wants the goods for a particular (and not customary) purpose; and (2) the buyer *relies on the seller's judgment* to recommend a suitable product.

Example: Consumer tells Shoe Dealer that he wants a pair of shoes for mountain climbing. Dealer recommends Brand X as having good traction. If the shoes don't have good traction, and Consumer falls, he can sue Shoe Dealer for breach of the implied warranty of fitness for a particular purpose.

IV. STRICT PRODUCT LIABILITY

A. **General rule:** Virtually all states apply the doctrine of *"strict product liability,"* and you should therefore assume that this doctrine applies on the MBE.

1. **Basic rule:** The basic rule of strict product liability is that a *seller* of a product is *liable without fault* for *personal injuries* (or other *physical harm*) caused by the product if the product is sold in a *defective condition.* Once a defect is shown to have existed, the seller is liable even though she *used all possible care*, and even though the plaintiff did not buy the product from or have any *contractual relationship* with the seller.

Example: Manufacturer makes a car with defective brakes. Manufacturer sells that car to Dealer, who resells it to Owner, who resells it to Consumer. Consumer is injured when the car crashes because the brakes don't work. Consumer can recover from Manufacturer in "strict tort liability," by showing that the brakes were in a defective condition unreasonably dangerous to users at the time the car left the plant. This is true even though Manufacturer used all possible care in designing and building the car, and even though Consumer never contracted with Manufacturer.

B. **Retailers and other non-manufacturers:** Strict product liability applies not only to the product's manufacturer, but also to its *retailer*, and any other person in the distribution chain (e.g., a *wholesaler*) who is in the business of selling such products.

Example: On the above example, Consumer can recover against Dealer, even though Dealer merely resold the product and behaved completely carefully.

1. **MBE tip on retailers:** On the MBE, you'll often see scenarios in which a consumer who is injured by a defective product sues the retailer who sold it to her. In such a scenario, remember that the retailer is strictly liable for selling the defective product, and that's true even if the retailer was *non-negligent* in *selecting, displaying and otherwise selling* the product, and in fact even if there was no possible way the retailer *could have discovered* the defect.

Example: Retailer, a large chain-store operator, sells washing machines in their original cartons. Retailer sells such a machine made by ManCo to Mom. Two years after sale, Mom's son Sam badly cuts himself while reaching into the washing machine to retrieve a wet sock. The injury was due to a sharp edge, which came into existence only because a blade on the machine broke after delivery to Mom, on account of poor product design by ManCo. No testing the results of which were available to Retailer would have indicated that there was any risk of such breakage or that the product was badly designed.

Assuming that the break-prone design constitutes a dangerous defect (which is likely), Retailer will be strictly liable to Sam, even though Retailer behaved non-negligently, and in fact even though there was nothing Retailer could have done to discover the risk of such a breakage at the time it sold the product to Mom.

a. **Retailer's fate linked to manufacturer's fate:** If the manufacturer of a product has strict liability (because the product is defective), then you can *count on the retailer's also being liable.* Sometimes the MBE examiners will phrase the question in a way that links the retailer's liability to the manufacturer's liability. This lets the examiners test you without their having to make sure that the fact pattern unambiguously establishes a "defect" — the correct answer may be something like "P can recover in strict liability against Retailer if she can recover against Manufacturer."

Example: Consumer buys from Store a widget manufactured by ManCo. Consumer is injured while using the widget, and sues both Store and ManCo in strict product liability. If Consumer can recover against ManCo, she can also recover against Store. (That's a true statement even if we don't know whether the product was defective, and therefore don't know whether Consumer can recover against either — we just know that both claims will turn out the same way.)

C. **Bystanders and other non-user plaintiffs:** *Any person who is injured* due to a dangerously defective product may recover, even if the plaintiff never bought the product. Thus *family members of buyers, bystanders,* even *rescuers,* may all recover if their injuries are proximately caused by the defect in the product. As the idea is sometimes put, "*privity*" is *not required* for strict product liability.

Example 1: Consumer buys a car from Dealer. The steering wheel fails due to a manufacturing defect, causing the car to swerve and hit Ped, a pedestrian walking on the sidewalk. Ped can recover from Dealer in strict product liability, because his physical injuries were proximately caused by a defective product sold by Dealer. The fact that neither Ped nor any member of his family ever purchased the product in question doesn't matter.

Example 2: X buys a sport parachute from SportsStore, a sporting goods retailer. Due to a manufacturing defect, the parachute opens 2 seconds too late during a sky dive by X. X hits the ground in a remote mountainous location and breaks his leg. (He would have landed on the target, and with no injury, had the chute opened on time). P, a paramedic, hikes with two others into the mountains to rescue X. While doing so, he falls into a crevasse and is injured.

P can recover from SportsStore in strict product liability — the defect in the product sold by SportsStore proximately caused P's injury (it was reasonably foreseeable that a parachute's failure to operate properly due to defective manufacture would cause a rescue effort in which the rescuer might be injured), so the fact that P wasn't a user, and wasn't injured directly by the product, won't matter. Nor will it matter that SportsStore had no way to know of the existence of the defect.

D. **Manufacturing, design and failure-to-warn defects:** There are three different types of defects that may exist: (1) a *manufacturing* defect; (2) a *design* defect; and (3) a *warning* defect. It's important to decide which type of defect is or may be at issue, because there are different rules of law governing what constitutes a defect of each type. Here's a brief summary of what each type of defect looks like:

1. **Manufacturing:** In a *manufacturing* defect, a particular instance of the product is *different from* — and more dangerous than — *all the others*, because the product *deviated from the intended design*.

    Example: D makes a bicycle which, because of an air bubble that gets into its front fork during manufacture, has an invisible crack that causes the fork to break while P is riding it. This is a manufacturing defect — this bike is different from the other bikes of the same model, in an unintended way.

2. **Design:** In a *design* defect, all of the similar products manufactured by D are *the same*, and they all bear a feature whose design is itself defective, and unreasonably dangerous. (Design defects are discussed beginning on p. 83.)

    Example: D makes a particular model step-ladder that, when more than 150 lbs. is placed on it, is likely to crack because the wood used is a poor grade. This is a design defect — all the ladders of this model have the same poor wood and the same risk of breakage when used for the intended purpose.

3. **Warning:** In a *failure-to-warn* case, the maker has neglected to give a warning of a danger in the product (or in a particular use of the product), and this lack of a warning makes an otherwise-safe product unsafe. Failure to warn is discussed beginning on p. 85.

    Example: D, a prescription drug maker, fails to warn users that the drug causes a serious allergic reaction in 2% of the people who take it.

E. **What product meets test:** A product gives rise to strict liability only if it is "*defective*."

1. **Meaning of "defective":** In the usual case of a manufacturing (as opposed to design) defect, a product is "defective" if the product "*departs from its intended design* even though *all possible care was exercised* in the preparation and marketing of the product." (Rest. 3d.)

F. **Unavoidably unsafe products:** A product will not give rise to strict liability if is *unavoidably unsafe*, and its benefits outweigh its dangers.

1. **Prescription drugs:** For instance, a *prescription drug* is not "defective" merely because it causes some side effects and may in an individual case cause more damage than it cures. This is also true of *vaccines*. In fact, under the new Third Restatement rule, drugs, vaccines, and medical devices will be non-defective (unavoidably unsafe) as long as there is *even a single group of patients* for whom the product's benefits outweigh its harms.

G. **Unknowable dangers:** Similarly, if the danger from the product's design was *"unknowable"* at the time of manufacture, there will be no liability. See Rest. 3d (P.L.), §2(d): a design defect will exist only "when the *foreseeable* risks of harm posed by the product could have been *reduced or avoided* by the adoption of a *reasonable alternative design*." So if the risk of harm from the design is unknowable at the time of manufacture, there was no "foreseeable risk" and thus no design-defect liability.

1. **Failure to warn:** Similarly, there can be no *"failure-to-warn"* liability (see *infra*, p. 85) for a danger whose existence was unknowable at the time of manufacture.

H. **Obvious dangers:** The fact that a danger is *"obvious"* may have an impact on whether the product is deemed defective, and thus on whether D is liable. The treatment of obviousness depends on whether the defect is a manufacturing defect, a design defect, or a failure to warn.

1. **Manufacturing defect:** Where the defect is a *manufacturing* defect, the fact that the danger or defect is obvious *won't* block P from recovering (though under comparative fault — generally applicable in product liability cases, see *infra*, p. 88 — it might reduce P's recovery).

Example: D makes a can of tuna fish, which contains a sliver of metal in it. P fails to notice the metal and is injured when he swallows it. Even if an ordinarily attentive consumer would have spotted the metal and not eaten it, the "obviousness" of the danger won't stop the product from being defective, and P will be able to recover. Furthermore, in a comparative-negligence jurisdiction (which is what you are to assume exists on the MBE unless you're told otherwise in the question), even P's negligent failure to notice the danger won't eliminate his recovery (though it may reduce it under comparative-negligence principles).

2. **Design defect:** If what's alleged is a *design* defect, under the modern view the obviousness of the defect is a *factor* bearing upon liability, but it *doesn't automatically* mean that P can't recover. Instead, the question is whether the design's *benefits outweigh its dangers*, considering possible alternative designs — if the answer is "no," P can recover even though the dangers were obvious.

   Example: Suppose that D manufactures cigarettes using a particular type of tobacco and a particular curing process, which together produce very high tar and nicotine, and thus high risk of cancer. P gets cancer from smoking D's cigarettes. Even if P was perfectly aware of how dangerous D's cigarettes were, this fact won't (in most courts) bar the court from finding that the cigarettes were "defective" and thus bar P from recovering in strict product liability. So, for instance, if P can show that a cigarette made with a different process would taste as good and have less cancer risk, P could win. (But the test will be a cost-benefit analysis: if P shows merely that a safer cigarette could have been made by reducing the elements that give the cigarette the flavor that most smokers expect, D's process won't be found to be "defective" and P will lose, since the safer cigarette won't have the same "benefits" as D's dangerous one.)

3. **Failure-to-warn liability:** If the defect or danger is obvious, this will normally *prevent failure-to-warn liability*. That's because if P is actually aware of the obvious danger, the warning won't add anything, and if P isn't aware of the obvious danger he's unlikely to notice or respond to the warning either.

V. DESIGN DEFECTS

A. **Definition of "design defect":** A *"design defect"* must be distinguished from a "manufacturing defect." In a design defect case, all the similar products manufactured by D are the same, and they all bear a feature whose design is itself defective, and unreasonably dangerous.

1. **Prima facie case:** In an MBE question that seems to involve a strict product liability claim based on an allegedly defective design, here are the elements of a plaintiff's *prima facie case:*

   ❑ That D was *in the business of selling* a product;

   ❑ That the product was *defectively designed* (with defectiveness measured vis-á-vis *reasonable alternative designs*, as discussed *infra*, p. 84);

   ❑ That the defective design made the product *not reasonably safe*;

   ❑ That *physical harm* to the plaintiff's person or property occurred;

   ❑ That the physical harm would not have occurred had the design not been defective;

   ❑ That the defective design proximately caused the physical harm.

B. **Negligence predominates:** Most design defect claims have a heavy *negligence* aspect, even though the complaint claims strict liability. As the Third Restatement puts it, a product has a defective design "when the *foreseeable risks of harm* posed by the product *could have been reduced or* *avoided by the adoption of a reasonable alternative design* by the seller or other distributor . . . and the omission of the alternative design *renders the product not reasonably safe*."

1. **Reasonable alternative design:** So P must show that there was a *"reasonable alternative design"* (*RAD*). In deciding whether P's proposed alternative qualifies as an RAD, the court will consider the *cost and utility* of the alternative, compared with the cost and utility of D's design.

    Example 1 (no practical alternative design): D makes a bullet-proof vest, the Model 101, that covers only the wearer's front and back, not sides. P, a police officer, is shot in the side while wearing a Model 101 vest. At trial, P says that a design with side protection was an RAD, and that the no-sides design is therefore "defective." Suppose that the side-protection design would have weighed five pounds more and cost twice as much. A court is likely to conclude that the side-protection design is not an RAD, because its cost-benefit ratio is not distinctly superior to the Model 101's, since many wearers would prefer the lighter cheaper design over the greater protection.

    Example 2 (practical alternative design): Manco, a manufacturer of paper cutters used by print shops, makes two models of manually operated electric cutters. Model 1 can be operated one-handed, and costs $3,000. Model 2 is comparable to Model 1 in all respects except that as a safety feature, both hands are required to be placed on the control panel (away from the cutting blade) before any cutting can occur. Model 2 costs $3,200, with the extra $200 representing the manufacturer's cost of including the safety feature. Manco's advertising materials state that Manco "strongly recommends Model 2 over Model 1 because of its greater safety." Printco, a print shop, buys a Model 1 in order to save the $200 differential. Model 1 contains a large red sign label affixed to the front saying, "WARNING: Place both hands on control panel when operating, to avoid danger of cutting off fingers." Work, an employee of Printco, is aware of the danger, but gets two fingers from his left hand cut off because he is momentarily distracted and forgets to put his left hand on the control panel, an accident that could not have happened with a Model 2.

    If Work sues Manco in strict product liability, the most likely outcome is that Work will win, because an alternative safer design was reasonably available. Since the safety risk was eliminated in the Model 2 at an extra cost of only $200 (compared with an overall product price of $3,000), it's clear that a safety-enabled model was a "reasonable alternative design." Furthermore, nothing in the facts suggest that there was any functionality trade-off in having the safety device (unlike, say, the police bullet-proof vest in Example 1 above, where greater protection would typically result in loss of mobility). So a trier of fact would be very likely to conclude that the lack of the alternative safety device made the Model 1 defective in design, thereby subjecting Manco to strict product liability.

2. **Component makers:** On the MBE, make sure that the defendant you're focusing on made (or was at least responsible for) the design in question. The examiners will sometimes give you a fact pattern in which one defendant (call him D1) makes a non-defective and properly-designed component, and the component is then incorporated by someone else (call her D2) into an assembled product that has a dangerously defective design. On these facts, D1 won't be liable for the design defect, since D1 did not sell a product containing the defective design, and had no connection with the process by which the defective design got incorporated into the final defective product.

    Example: Turbine Co. makes a jet engine turbine that it sells to Engine Co. Engine Co. sells a complete engine (including the turbine) to PlaneCo. PlaneCo designs the overall aircraft in such a way that there is a dangerous risk that the engine will fall off in flight, for reasons having nothing to do with Turbine's design or manufacture of the turbine. One such engine does fall off, causing the plane to crash, killing P. P's estate will not be able to recover in strict liability from Turbine Co. on a design-defect (or any other) theory. That's because Turbine didn't make the design that was defective, or sell a product that, at the time of the sale, was defective.

C. **Types of claims:** Two types of common design-defect claims are as follows:

1. **Structural defects:** P shows that because of D's choice of materials, the product had a *structural weakness*, which caused it to break or otherwise become dangerous.

2. **Lack of safety features:** P shows that a *safety feature* could have been installed on the product with so little expense (compared with both the cost of the product and the magnitude of the danger without the feature) that it is a defective design not to install that feature.

a. **State of the art:** D will be permitted to rebut this by showing that competitive products sold at the same time similarly lacked the safety feature. This is the *"state of the art"* defense. But such a showing will *not* be *dispositive* — the trier of fact is always free to conclude that all products sold in the marketplace at the time were defective due to lack of an easily-added feature.

VI. DUTY TO WARN

A. **Significance of the duty to warn:** The *"duty to warn"* is essentially an *extra* obligation placed on a manufacturer or seller of goods.

1. **Manufacturing defect:** Thus if a product is *defectively manufactured, no warning can save D from strict liability.*

2. **Design defect:** Similarly, if a product is *defectively designed*, a warning will generally *not* shield D from strict product liability.

3. **Properly manufactured and designed product:** If a product is *properly designed* and *properly manufactured*, D must nonetheless give a warning if there is a *non-obvious* risk of personal injury from using the product. Similarly, in this situation, D may be liable for not giving *instructions concerning correct use*, if a reasonable consumer might misuse the product in a foreseeable way.

Examples: Prescription drugs, even when properly designed and properly manufactured, must contain warnings about side effects. Similarly, a household utility like a lawn mower, if it poses a non-obvious risk of personal injury such as cutting a foot, must contain instructions concerning correct use.

a. **"Learned intermediary" doctrine for drugs:** In the case of prescription drugs, the warning generally needs to be given only to the *physician* — who is a *"learned intermediary"* between manufacturer and user — not to the user.

B. **Risk-utility basis for liability:** Liability for failure to warn is usually based on a negligence-like *risk-utility analysis.* Thus under the Third Restatement, a product will be deemed defective on account of "inadequate instructions or warnings" "when the *foreseeable risks of harm* imposed by the product could have been *reduced or avoided* by the provision of *reasonable instructions or warnings* . . . and the omission of the instructions or warnings renders the product *not reasonably safe*." Rest. 3d (P.L.), §2(c).

C. **Unknown and unknowable dangers:** If D can show that it *neither knew* nor, in the exercise of reasonable care *should have known,* of a danger at the time of sale, most courts hold that there was *no duty to warn* of the unknown danger.

1. **Restatement 3d applies:** This principle is applied by the Third Restatement. The provision (§2(c)) quoted in Par. (B) above makes a failure to warn a defect only if it related to "foresee-

able risks of harm"; this language suggests that if the risks are not reasonably foreseeable at the time of sale, failure to warn of those risks will not cause the product to become defective no matter how dangerous those risks might eventually turn out to be.

Example: D manufactures and sells fire-resistant roof construction materials, exposure to which turns out, decades later, to materially increase the risk of a particular type of Acute Lymphocytic Leukemia (ALL). Assume that this risk was not reasonably foreseeable to one in D's position at the time D sold the product to Contractor, who installed it in P's house. Years later, P gets ALL that can be traced to his exposure to the material sold by D. If P brings a suit for failure to warn, in most courts P will not prevail, because D had no duty to warn of a risk that was not, at the time of sale, foreseeable.

2. **Check adequacy of warning:** Even if the manufacturer gives warnings, be sure that the warnings were *adequate* — if they're not, they will not negate failure-to-warn liability. So, for instance, the warning may not quite cover the situation at hand, or may not indicate just how dangerous the eventuality being warned of may turn out to be.

D. **Danger to small number of people:** If the manufacturer knows that the product will be dangerous to a *small number* of people, the need for a warning will usually turn on the *magnitude* of the danger; if the danger is great enough, even a small number of potential bad results will require a warning.

E. **Hidden causation issue:** In any MBE failure-to-warn scenario, be sure to check that the requirement of a *causal link* between the failure to warn and the resulting injury is satisfied. If the provision of a warning *would not have prevented the accident* from occurring, then the defendant will *not* be liable for failing to warn. The MBE examiners love to slip a causation issue into fact patterns involving failure to warn or failure to give instructions.

1. **Plaintiff who does not read warnings or ignores them:** For example, in a case in which the injured plaintiff is the one who was the user of the product, and the claim is based upon the defendant manufacturer's failure to place a warning label on the product, evidence that the plaintiff *never read any warning labels* would prevent failure-to-warn liability. Similarly, if there is evidence that even had plaintiff read the warning, plaintiff would have *ignored the warning* and used the product in the same way so that the accident would have happened anyway, failure to warn will not be the basis for liability.

Example: D manufactures a hand-operated power saw that is sold to P, a professional carpenter. P cuts off one of the fingers of his left hand while holding the saw with his right hand only. The saw contains a bold-faced warning label, but the warning label does not specify that the saw should only be operated with two hands. P sues D in strict product liability, alleging that the failure of the warning label to specify a need for two-handed operation rendered the product dangerously defective. D presents evidence at trial that P had over the course of his career used many similar hand saws, that most of them had a label warning against one-handed use, and that P very frequently ignored such warnings by operating the saws with one hand only.

If the jury is convinced that P would have ignored a two-hands-only label had one been present, then P will not be permitted to recover for failure to warn.

VII. WHO MAY BE A DEFENDANT

A. **Chattels:** In any case involving a *"good"* or *"chattel,"* both strict and warranty liability will apply to *any seller* in the *business* of selling goods of that kind.

1. **Retailer:** This means that a *retail dealer* who sells the good, but has not manufactured it, will have strict liability as well as warranty liability, even if she could have done nothing to discover the defect. But this is true only if the seller is in the *business of selling goods of that type* (so that

a *private individual* selling a good, or a business person selling outside of the usual course of his business, will not have liability).

a. **Indemnity:** If the retailer is held liable in this way, she will be entitled to *indemnity* from the manufacturer or wholesaler, as long as the retailer was not herself negligent. See *supra*, p. 51.

B. **Services:** One who sells *services*, rather than goods, generally does *not* fall within standard strict liability nor within the UCC implied warranties.

1. **MBE Tip:** The MBE examiners like to test this point: they'll give you a scenario involving a service provider, who delivers a patently defective (and dangerous) service. They'll try to trick you into thinking that strict product liability applies — it doesn't, because such liability applies only to goods, not services.

a. **Electric utilities:** Electric utilities, and others who *supply electricity* as some aspect of the service they sell, are good examples. At least where the electricity has not yet been delivered to the customer (e.g., at the time of the accident it's passing through a telephone pole or power station maintained by the utility), a plaintiff bystander who gets *electrocuted* will have to show that the utility or service provider behaved negligently.

Example: Utility puts up a wooden pole next to the street, containing high-voltage power lines. Due to a defect in the insulation on a bolt that Utility fastens at shoulder height onto the pole, the bolt carries a high-voltage charge. When P, a passerby, touches the bolt, he is electrocuted.

P will not be able to recover in strict product liability against Utility, because Utility sold a service (electricity), not a defective product (the pole or the bolt). (Operation of high-voltage lines might be held to be an ultrahazardous activity leading to strict liability on that count, but that wouldn't be strict "product" liability. Also, if the electricity had already passed into the house of a customer before the accident, a court might hold that the electricity had become a "product" that could give rise to strict product liability.)

b. **Construction workers:** Another good illustration of the principle that service providers won't have strict product liability is *construction work.* You'll sometimes see on the MBE a scenario in which a construction company (call it Contractor) does work using a construction product that is not being "sold" by Contractor to the customer, and some bystander is injured. Contractor won't have strict product liability, because it didn't sell the defective product.

Example: Contractor does tiling in Customer's apartment. In doing so, Contractor uses a high-temperature torch made by Manco. The torch, due to a design defect, sprays its flame too widely, and ignites a piece of pre-existing wall. The resulting fire releases toxic fumes that leak into the neighboring apartment, injuring Neighbor. Neighbor won't be able to recover against Contractor in strict product liability, because Contractor didn't "sell" the torch, making the fact that the torch was defective irrelevant. (But Neighbor could recover in strict product liability against Manco, because the torch was defective, was at some point in the distribution chain sold by Manco, and proximately caused the injury to Neighbor.)

2. **Product incorporated in service:** However, if a product is furnished to a customer *in combination with a service*, then most courts (and the Restatements) *will* apply strict liability if the product turns out to be defective.

Example: P goes to D's beauty parlor to get a permanent. D uses a solution made by a cosmetics company, which badly burns P's scalp. A court will probably hold D strictly liable for the defective solution, even though the product is being furnished in combination with services.

a. **Services by professionals:** But where the services are rendered by a *health professional,* she will almost never be liable in either strict tort or warranty, even if the service incorporates a product that is defective.

Example: D is a surgeon who puts a defective pacemaker into P's heart. D will almost certainly not be held strictly liable for the product defect.

VIII. DEFENSES BASED ON PLAINTIFF'S CONDUCT

A. **General rule of plaintiff's negligence applies:** *Whatever* the jurisdiction's standard method of dealing with plaintiff's negligence is (typically comparative negligence of one sort or another), *that method generally applies to product-liability actions.*

1. **Consequence on MBE:** Therefore, in a *comparative-negligence* jurisdiction (which is what you are to *assume* exists on the MBE unless the particular question specifies otherwise) P's comparative negligence in using an obviously defective product will *reduce, but not eliminate*, D's liability in a strict product liability action.

Example: P drinks a bottle of clear soda, which contains a sizeable decomposed beetle. P becomes ill as a result. A consumer using an ordinary degree of attentiveness would have seen the beetle before ingesting it. P didn't see it because he was drunk. On an MBE question in which you're told nothing about the jurisdiction's rule of comparative-vs-contributory negligence, P's carelessness will not prevent him from recovering in strict liability from the retailer who sold him the soda. This follows because you would assume that comparative negligence is in force, and under comparative negligence P's recovery might (though not necessarily) be reduced but would certainly not be eliminated.

B. **Different types of negligence by P:** There are a number of different ways in which a plaintiff might behave negligently with respect to a product.

1. **Failure to discover the risk:** First, P might *"negligently" fail to discover that there is a defect at all.* Here, if P's only fault is to fail to discover the defect, this is probably *not really "negligence" at all,* since a person is normally entitled to assume that a product is not defective. Therefore, in the ordinary case P's failure to discover the defect *will not cause any reduction* in her recovery. But even if the defect is so obvious that a trier of fact decided that not discovering it was negligence, P's failure to discover it would at most *reduce* her risk under comparative negligence, not eliminate it. (See the above beetle-in-the-soda example.)

2. **Knowing assumption of risk:** Second, P might be fully aware of a product's defectiveness (whether of a manufacturing or design nature), yet voluntarily and unreasonably decide to *"assume the risk"* of that defect. In this situation, the modern trend is to *treat assumption-of-risk as a form of comparative negligence*: to the extent that P's decision to use the product in the face of the known risk was *unreasonable*, it will cause plaintiff's recovery to be reduced proportionately (and will *not* serve as an *absolute bar* to recovery).

a. **Ignoring of safety precaution:** Suppose P *consciously fails to use an available safety device*, and is then injured by a product defect that would not have led to injury had the safety device been used. In some situations, the safety device is one provided by the manufacturer of the defective product; in other cases, it is provided by a third party. The analysis is pretty much the same in both types of situations — in most courts the plaintiff's failure to use an available safety device is generally fault that *reduces* (but does *not eliminate*) plaintiff's recovery.

Example: P, a consumer, purchases a Slicer-Dicer made by D. The Slicer-Dicer is designed to slice, dice, chop, and puree a variety of household products. The Slicer Dicer comes with a hand guard, which when installed prevents the user's hand from getting near the cutting blades. The hand guard is purposely designed to be removable for easy cleaning; the device and its instruction manual both contain a bold-faced warning that the device should not be operated without the hand guard. P removes the hand guard because he finds it easier to use the machine without it; he realizes that there is a greater danger of cutting his hand, but decides to risk it. P's hand slips, and is severely cut by the blades. P sues D on the theory that D's permitting the guard to be removed for separate cleaning constituted a design defect.

In a comparative-negligence jurisdiction the court will probably hold that P's use of the product without the guard should reduce, but not eliminate, his recovery.

3. **Use for unintended purpose:** Even if P totally *misuses* the product, D will not be relieved from liability unless the misuse was so *unforeseeable* or *unreasonable* that either: (1) the misuse *couldn't reasonably be warned against or designed against*, or (2) the misuse is found to be *"superseding."*

Example: D makes a chair with bars across the back. The chair is designed for seating, not climbing. P takes the chair and uses the bars across the back as a step-ladder; he then falls and hurts himself badly. A court would probably hold that the misuse here was so unforeseeable and unreasonable that the risks the design presents (the risk of unsafe climbing) need not be designed against or warned against.

a. **Extreme misuse required:** But it takes a *very extreme misuse* to be superseding in a strict product liability case. The mere fact that the defendant *warned against* a particular use won't be enough to establish misuse when the plaintiff engages in that use. And in any event, courts will narrowly construe warnings.

Example: D manufactures an all-electric sports car that can go from 0 to 90 mph in 4.7 seconds. The user's manual states in bold letters on the cover, "Using the full acceleration capability of this car is dangerous. Do not accelerate faster than 0-80 in 5.0 seconds, because any faster rate will impose G-forces in excess of 2, which may cause neck and spine injuries." P reads the manual, doesn't focus on this cover language, and figures, "Let's see how fast this can accelerate." P floors it, and his head snaps back when he accelerates at 3 G-forces. Due to a lack of a head rest that would accommodate the accelerations of which the car is capable, P's neck is fractured. He sues D in strict product liability, claiming that the lack of a proper head rest was a design defect.

A court would be *unlikely* to hold that P's conduct, including the ignoring of the warnings, constituted misuse of the sort that would be superseding. Since the car was manufactured in a way capable of acceleration more rapid than the head rest could support, any misconduct by P would be classified as comparative negligence that will reduce his recovery, not as a superseding cause that would negate recovery entirely.

CHAPTER 15

NUISANCE

I. NUISANCE GENERALLY

A. Type of injury: The term "nuisance" refers not to a type of tort, but to a *type of injury* which P has sustained. In the case of "public nuisance," the injury is the loss of any right that P has by virtue of being a "member of the public." In the case of "private nuisance," P's injury is interference with his *use or enjoyment of his land.*

1. **Three mental states:** A suit for nuisance may be supported by any of the three standard mental states for a defendant: (1) intentional interference with P's rights; (2) negligence; or (3) abnormally dangerous activity or other conduct giving rise to strict liability. There is *no general strict liability for causing a nuisance.*

II. PUBLIC NUISANCE

A. **Definition:** A *"public nuisance"* is an interference with a *"right common to the general public."*

1. **Examples:** Examples of things that have been held to constitute public nuisances include: *health hazards*, maintenance of *improper businesses* (e.g., an unlicensed bar or house of prostitution), and *obstruction* of public streets.

2. **Factors:** Courts look at a number of factors in deciding whether something is a public nuisance, including the *type of neighborhood*, the frequency/duration, the degree of damage, and the social value of the activity.

   a. **Substantial harm required:** A public nuisance will not be found to exist unless the harm to the public is *substantial.*

   b. **Must injure public at large:** P must show that there has been actual injury, or possibility of injury, to the *public at large* (not just P himself).

3. **Need not be a crime:** It is not the case that for conduct to be actionable as a public nuisance, it must also be a *crime* (though the fact that the conduct *is* a crime will make it more likely to be held to be a public nuisance).

B. **Requirement of particular damage:** A private citizen may recover for his own damages stemming from a public nuisance, but only if he has sustained damage that is *different in kind*, not just degree, from that suffered by the public generally.

Example: An oil tanker runs aground, discharging oil onto the beach. Fishermen and clam diggers have suffered the requisite "damage different in kind." But operators of tourist businesses, who have suffered only indirect interference based on the drying up of tourism, have suffered only damage "greater in degree," not different in kind, so they may not recover in public nuisance. [*Burgess v. M/V Tamano*]

1. **Magnitude of monetary loss irrelevant:** In determining whether P's damage is different in kind from that suffered by the public generally, the *magnitude* of the financial harm is usually *irrelevant.*

2. **Injunction:** The requirement of a "different kind" of harm will *not* necessarily be imposed in suits for an *injunction*, as opposed to one for damages.

C. **MBE Tip:** Nuisance liability on the MBE is much more likely to be for *private* nuisance (below) than for public nuisance.

III. PRIVATE NUISANCE

A. **Nature of private nuisance:** A *private nuisance* is an *unreasonable interference* with P's *use and enjoyment* of his *land.*

1. **Must have interest in land:** P can sue based on a private nuisance only if he has an *interest in land* that has been affected.

Example: An ocean fisherman who is injured by an oil spill cannot sue for private nuisance, because no interest in land held by him is affected.

a. **Tenants and family members:** But a fee simple is not necessary — a *tenant*, or members of the *family* of the owner or tenant, may sue.

2. **Elements:** P must demonstrate *two* elements in order to recover: (1) that her *use and enjoyment of her land* was interfered with in a *substantial way*; and (2) that D's conduct was either *negligent*, *abnormally dangerous*, or *intentional*.

B. **Interference with use:** The interference with P's use and enjoyment must be *substantial*. If P's damage is merely a small *inconvenience* (e.g., somewhat extra noise, mildly unpleasant smells), there will be no recovery.

Example: P and D run businesses that are next door to each other in a commercial district. D's business, a factory, makes some amount of noise. P's business is also a factory, but a quiet one. Even if D unreasonably chooses louder machinery than needed, unless the interference with P's business is "substantial," P cannot recover for nuisance.

C. **Defendant's conduct:** There is *no general rule of "strict liability" in nuisance*. P must show that D's conduct fell within one of the three classes for tortious defendant conduct: *negligence*, *intent*, or *abnormal dangerousness*.

Example: D, a utility, suddenly spews polluted smoke onto the land of P, a nearby owner. Unless P can show that D was careless in allowing the pollutants, intended to pollute, or was carrying out an abnormally dangerous activity, P cannot recover for private nuisance.

1. **Intentional:** In nuisance cases, D's conduct will be deemed "intentional" even though D did not *desire* to interfere with P's use and enjoyment of her land, as long as D *knew with substantial certainty* that such interference would occur.

Example: In the above example, if P put D on notice that pollution was occurring, and D continued with the conduct, the continuing conduct would be deemed intentional, and D could be liable for nuisance.

D. **Unreasonableness:** D's interference with P's interest must be *"unreasonable."*

1. **Test for unreasonableness:** The interference will be deemed unreasonable if *either*: (1) the *harm* to P *outweighs the utility* of D's conduct; *or* (2) the harm caused to P is greater than P should be *required to bear without compensation.*

Example: On the above pollution example, even though operation of a utility is socially beneficial, and even if the social benefits outweigh the damage to P from the pollutants, D probably will have to pay for the ongoing polluting, because it is not fair that P should have to bear the burden of this pollution without compensation.

a. **Noise and unattractive sights:** Excessive *noise* and unattractive *sights* are especially common sources of nuisance on MBE questions.

Example: P's house is in a residential neighborhood, but adjacent to a commercial neighborhood. D opens up a stone-cutting business immediately across the street (in the commercial neighborhood), which uses machines that make a loud sound that is deafening to anyone sitting in P's backyard. A court would likely hold that D's use of these loud machines constitutes a nuisance, because it unreasonably interferes with P's use and enjoyment of his property.

2. **Action taken for spite:** An action taken by the defendant for *spite* — that is, an action of *little or no benefit to the defendant*, and taken for the *purpose* of *annoying or injuring* the plaintiff — is especially likely to be found to be unreasonable and thus a nuisance.

   Example: P and D, who are neighbors, quarrel. Out of anger at P, D then puts up bright lights and a large "spite fence," both of which are of little benefit to D and a major detriment to P's enjoyment. The cost/benefit analysis, coupled with D's harmful intent, will likely lead the court to conclude that D's conduct was "unreasonable." If so, D will be found to have created a nuisance.

3. **Nature of neighborhood:** One important factor in determining whether D's conduct is "unreasonable" is the kind of *neighborhood* in which D and P are located — the more commercial or industrial the neighborhood, the less likely given conduct is to be a nuisance.

4. **Hypersensitive plaintiff:** Even if the harm to the plaintiff's use or enjoyment of the property is great, there will be no nuisance liability unless the use and enjoyment of a person in a community having *normal sensitivity* would be seriously harmed. So a *"hypersensitive plaintiff"* will *not* be able to recover for nuisance no matter how great the harm to the plaintiff's use and enjoyment, if an ordinarily sensitive person would not be unduly bothered. Rest. 2d, §821F, Comm. d and Illustr. 1.

   Example: P is an invalid who is thrown into convulsions by the ringing of a nearby church bell, the sound of which would not be disturbing to an ordinary member of the community whose house was located the same distance from the church as P's. P cannot recover for nuisance, because he is hypersensitive.

5. **Interference with water:** Where a landowner has a stream, lake, pond, or other *water* on or adjacent to her property, she has a right to be free of interference with her continued use and enjoyment of that water. Interferences are evaluated by reasonableness rules similar to those applicable to nuisance.

   a. **Restatement test:** Thus the Restatement evaluates one landowner's interference with another's use and enjoyment of water use by considering such nuisance-like factors as:

      - ❑ the *purpose* of the competing uses;
      - ❑ the *suitability* of the uses to the stream, lake, etc.;
      - ❑ the *economic value* of the uses;
      - ❑ the *social value* of the uses;
      - ❑ the practicality of *avoiding the harm* by *adjusting the use or quantity* being made by one owner or the other;
      - ❑ the need to *protect the existing value* of land;

      and the like. Rest. 2d, §850A.

      Example: A stream runs from D's property to P's property next door, and has done so for years. Both are vacation homes. P has never physically entered the stream, but enjoys looking at it. Recently, D built a dam that created an ornamental pond on D's land, but that completely stopped the flow of water to P's property.

      A court will likely enjoin the dam (i.e., require D to remove it), on a nuisance-like theory that D has unreasonably interfered with P's use and enjoyment of her property.

E. **Remedies:** P may be entitled to one or both of the following *remedies* for private nuisance:

   1. **Damages:** If the harm has already occurred, P can recover *compensatory damages*.

2. **Injunction:** If P can show that damages would not be a sufficient remedy, she may be entitled to an *injunction* against continuation of the nuisance. (But to get the injunction, P probably has to show that the harm to her and to all others similarly situated *outweighs* the utility of D's conduct.)

F. **Assumption of risk:** The defense of *assumption of risk* is generally applicable to nuisance cases, but it is a very hard defense for a defendant to establish.

1. **"Coming to the nuisance":** Most commonly, the defense arises where D claims that P *"came to the nuisance,"* i.e., that P purchased his property with *advance knowledge* that the nuisance existed. Today, "coming to the nuisance" is *not* an absolute defense, but merely *one of numerous factors* to be considered in determining whether P should win.

Example: P, a developer, buys a parcel next to D's cattle feed lot, and sells off some of the parcels as homesites. D will be enjoined from operating the feed lot — the manure from which creates flies and odor — even though P came to the nuisance, because the rights of innocent parties, including the homeowners, are at stake. [*Spur Industries, Inc. v. Dell E. Webb Development Co.*]

a. **No significance to plaintiff being first:** By the way, in the opposite scenario — where the plaintiff occupied the location *before* the defendant (or before the defendant's allegedly tortious use) — plaintiff's priority of use is completely *irrelevant*. In other words, the fact that the plaintiff's use was the prior one does not help the plaintiff's case.

CHAPTER 16

MISREPRESENTATION

I. INTENTIONAL MISREPRESENTATION ("DECEIT")

A. **Definition:** The common-law action of *"deceit"* or "fraud" corresponds to what we today call *"intentional misrepresentation."*

1. **Elements:** To recover for intentional misrepresentation or deceit, P must establish the following elements:

a. A *misrepresentation* by D;

b. *Scienter* (i.e., a culpable state of mind — either knowledge of the statement's falsity or reckless indifference to the truth);

c. An *intent to induce the plaintiff's reliance* on the misrepresentation;

d. *Justifiable reliance* by P; and

e. *Pecuniary damage* to P, stemming from the reliance.

B. **Misrepresentation:** D must make a *misrepresentation* to P. Normally, this will be in *words*.

1. **Actions:** But D's *actions* may also constitute a misrepresentation.

Example: A used car dealer turns back the odometer on a car. This is a misrepresentation.

2. **Concealment:** If D intentionally *conceals* a fact from P, he will be treated the same way as if he had affirmatively misstated that fact.

3. **Non-disclosure:** If D simply *fails to disclose* a material fact (as opposed to taking positive steps to conceal it), it is harder for P to establish the requisite misrepresentation.

a. **General rule:** The *general rule* is that *failure to disclose by itself does not constitute misrepresentation.*

Example: D proposes to buy a parcel of rural land from its absentee owner, P. D, who is a petroleum engineer, knows that oil has recently been discovered beneath adjacent lands. P does not know this. D offers a price about equal to the market value the land would have as farmland, which is far below what an oil company would now pay given the local oil discoveries. D says nothing about the discoveries, nor makes any other statement about the value of the land. P agrees to sell, closes on the sale, and then discovers that D knew about the oil discovery. P sues D for intentional misrepresentation.

P will lose. This scenario falls within the general rule that one party to a proposed transaction ordinarily has no duty to make disclosure to the other about a material fact which the former knows and the other does not. There are exceptions (see *infra*, p. 94) but none applies here. (But if D said, "I'm an oil engineer, and I can tell you that no oil has been or is likely to be discovered around here," that's an affirmative misrepresentation that *would* be the basis for liability.)

b. **Exceptions:** But there are some important *exceptions* to the general rule that nondisclosure will not trigger liability for deceit. These exceptions include:

[1] matters which must be disclosed because of a *fiduciary relationship* between the two parties (e.g., lawyer/client);

[2] matters which must be disclosed in order to prevent a *partial* statement of the facts from being misleading;

[3] *newly acquired* information, which, if not disclosed, would make a *previous statement* misleading; and

[4] facts *basic to the transaction*, if the party with knowledge knows of the other's reliance and knows that the other would reasonably expect a disclosure of those facts.

Example of [4]: A homeowner who fails to disclose to the buyer the presence of termites will today usually be found to have made a misrepresentation — this is a fact basic to the transaction that, as the seller should know, a buyer would normally expect to be told about. This represents a change from the common-law rule. [*Obde v. Schlemeyer*]

C. **Scienter:** P must show that D had that culpable state of mind called *"scienter."* D acts with scienter if he either: (1) *knew or believed* that he was not telling the truth; (2) did not have the *confidence* in the accuracy of his statement that he stated or implied that he did; or (3) knew that he *did not have the grounds* for a statement that he stated or implied that he did.

1. **Negligence not enough:** Scienter does not exist where D was merely *negligent* in making the misrepresentation. (In this instance, a claim for negligent misrepresentation, discussed below, must be brought.)

D. **Third-party recovery:** Where the fraudulent misrepresentation was not made to P, but to some *third person*, P can recover if she can show that:

[1] she is a member of a class which D had *reason to expect* would be induced to rely; and

[2] the transaction is of the *same sort* that D had reason to expect would occur in reliance.

Example: D falsely claims to have good title in an auto, and sells the car to X, who D knows is wholesaler. X resells to P, repeating the misrepresentation. Under modern law, P could recover against D, because P is a member of a class — ultimate buyers — whom D had reason to expect might rely on the misrepresentation, and the transaction is of the same sort — sale of the car — as D had reason to expect would occur in reliance. [*Varwig v. Anderson-Behel Porsche/Audi*]

E. Justifiable reliance: P must also show that he in fact *relied* on the misrepresentation, and that his reliance was *justifiable*.

1. **Investigation by P:** If, after receiving D's misrepresentation, P makes his *own investigation*, and *relies totally* or almost totally upon this investigation, P will be held not to have met the reliance requirement. (But if the misrepresentation is a *substantial factor* in inducing the reliance, P can recover even though his own investigation was also a substantial factor.)

2. **Justifiability:** P must show that his reliance was *justifiable*.

   a. **No general duty to investigate:** But P has no *duty to investigate* on his own, even where an investigation could be easily done, and would disclose the falsity of D's statements. In other words, P's failure to investigate does not by itself make the reliance unjustifiable. (But P may not overlook the *"obvious"* — if he does, his reliance is unjustifiable.)

3. **Materiality:** P must show that the fact that he relied on was *material* to the underlying transaction.

F. Opinion: It is hard for P to recover for a statement that is fairly characterizable as an *"opinion."*

1. **Adverse party:** It is especially hard for P to recover where D was an *"adverse party"* to P at the time of the misstatements. But even here, P may be justified in relying on D's expression of opinion if: (1) D purports to have *special knowledge* that P does not have; (2) D stands in a *fiduciary* relationship to P; or (3) D knows that P is especially *gullible*.

   a. **"Puffing" still not actionable:** *"Puffing"* or *"trade talk"* is *not* actionable.

   Example: Car Dealer says to Consumer, "This is the best two-door car for the money." In fact, Car Dealer believes that the car is a terrible value. Consumer cannot recover for intentional misrepresentation, because Car Dealer's statement is obviously "puffing."

2. **Opinion of apparently disinterested person:** If the opinion is expressed not by one of the parties to a business deal, but by someone whom the plaintiff reasonably perceives as being *"disinterested,"* it is *easier* for P to recover.

3. **Opinion implying fact:** The above rules apply only to statements of "pure" opinion. Where an opinion either *expresses* or *implies facts separate from the opinion*, P can recover for misstatement of the underlying facts.

   a. **Lack of knowledge of inconsistent facts:** Thus an opinion often contains the implied statement that its maker knows of no facts *incompatible* with that opinion. If P can show that D really knew facts incompatible with his opinion, P can recover.

   Example: Seller tells Buyer, "In my opinion, this house is structurally sound." Seller really knows that the foundation is badly cracked. Buyer can recover. That's because Seller's statement includes an implied statement, "I don't know of any facts incompatible with the opinion I've just expressed." In fact, Seller does know of such incompatible facts (cracked foundation), so the implied statement is factually untrue, and will give rise to liability for deceit.

G. Statements about law: Today, statements involving *legal principles* are generally treated the same as any other statement. Thus if D's representation of law includes an implied statement about *factual* matters, P may rely upon the factual part of the statement.

Example: Seller tells Buyer that the house to be sold meets all applicable zoning regulations. If Seller knows that the house violates the local set-back rules, Buyer can recover.

H. Damages: In a deceit action, plaintiff can recover *only* for *pecuniary* (i.e., *financial*) loss.

1. No recovery for emotional distress: Thus plaintiff *cannot* recover for *emotional distress* that resulted from the deceit.

Example: D, offering to sell P D's rural land for $100,000, tells P that oil has been discovered on nearby parcels. P knows that this would be a cheap price if oil had really been discovered nearby. P gets very excited about his wonderful prospective purchase. Before signing a contract, P performs due diligence, and discovers that no oil has been discovered nearby, and that D knowingly misrepresented that oil had been discovered. P suffers great emotional distress at the loss of the opportunity he thought he had. P never signs a contract for the land, but sues D for deceit.

P cannot recover, because he has suffered no pecuniary loss, and damages for emotional distress (as distinguished from pecuniary loss) may not be recovered in a deceit action.

2. Benefit of the bargain: If the misrepresentation was made directly by D to P and a contract resulted, most courts give P the *"benefit of the bargain"* measure of damages.

II. NEGLIGENT MISREPRESENTATION

A. General: At common law, there was no action for "negligent misrepresentation." Unless P suffered personal injury or direct property damage (thus enabling her to bring a conventional negligence action), P was out of luck. But today, most courts *do* allow recovery for negligent misrepresentation, even where only *intangible economic harm* is suffered.

1. Same requirements: Most requirements for a negligent misrepresentation action are the same as for an intentional misrepresentation action.

B. Business relationship: Courts are quickest to allow recovery for negligent misrepresentation where D's statements are made in the course of his *business or profession*, and D had a *pecuniary interest* in the transaction. (Thus if D is P's friend, and makes a representation that is not in the course of D's business, P cannot recover.)

C. Liability to third persons: The maker of a negligent misrepresentation is liable to a much *narrower class* of third persons than is the maker of a fraudulent misstatement.

1. Persons intended to be reached: According to the prevailing rule, D is liable for negligent misrepresentation to a *"limited group of persons"* whom D either: (1) *intends to reach* with the information; or (2) knows the *recipient intends to reach*.

Example: D runs a stock ticker service, which negligently reports that X Corp has declared higher earnings, when in fact its earnings are lower. P, an investor, learns of the "higher" earnings from a subscriber to D's service, and buys the stock, losing money. P cannot recover from D, since they were not in contractual privity, and since P was not a member of a "limited group of persons" whom D intended to reach or who D knew that its subscriber intended to reach.

a. Persons covered: Even though the class of third persons covered is narrow, it is still important.

Examples where liability might attach include:

[1] a *surveyor* knows or should know that his survey will be given to a *prospective purchaser*, and a purchaser relies on the survey in buying the property;

[2] a *lawyer* drafts a *will* negligently cutting out a particular intended *heir*, and the heir sues

the lawyer;

[3] an *accountant* negligently certifies the *books* of X Corp, knowing that X Corp plans to seek a loan from Bank; Bank makes the loan, X Corp goes bankrupt, and Bank sues the accountant.

D. Damages limited to pecuniary harm: Damages for negligent misrepresentation are limited to *pecuniary harm.* This principle has several important consequences:

[1] Plaintiff *cannot* recover for *emotional harm* suffered as the result of the misrepresentation.

Example: D offers P a contract to purchase stock in D's new startup company, telling P that D is about to sign a large and profitable contract with the U.S. government. P signs the contract, and anticipates making millions of dollars on his investment. Before P has closed on the contract or paid money to D, the U.S. government rejects the proposed deal. D honestly (but negligently) believed that the deal would go through when he made the statement to P. D allows P to rescind the agreement. P suffers severe emotional distress from having his hopes of profit dashed. If the contract had gone through, P would indeed have made an enormous return on his investment.

P cannot recover for negligent misrepresentation, because he has suffered only emotional, not pecuniary, loss.

[2] Plaintiff *cannot* recover for the *"benefit of her bargain."* That is, if the misrepresentation relates to a contract, P may not recover the difference between the actual value received by P and the value that P would have received that the facts been accurately stated.

Example: On the facts of the above example, P cannot recover the difference between the price of the stock he contracted to buy and the value the stock would have had if D's representation about the government contract had been true.

[3] But plaintiff *can* recover the difference between the *value* of what P has *received* and what P *paid* in purchase price or other value.

Example: On the facts of the above Example, if P had paid $100,000 for the stock, and without the government contract the stock was worthless, P would be entitled to a return of the $100,000 as damages for negligent misrepresentation.

See generally Rest. 2d, §552B.

III. STRICT LIABILITY

A. Not generally allowed: Generally, a person has no liability for an *"innocent"* misrepresentation. In other words, as a general rule there is *no strict liability* for misrepresentations — misrepresentations must be intentional or negligent to be actionable. But there are two significant exceptions:

1. Sale, rental or exchange: If two parties are involved in a *sale*, *rental* or *exchange* transaction, and one makes a material misrepresentation to the other in order to close the deal, he will be liable even if the misrepresentation is innocent.

a. Warranty: Usually, the buyer can get as much relief from a claim of *breach* of express warranty as from the tort claim of strict liability for misrepresentation. But P may avoid certain contract defenses by relying on the tort theory rather than the warranty theory (e.g., the parol evidence rule).

2. **Sale of chattel:** A seller of goods who makes any misrepresentation on the label, or in public advertising, will be strictly liable for any *physical injury* or *property damage* which results, even if the injured person did not buy the product directly from D.

CHAPTER 17

DEFAMATION

I. GENERAL PRINCIPLES

A. **Meaning of "defamation":** The tort called *"defamation"* is actually two sub-torts, "libel" and "slander." These both protect a person's interest in his *reputation.* A state's freedom to define these torts as it wishes is sharply curtailed by the First Amendment.

B. **Prima facie case:** To establish a prima facie case for either libel or slander, P must prove:

1. **Defamatory statement:** A *false* and *defamatory* statement concerning P;
2. **Publication:** A *communicating* of that statement to a person other than P (a *"publication"*);
3. **Fault:** *Fault* on the part of D, amounting to at least *negligence*, and in some instances a greater degree of fault;
4. **Special harm:** Either *"special harm"* of a pecuniary nature, or the actionability of the statement despite the non-existence of such special harm.

II. DEFAMATORY COMMUNICATION

A. **Injury to reputation:** To be defamatory, a statement must have a tendency to *harm the reputation* of the plaintiff.

1. **Reputation not actually injured:** For the statement to be defamatory, it need not have *actually* harmed P's reputation. It must simply be the case that, *if the statement had been believed*, it would have injured P's reputation. (But in most cases of slander, P has to prove "special damage," i.e., that his reputation was in fact damaged and caused him pecuniary harm — this is not part of the definition of "defamatory," however.)

B. **Reference to plaintiff:** P must show that the statement was reasonably interpreted by at least one recipient as *referring to P.*

1. **Intent irrelevant:** But P does not necessarily have to show that D *intended* to refer to him, rather than to someone else. As a common-law matter (putting aside constitutional decisions), even if D behaved non-negligently and intended to refer to someone else entirely, P can still sue.
2. **Groups:** If D's statement concerns a *group*, and P is a member of that group, P can recover only if the group is a *relatively small one.*

   Example: The statement, "All lawyers are shysters," would not be defamatory as to any particular lawyer, assuming there was no evidence indicating that the statement was intended to refer to P in particular.

3. **Reference need not be by name:** If a non-explicit reference to P is reasonably understood as in fact referring to P, it does not matter that P is referred to by a *different name* or characterization. This is true even if the publication is labelled a "novel."

C. **Truth:** A statement is *not defamatory* if it is *true.*

1. **Substantial truth:** For truth to be a barrier to recovery, it is not necessary that the statement be *literally* true in all respects. Instead, the statement must merely be *"substantially"* true.

D. Opinion

1. **Pure opinion:** A statement of *pure opinion* can never be defamatory.

   Example: D says, "I think Smith is a disgusting person," without expressly or impliedly giving any factual basis for this statement. This is pure opinion, and therefore can't be defamatory.

2. **Implied facts:** But if a statement of opinion *implies undisclosed facts*, and a statement of those facts would be defamatory, then the statement will be itself treated as defamatory.

   Example: D says, "Based on my observations of P, I think she must be an alcoholic." This statement is probably actionable, because it implies that the speaker knows precise facts about P's alcohol consumption that would justify an opinion of alcoholism.

3. **Multiple possible interpretations:** A statement can be subject to *multiple plausible interpretations.* When an ambiguous statement is alleged to be defamatory, the meaning will be "that which the recipient correctly, or mistakenly but reasonably, *understands* that it was intended to express." Rest. 2d, §563.

   a. **Applicable to statement of opinion:** The examiners sometimes test this principle together with the principle that an opinion will be actionable if it falsely implies undisclosed facts, the statement of which would be defamatory. Thus the examiners give you an opinion which might imply unstated facts; if the only reasonable interpretation of the opinion, given the context, is that the speaker is *not* asserting undisclosed facts (or is asserting undisclosed facts that would *not* be defamatory), the statement can't be defamatory.

   Example: P is the mayor of City, and is defending his recent vote to raise local sales taxes on gasoline. D pickets an address by P, carrying a sign saying, "P has stolen our gas money." If (as seems likely), the only reasonable interpretation of this sign is that D is referring to the gas-tax increase, then the sign is not defamatory and P cannot recover for it (even if he could somehow show "actual malice"; see *infra*, p. 101). That's because: (1) pure opinions can't be defamatory; and (2) the only reasonable interpretation of what D is saying — that D is referring to the tax increase — results in D's statement being a pure opinion, not a reference to undisclosed facts that if repeated would be false and defamatory.

III. LIBEL vs. SLANDER

A. Significance of distinction: Distinguish between "libel" and "slander." This distinction makes a difference only with respect to the requirement of *special harm*: to establish slander, P must show that he suffered pecuniary harm (unless the statement falls into one of four special categories). To prove libel, by contrast, P does not have to show such special harm (except, in some courts, if the defamatory nature of the statement is not evident on its face).

B. Libel: Libel consists mainly of all *written or printed matter*.

1. **Embodied in physical form:** Most states hold that it also includes any communication embodied in *"physical form."*

   Examples: A phonograph record, or a computer tape, would be libel in most courts.

2. **Radio and TV:** Where a program is *broadcast* on radio or TV:

a. **Written script:** If it originated with a *written script*, all courts treat it as libel.

b. **No script:** If the program is "ad libbed" rather than coming from a written script, courts are split as to whether it is libel or slander.

C. **Slander:** All other statements are *slander*. An ordinary non-broadcast *oral statement*, for instance, is slander.

D. **Special harm:** P may generally establish slander only if he can show that she has sustained some *"special harm."* This harm generally must be of a *pecuniary nature*.

Example: P shows only that his friends believed D's defamatory statements, and the friends now socially reject P. If the statement is slander, and does not fall within one of the four "slander per se" categories, P cannot recover.

1. **"Slander per se":** There are four kinds of utterances which, even though they are slander rather than libel, require *no showing* of special (i.e., pecuniary) harm:

a. **Crime:** Statements imputing morally culpable *criminal behavior* to P.

b. **Loathsome disease:** Statements alleging that P currently suffers from a *venereal* or other loathsome and communicable disease.

c. **Business, profession, trade or office:** An allegation that adversely reflects on P's fitness to conduct her *business, trade, profession or office.*

Example: P is a storekeeper. D tells a friend F, "P cheats his customers." Since this statement reflects on P's fitness to conduct her business, P can recover without showing any pecuniary loss from the statement. So as long as P can show emotional distress (e.g., from when F repeats the remark to P), P can recover even though there's no evidence that F believed the statement, or that anyone stopped patronizing P's store.

d. **Sexual misconduct:** Statement imputing serious *sexual misconduct* to P.

2. **Libel:** In the case of *libel*, at common law courts do not require proof of actual harm, and can award *"presumed"* damages even without a showing of actual harm. However, recent Supreme Court decisions cut back on the states' ability to do this:

a. **Matters of public concern:** If the statement involves a matter of public concern or a public figure, and recovery is allowed without proof of "actual malice," presumed damages may *not* constitutionally be awarded (because to allow such damages would violate D's First Amendment rights).

b. **Matter of private concern:** But if the defamatory statement does *not* involve a matter of "public concern," presumed damages *may* be allowed, even without a showing of "actual malice."

Example: D, a credit reporting agency, sends a subscriber a written report falsely stating that P is insolvent. Since the statement is not of "public interest," P may recover $50,000 presumed damages without showing any financial loss, and without showing that D knew of the falsity or recklessly disregarded the truth. [*Dun & Bradstreet v. Greenmoss Builders*]

c. **Actual malice:** If P does show "actual malice" (that D either knew of the falsity or recklessly disregarded the truth), presumed damages may probably be constitutionally awarded, even if P is a public figure and the matter is one of public interest.

IV. PUBLICATION

A. Requirement of publication generally: P must show that the defamation was *"published."* "Publication" means, essentially, *"seen or heard by someone other than the plaintiff."*

1. Must be intentional or negligent: D's publication must have been *either intentional or negligent.* Thus there is *no "strict liability"* as to the publication requirement.

a. MBE tip: The MBE examiners love to test this point — they give you a fact pattern in which D makes the false and defamatory remark to P, and doesn't realize (or have reason to realize) that a third person can overhear it. There's *no liability* in this scenario, even if the third person does overhear the remark.

Example: While D and P are dining together alone in a restaurant, D calls P a thief for stealing a sum that D invested with P. A waiter overhears and understands the remark. Unless D knew or should have known that the waiter (or at least someone other than P) would likely hear the remark, D can't be liable to P for defamation even if the statement was false.

2. Must be understood: The publication requirement means that someone other than the plaintiff must not only have heard or seen the communication, but *understood* it. The MBE examiners will sometimes test on this element, perhaps by stipulating that a foreign language was used.

Example: P and D speak a rarely-spoken foreign language, Xi. In a public place, D makes a defamatory statement in Xi to (and about) P, which P understands. Unless P can show that someone else present heard and understood the communication, P can't recover for defamation, because the publication element will not have been satisfied.

B. Repeater's liability: One who *repeats* a defamatory statement made by another is held to have published it, and is liable as if he were the first person to make the statement. This is true even if he indicates the source, and indicates that he himself does not believe the statement.

Example 1: D says, "X told me that P is a thief who steals from his customers, though I doubt it." D has published the defamatory statement, and can be liable to P.

Example 2: D, a newspaper, publishes X's letter-to-the-editor, in which X says, "P embezzled funds from me." D has published the defamatory statement, and can be liable, even though D does not indicate that it believes that X is telling the truth.

V. FAULT

A. Common-law strict liability: At common law, libel and slander were essentially *strict liability* torts. P had to show that the *publication* occurred due to D's intent or negligence, but did not have to show intent or negligence as to any of the other aspects. For instance, it was irrelevant that D had every reason to believe that the statement was *true.*

B. Constitutional decisions: But Supreme Court decisions on the First Amendment have eliminated courts' right to impose strict liability for defamation. The precise mental state which D must be shown to have met depends on whether P is a public figure:

1. Public figure and the "actual malice" requirement: If P is a *"public figure,"* she can recover only if she shows that D made the statement with either: (1) *knowledge that it was false*; or (2) *"reckless disregard"* of whether it was true or false. [*New York Times v. Sullivan*] (These two alternate states of mind are collectively called *"actual malice,"* which is a term of art.)

a. **Meaning of "reckless disregard":** For P to show that D "recklessly disregarded" the truth, it is *not* enough for P to show that a "reasonably prudent person" would not have published, or would have done further investigation. Instead, P must show that D *in fact entertained serious doubts* about the truth of the statement.

2. **Private figures:** But if P is *neither* a public official nor a public figure, she is *not constitutionally required* to prove that D knew his statement was false or recklessly disregarded whether it was true or false. [*Gertz v. Robert Welch, Inc.*]

a. **P must prove at least negligence:** However, even if the plaintiff is a private figure, she cannot recover unless she can show *at least negligence* by the defendant regarding the truth of the statement. So if the defendant *reasonably but mistakenly believes* that his statement is true, courts universally *refuse* to allow the plaintiff to recover. Rest. 2d, §580B(c). (In fact, at least where the defendant is a member of the media, the First Amendment prevents the states from imposing strict liability for defamation, even if the plaintiff is a private figure. *Gertz*, *supra*.)

Example: D fires P. P seeks a new job from X. X asks D for a reference. D writes back, "We fired P because P sexually harassed a co-worker." If D's belief that P harassed a co-worker was reasonable, P cannot recover from D for libel, even if P can prove that the accusation was completely false.

i. **MBE tip:** Since even private figures must prove at least negligence, the examiners can give you a fact pattern in which P will lose by not proving the requisite level of fault, without it even being clear whether P is or isn't a public figure. Just remember, *whether P is a public or private figure, P will always have to prove, at the least, that D was negligent in not ascertaining that the statement was false.*

Example: P is a locally prominent shop owner. D, the local newspaper, writes a story that P has been accused by X, a customer, of having defrauded P. X really made the accusation, but it was false. P rests his defamation case at trial with no evidence from which a jury could find either that D believed the accusation was false or that D was negligent in not determining whether it was true.

P cannot recover for defamation even if he is not a public figure. In other words, you can determine that P must lose, without ever determining whether P's local prominence made him a "public figure" for constitutional purposes (in which case he would have to show "actual malice").

ii. **P may recover for negligence:** Conversely, if plaintiff *does* prove that defendant was negligent in not ascertaining that the communication was false, most states *allow plaintiff to recover,* if plaintiff is not a public figure.

Example: Same shop-owner example as above. Now, however, P presents unrebutted evidence that D knew or should have known that X was an inveterate liar who had often, prior to the article, made false accusations against local merchants. Assume that P is not a public figure. P may recover even though D had merely negligently — not recklessly — failed to check out the truth of X's allegations.

iii. **"Actual malice" doesn't apply:** Don't be mousetrapped into thinking that the *NY Times "actual malice"* standard applies to a suit brought by a private figure — it *doesn't* (though as noted the plaintiff must at least prove negligence). The MBE examiners like to give you a private-figure scenario, then give you a (wrong) choice that says that plaintiff can't recover unless she shows knowledge of falsity or reckless disregard of the truth. Thus in the above shop-owner example, an incorrect choice might say, "P cannot recover because he has not established that D believed the accusations were false or recklessly disregarded whether they were true."

iv. **Serious doubts about statement's truth:** Conversely, if plaintiff shows that defendant did in fact have *significant doubts about the statement's accuracy*, but made it anyway, then this clearly meets the negligence requirement (and indeed probably meets the "actual malice" requirement if plaintiff is a public figure). So anytime on the MBE you have a fact pattern in which D passes on a *rumor* whose truth D doubts, D meets the fault requirement for defamation.

Example: Paul, who is not a public figure, used to work for Dave. Paul then went to work for Bob. Ultimately, Paul left Bob's employ and applied for a job with Sara. Sara asked Dave her opinion about Paul's integrity. Dave responded, "I had no problem with Paul, but I heard that Bob fired Paul because he suspected that Paul may have embezzled from him." Dave knew that he (Dave) had heard this rumor third-hand, and Dave had substantial doubts about whether it was true, but he figured he'd pass it on anyway because he liked Sara and wanted to help her. In fact, Bob had not fired Paul or suspected him of any wrongdoing.

Dave is liable for defamation. His making of the statement to Sara, while having serious doubts about its truth, is enough to establish that he was negligent as to the truth or falsity of his statement. Since a private figure plaintiff does not have to prove more than negligence, the fault requirement is met. (In fact, even if Paul were a public figure, Dave's repetition of the statement while having serious doubts about its truth probably meets the "actual malice" requirement, i.e., shows reckless disregard of the statement's truth, which is one of the two ways of behaving with actual malice [the other being knowledge of the statement's falsity].)

VI. PRIVILEGES

A. **Absolute privileges:** An *"absolute"* privilege applies even if D was motivated solely by malice or other bad motives. The following classes of absolute privilege are usually recognized:

1. **Judicial proceedings:** Judges, lawyers, parties and witnesses are all absolutely privileged in what they say during the course of *judicial proceedings*, regardless of the motives for their statements.

   Example: D, in a pleading in a civil lawsuit between him and P, calls P a crook. P cannot recover from D for defamation, even if P shows that D knew D's statement was a lie.

2. **Legislative proceedings:** *Legislators* acting in furtherance of their legislative functions are absolutely privileged.

3. **Government officials:** Many *government officials* have absolute immunity for statements issued in the course of their jobs. Thus all federal officials, and all high state officials, have this privilege.

4. **Husband and wife:** Any communication between a *husband and wife* is absolutely privileged.

5. **Consent:** Any publication that occurs with the *consent* of the plaintiff is absolutely privileged. Rest. 2d, §583. Sometimes, the concept is expressed by saying that the plaintiff *"invited"* the defamation.

   a. **Scope of consent:** The plaintiff may be deemed to have consented to the publication even if the plaintiff *doesn't know the precise scope* of the communication that will be published, but has reason to know of its *general nature.*

i. **Publication of basis for prior decision by defendant:** Thus consent will likely be found where the defendant has made some decision unfavorable to plaintiff, and the plaintiff asks for a *public clarification* of the basis for the defendant's decision.

Example: P works for D Corp. D fires P, telling P that D has received complaints that P has engaged in sexual harassment of a subordinate. P seeks a new job from X, and X asks P to get a letter from D clarifying the circumstances behind P's firing. P asks D to write the letter. D then writes a detailed letter to X, listing the name of the accuser and the precise allegations. Even if P can prove that the allegations by the accuser were completely untrue (and that D was unreasonable in believing them), P will be deemed to have consented to the publication of the libel in the form of the letter to X, and will therefore be absolutely barred from recovery against D.

B. **Qualified privilege:** Other privileges are merely *"qualified"* or "conditional" ones. A qualified privilege will be lost if D is acting primarily from *malice*, or from some other purpose not protected by the privilege. Qualified privileges tend to be tested more often on the MBE than absolute privileges.

1. **Protection of publisher's interests:** D is conditionally privileged to *protect his own interests*, if these are sufficiently important, and if the defamation is directly related to those interests.

Example: If D reasonably believes that his property has been stolen by P, he may tell the police of his suspicions of P. If D's belief is reasonable, he is protected against a slander action by P, even if his suspicions are wrong.

2. **Interest of others:** Similarly, D may be qualifiedly privileged to act for the protection of the *recipient* of his statement, or some other third person. The issue is whether D's statement is "within the generally accepted standards of *decent conduct*."

a. **Old boss to new boss:** Thus an ex-employer generally has the right to give information about his *ex-employee* P to a new, prospective employer if asked by the latter. This is a scenario that is often tested on the MBE.

i. **"Malice" standard:** The ex-employer is *protected* by the qualified privilege as long as she is *not acting maliciously* or for some other clearly-improper purpose. So, for instance, the fact that the ex-employer *negligently believes* that information she is repeating about the ex-employee is or may be true won't take away the privilege, as long the ex-employer's belief is not in "reckless disregard" of the truth. See Rest. 2d, §600, Comm. b.

Example: P used to work as a cashier at a store in which D was the manager. X, who is trying to decide whether to hire P, contacts D for a reference. D tells X, "We had suspicions that P was occasionally letting her friends take an item without paying for it, but we never actually caught her red-handed. Anyway, we fired P because of these suspicions." X repeats D's comments to P, and P sues D for slander.

As long as D actually believed that P was or may have been behaving dishonestly, and that these suspicions of dishonesty were the reason the store fired P, D will be protected by the qualified privilege, so that P can't recover. That's true even if P can show that D was negligent in suspecting P of dishonesty. (But if D "recklessly disregarded" the accuracy of the information that he was passing on — for instance, by repeating some fourth-hand gossip about P's dishonesty at a different employer that D incorrectly thinks he remembers hearing years ago — then the qualified privilege would be deemed abused and lost, and P could recover.)

3. **Public interest:** D may be conditionally privileged to act in the *public interest*.

Example: A private citizen's reasonable but mistaken accusation made to the police that P committed a crime would be covered.

4. **Report of public proceedings:** There is a conditional privilege to report on *public proceedings*, such as court cases, legislative hearings, etc.

   Example: D, a newspaper, accurately reports that in a lawsuit, X has called P a crook and a liar. Even if X's statement is completely untrue and was made with malice, D has a qualified privilege to make the report of the public proceeding, and therefore may not be sued for libel.

C. **Abuse of qualified privilege:** Even where a qualified privilege exists, it may be *abused* (and therefore forfeited) in a number of ways.

1. **Actual malice:** Most importantly, the privilege will be lost if D *knew that his statement was false*, or acted in *reckless disregard* of whether it was true.

   Example: D, P's ex-employer, is asked for information by X, P's new prospective employer, concerning P's work. D's clerk negligently misreads the file, and asserts that P was fired for dishonesty, when in fact P quit voluntarily. If the clerk is shown to have behaved recklessly, D's qualified privilege — to protect the interest of a third person by commenting on an employee's fitness — will be deemed abused and thus forfeited. But if the clerk was only negligent, the privilege will probably not be lost.

2. **Excessive publication:** The privilege is abused if the statement is made to persons to whom publication is *not reasonably necessary* to protect the interest in question, or if more damaging information is stated than is reasonably needed.

CHAPTER 18

INVASION OF PRIVACY

I. INVASION OF PRIVACY

A. **Four torts:** The so-called *"invasion of privacy"* cause of action is essentially four distinct mini-torts. They all involve P's "right to be let alone." The four are:

[1] *misappropriation* of P's name or picture;

[2] *intrusion* on P's solitude;

[3] undue publicity given to P's *private life*; and

[4] the placing of P in a *false light*.

We consider each one in turn below.

B. **Misappropriation of identity:** P can recover if her *name or picture* has been *misappropriated* by D for his own financial benefit.

Example: D, a cereal maker, runs an ad containing a photo of P eating D's cereal. P does in fact eat D's cereal, but has never agreed to endorse it. P can recover for appropriation of his picture.

C. **Intrusion:** P may sue if his *solitude* is *intruded upon*, and this intrusion would be *"highly offensive* to a reasonable person."

Example: To gain derogatory information about P to use in their upcoming civil case, D hires a detective to wiretap P's home, and to eavesdrop on P using a directional microphone pointed at P's front window. P has an invasion-of-privacy claim against D of the "intrusion upon solitude" variety.

1. **Must be private place:** This "intrusion upon solitude" branch is triggered only where a *private place* is invaded. Thus if D takes P's picture in a public place, this will normally not be enough.

D. Publicity of private life: In most (but not all) courts, P may recover if D has *publicized* the details of P's *private life*. The effect must be "*highly offensive to a reasonable person.*" Rest. 2d, §652D.

Example: D, a sensationalist newspaper, prints the details of the extramarital sex life of P, who is wealthy but not a public figure. P may be able to recover against D for publicity of private life.

1. **Not of legitimate public concern:** But the First Amendment requires that recovery for the "publicity of private life" be allowed only if the material publicized is *not of legitimate public concern* or *"newsworthy."* Rest. 2d, §652D, Comm. d.

   Example: If P is on trial for murder, it is not an invasion of his privacy for newspapers to give reports on even minor private details of his past life, such as his sexual history.

2. **Already-public information:** Also, recovery is not allowed where the information is *already known or available to the public*, and defendant merely gives extra publicity to this publicly-available information. Rest. 2d, §652D, Comm. b.

   Example: At a public meeting of the Muni Zoning Board, Fred complains that his next-door neighbor Nan has been sunbathing nude, and getting drunk, in her outdoor hot tub, which Fred (and only Fred) can see from a particular window in his house. Newspaper, whose reporter is present, accurately reports Fred's remarks, identifying Nan. Nan cannot recover for publicity-of-private-life against Newspaper, because the information had already been made public at the zoning meeting.

3. **More than small group of people:** The matter must be made *"public."* This requires that it be communicated "to the public at large, or to so many persons that the matter must be regarded as substantially certain to become one of public knowledge." Rest. 2d, §652D, Comm. a. So it's not publicity-of-private-life if the defendant communicates the material "to a single person or even to *a small group of persons*." *Id.*

   Example: D and P are co-workers at an office. D tells three co-workers about an episode from P's private sex life about which P has confided to D, with instructions not to tell anyone else. Unless there's reason to believe that the three co-workers will spread the information further, P can't recover from D for publicity-of-private-life.

E. False light: P can recover if he is placed before the public eye in a *false light*, and this false light would be highly offensive to a reasonable person.

Example: P is a war hero. D makes a movie about P's life, including fictitious materials such as a non-existent romance. D is liable for invasion of privacy, of the "false light" variety.

1. **Actual malice:** But at least where P is a public figure, he can recover for "false light" only if he can show that D knew the portrayal was false, or acted in reckless disregard of whether it was. In other words, the *New York Times v. Sullivan "actual malice"* standard *applies* to false light actions by public figures. [*Time, Inc. v. Hill*]

   a. **Private figures:** Probably private figures do *not* have to meet this "actual malice" standard.

MBE-STYLE QUESTIONS ON TORTS

TORTS QUESTIONS

These questions are the Torts questions from the Self-Assessment Test. They are presented here in approximately the order in which the main topic or theme of the question is treated in the substantive outline earlier in this book. Thus questions focusing on Intentional Torts and Defenses come first, followed by questions on Negligence, etc.

The NCBE examiners tell you to assume that joint-and-several liability, with pure comparative negligence, is the relevant rule unless otherwise indicated. You should answer these questions on that same assumption unless the text of the question indicates otherwise.

26 min
16/17

1. A bus passenger was seated next to a woman whom he did not know. The woman stood to exit the bus, leaving a package on the seat. The passenger lightly tapped the woman on the back to get her attention and to inform her that she had forgotten the package. Because the woman had recently had back surgery, the tap was painful and caused her to twist and seriously injure her back.

   If the woman sues the passenger to recover for the back injury, will she prevail?

   (A) No, because she is presumed to have consented to the ordinary contacts of daily life.

   (B) No, because she was not put in apprehension because of the touching.

   (C) Yes, because the passenger intentionally touched her.

   (D) Yes, because the passenger's intentional touching seriously injured her.

   [Q7063]

2. The plaintiff suffered a serious injury while participating in an impromptu basketball game at a public park. The injury occurred when the plaintiff and the defendant, on opposing teams, each tried to obtain possession of the ball when it rebounded from the backboard after a missed shot at the basket. During that encounter, the plaintiff was struck and injured by the defendant's elbow. The plaintiff now seeks compensation from the defendant.

   At the trial, evidence was introduced tending to prove that the game had been rough from the beginning, that elbows and knees had frequently been used to discourage interference by opposing players, and that the plaintiff had been one of those making liberal use of such tactics.

   In this action, will the plaintiff prevail?

   (A) Yes, if the defendant intended to strike the plaintiff with his elbow.

   (B) Yes, if the defendant intended to cause a harmful or offensive contact with the plaintiff.

   (C) No, because the plaintiff impliedly consented to rough play.

   (D) No, unless the defendant intentionally used force that exceeded the players' consent.

   [Q3017]

GO ON TO THE NEXT PAGE

3. A thirteen-year-old girl was a member of a national young people's scouting organization. As part of a scouting project, she planned to spend an entire weekend camping alone in the woods. The defendant, who knew about the project, phoned the scout's mother the day after the scout left home. The defendant said, "We have your daughter. We've already beaten her up once, just to hear her scream. Next time, we might kill her." The defendant instructed the mother to deliver a cash ransom to a specified location within one hour. Since there was no way to locate the scout's campsite in the woods, the mother could not find out whether the defendant was telling the truth. Horrified that her daughter might be beaten and injured or killed, she delivered the ransom as instructed. She remained in a hysterical state until the scout returned from her camping trip, and the mother realized that the ransom demand had been a hoax. The mother, who already suffered from a heart ailment, had a heart attack the day after the scout's return.

   If the mother asserts a claim against the defendant for assault, the court should find for

   (A) the mother, because the defendant was aware that his conduct would frighten her.

   (B) the mother, because the court will transfer the defendant's intent.

   (C) the defendant, because the mother did not perceive injury being inflicted upon the scout.

   (D) the defendant, because the mother had no reason to expect to be touched by the defendant.

   [Q5018]

4. The defendant and the plaintiff had been friends for years, and worked in the same office. Ever since they were children, they had enjoyed playing "practical jokes" on each other. Frequently, they would spend hours together, laughing about the tricks they had played on each other. One day, planning to have some fun with the plaintiff, the defendant bought a large rubber spider from a toy store. Knowing that the plaintiff was horrified of spiders, the defendant came into work early, and placed the toy spider in the top drawer of the plaintiff's desk. Later, when the plaintiff arrived at work, he opened his top drawer to get out a letter opener and saw the rubber spider. Believing it to be real, and terrified that it would bite him, the plaintiff screamed in fear, fainted, and fell to the floor. As he fell, he struck his head on the corner of his desk, sustaining a serious fracture of the skull.

   If the plaintiff asserts a claim for assault against the defendant for the injury which he sustained in the fall, which of the following arguments would be most effective in the defendant's defense?

   (A) The plaintiff's fear of being bitten by a spider was not apprehension of a battery.

   (B) A reasonable person in the plaintiff's position would not have become apprehensive at the sight of a spider.

   (C) The plaintiff impliedly consented to the prank by engaging in a course of practical joking with the defendant.

   (D) The defendant was not substantially certain that the plaintiff would be injured as a result of the joke.

   [Q5112]

GO ON TO THE NEXT PAGE

5. A law student rented a furnished apartment. His landlord began to solicit his advice about her legal affairs, but he refused to provide it. The landlord then demanded that he vacate the apartment immediately. The landlord also engaged in a pattern of harassment, calling the student at home every evening and entering his apartment without his consent during times when he was at school. During these unauthorized visits she removed the handles from the bathroom and kitchen sinks, but did not touch anything belonging to the student. The lease has a year to run, and the student is still living in the apartment. The student has sued the landlord for trespass to land.

   Is he likely to prevail?

   (A) No, because he has no standing to sue for trespass.

   (B) No, because the landlord caused no damage to his property.

   (C) Yes, for compensatory damages only.

   (D) Yes, for injunctive relief, compensatory damages, and punitive damages.

   [Q7088]

6. A driver was driving his car near an owner's house when the owner's child darted into the street in front of the driver's car. As the driver swerved and braked his car to avoid hitting the child, the car skidded up into the owner's driveway and stopped just short of the owner, who was standing in the driveway and had witnessed the entire incident. The owner suffered serious emotional distress from witnessing the danger to his child and to himself. Neither the owner nor his property was physically harmed.

   If the owner asserts a claim for damages against the driver, will the owner prevail?

   (A) Yes, because the driver's entry onto the owner's land was unauthorized.

   (B) Yes, because the owner suffered serious emotional distress by witnessing the danger to his child and to himself.

   (C) No, unless the driver was negligent.

   (D) No, unless the owner's child was exercising reasonable care.

   [Q3149]

7. A neighbor, who lived next door to a homeowner, went into the homeowner's garage without permission and borrowed the homeowner's chain saw. The neighbor used the saw to clear broken branches from the trees on the neighbor's own property. After he had finished, the neighbor noticed several broken branches on the homeowner's trees that were in danger of falling on the homeowner's roof. While the neighbor was cutting the homeowner's branches, the saw broke.

   In a suit for conversion by the homeowner against the neighbor, will the homeowner recover?

   (A) Yes, for the actual damage to the saw.

   (B) Yes, for the value of the saw before the neighbor borrowed it.

   (C) No, because when the saw broke, the neighbor was using it to benefit the homeowner.

   (D) No, because the neighbor did not intend to keep the saw.

   [Q3003]

GO ON TO THE NEXT PAGE

8. A landowner was hunting rattlesnakes on his land with a pistol when he saw a hunter carrying a shotgun and attempting to enter the owner's land by crawling under the barbed wire fence which surrounded it. The owner waited until the hunter had gotten past the fence and then approached the hunter, telling him that he was trespassing and ordering him to leave. The hunter said, "I only want to shoot some birds. I got a right to do that if I want to, don't I?" After the hunter said this, the owner placed his hand on the hunter's chest and pushed him gently backward, repeating his demand that the hunter leave. The hunter shoved the owner away from him and pointed his shotgun at the owner, saying, "Nobody pushes me, Mister." The owner immediately drew his pistol from the holster on his belt and fired at the hunter, striking him in the arm and causing him to drop his shotgun.

   If the hunter asserts a claim against the owner for battery, the court should find for

   (A) the owner, if he reasonably believed that no lesser force would safely cause the hunter to leave his property.

   (B) the owner, if he reasonably believed that no lesser force would safely prevent the hunter from firing the shotgun at him.

   (C) the hunter, because the owner made the first use of force.

   (D) the hunter, because the owner did not use force against him until the hunter's entry onto the realty was complete.

   [Q5052]

9. As an encyclopedia salesman approached the grounds on which a reclusive homeowner's house was situated, he saw a sign that said, "No salesmen. Trespassers will be prosecuted. Proceed at your own risk." Although the salesman had not been invited to enter, he ignored the sign and drove up the driveway toward the house. As he rounded a curve, a powerful explosive charge buried in the driveway exploded, and the salesman was injured.

   Can the salesman recover damages from the homeowner for his injuries?

   (A) Yes, if the homeowner was responsible for the explosive charge under the driveway.

   (B) Yes, unless the homeowner, when he planted the charge, intended only to deter, not to harm, a possible intruder.

   (C) No, because the salesman ignored the sign, which warned him against proceeding further.

   (D) No, if the homeowner reasonably feared that intruders would come and harm him or his family.

   [Q3195]

10. A trucker was driving a truckload of gravel over a highway in a rural part of the state, when through no fault of her own, one of the tires on her truck blew out, causing the truck to go out of control. The truck overturned, spilling the gravel onto the land of a private landowner that was adjacent to the road. The trucker, who was unhurt, returned later with another truck and a tractor equipped with a power shovel. Using the power shovel, the trucker scooped up the spilled gravel and loaded it onto the other truck.

   If the landowner asserts a claim against the trucker for trespass to land, the court should award the landowner a judgment for

   (A) nominal damage only.

   (B) all damage resulting from the spilling of gravel onto the landowner's land.

   (C) only the damage caused by the trucker's removal of the gravel from the landowner's land.

   (D) no damage.

   [Q5075]

11. A customer fell and injured himself when he slipped on a banana peel while shopping at a grocer's store. The banana peel was fresh and clean except for a mark made by the heel of the customer's shoe. In an action brought by the customer against the grocer, these are the only facts in evidence.

Should the trial judge permit the case to go to the jury?

(A) No, because the customer had an obligation to watch where he stepped.

(B) No, because there is not a reasonable basis for inferring that the grocer knew or should have known of the banana peel.

(C) Yes, because it is more likely than not that the peel came from a banana offered for sale by the grocer.

(D) Yes, because the grocer could foresee that a customer might slip on a banana peel.

[Q7083]

12. A bright nine-year-old child attended a day care center after school. The day care center was located near a man-made duck pond on the property of a corporation. During the winter, the pond was used for ice skating when conditions were suitable. At a time when the pond was only partially frozen, the child sneaked away from the center and walked out onto the ice covering the pond. The ice gave way, and the child fell into the cold water. He suffered shock and would have drowned had he not been rescued by a passerby. At the time of the incident, the pond was clearly marked with signs that stated, "THIN ICE - NO SKATING." When the child left the day care center, the center was staffed with a reasonable number of qualified personnel, and the center's employees were exercising reasonable care to ensure that the children in their charge did not leave the premises. The jurisdiction follows a rule of pure comparative negligence.

In a suit brought on the child's behalf against the day care center, who is likely to prevail?

(A) The child, because he left the center while he was under the center's care.

(B) The child, because the day care center is located near a pond.

(C) The day care center, because it was not negligent.

(D) The day care center, because the child was a trespasser.

[Q7094]

13. A car owner washed her car while it was parked on a public street, in violation of a statute that prohibits the washing of vehicles on public streets during rush hours. The statute was enacted only to expedite the flow of automobile traffic. Due to a sudden and unexpected cold snap, the car owner's waste water formed a puddle that froze. A pedestrian slipped on the frozen puddle and broke her leg. The pedestrian sued the car owner to recover for her injury. At trial, the only evidence the pedestrian offered as to negligence was the car owner's admission that she had violated the statute. At the conclusion of the proofs, both parties moved for a directed verdict.

How should the trial judge proceed?

(A) Deny both motions and submit the case to the jury, because, on the facts, the jury may infer that the car owner was negligent.

(B) Deny both motions and submit the case to the jury, because the jury may consider the statutory violation as evidence that the car owner was negligent.

(C) Grant the car owner's motion, because the pedestrian has failed to offer adequate evidence that the car owner was negligent.

(D) Grant the pedestrian's motion, because of the car owner's admitted statutory violation.

[Q7020]

14. In a civil action, the plaintiff sued a decedent's estate to recover damages for injuries she suffered in a collision between her car and one driven by the decedent. At trial, the plaintiff introduced undisputed evidence that the decedent's car swerved across the median of the highway, where it collided with an oncoming car driven by the plaintiff. The decedent's estate introduced undisputed evidence that, prior to the car's crossing the median, the decedent suffered a fatal heart attack, which she had no reason to foresee, and that, prior to the heart attack, the decedent had been driving at a reasonable speed and in a reasonable manner. A statute makes it a traffic offense to cross the median of a highway.

In this case, for whom should the court render judgment?

(A) The decedent's estate, because its evidence is undisputed.

(B) The decedent's estate, because the plaintiff has not established a prima facie case of liability.

(C) The plaintiff, because the accident was of a type that does not ordinarily happen in the absence of negligence on the actor's part.

(D) The plaintiff, because the decedent crossed the median in violation of the statute.

[Q7059]

15. A traveler was a passenger on a commercial aircraft owned and operated by an airline. The aircraft crashed into a mountain, killing everyone on board. The flying weather was good.

The traveler's legal representative brought a wrongful death action against the airline. At trial, the legal representative offered no expert or other testimony as to the cause of the crash.

On the airline's motion to dismiss at the conclusion of the legal representative's case, the court should

(A) grant the motion, because the legal representative has offered no evidence as to the cause of the crash.

(B) grant the motion, because the legal representative has failed to offer evidence negating the possibility that the crash may have been caused by mechanical failure that the airline could not have prevented.

(C) deny the motion, because the jury may infer that the aircraft crashed due to the airline's negligence.

(D) deny the motion, because in the circumstances common carriers are strictly liable.

[Q3161]

16. A construction company was digging a trench for a new sewer line in a street in a high-crime neighborhood. During the course of the construction, there had been many thefts of tools and equipment from the construction area. One night, the construction company's employees neglected to place warning lights around the trench. A delivery truck drove into the trench and broke an axle. While the delivery driver was looking for a telephone to summon a tow truck, thieves broke into the delivery truck and stole $350,000 worth of goods. The delivery company sued the construction company to recover for the $350,000 loss and for $1,500 worth of damage to its truck. The construction company stipulated that it was negligent in failing to place warning lights around the trench, and admits liability for damage to the truck, but denies liability for the loss of the goods.

On cross-motions for summary judgment, how should the court rule?

(A) Deny both motions, because there is evidence to support a finding that the construction company should have realized that its negligence could create an opportunity for a third party to commit a crime.

(B) Grant the construction company's motion, because no one could have foreseen that the failure to place warning lights could result in the loss of a cargo of valuable goods.

(C) Grant the construction company's motion, because the criminal acts of third persons were a superseding cause of the loss.

(D) Grant the delivery company's motion, because but for the construction company's actions, the goods would not have been stolen.

[Q7032]

17. The Rapido is a sports car manufactured by the defendant, a car maker. The Rapido has an excellent reputation for mechanical reliability with one exception, which is that the motor may stall if the engine has not had an extended warm-up. The plaintiff had just begun to drive her Rapido in city traffic without a warm-up when the engine suddenly stalled. Behind the plaintiff, a car driven by an elderly man tried to stop, but rear-ended the plaintiff's car. The plaintiff suffered no external physical injuries as a result of the collision. However, the shock of the crash caused her to suffer a severe heart attack.

The plaintiff brought an action against the defendant based on strict liability in tort. During the trial, the plaintiff presented evidence of an alternative engine design of equal cost that would eliminate the stalling problem without impairing the functions of the engine in any way. The defendant moves for a directed verdict at the close of the evidence.

This motion should be

(A) denied, because the jury could find that an unreasonably dangerous defect in the engine was a proximate cause of the collision.

(B) denied, if the jury could find that the Rapido was not crashworthy.

(C) granted, because the elderly man's failure to stop within an assured clear distance was a superseding cause of the collision.

(D) granted, if a person of normal sensitivity would not have suffered a heart attack under these circumstances.

[Q3146]

18. A four-year-old child sustained serious injuries when a playmate pushed him from between two parked cars into the street, where he was struck by a car. The child, by his representative, sued the driver of the car, the playmate's parents, and his own parents. At trial, the child's total injuries were determined to be $100,000. The playmate's parents were determined to be 20% at fault because they had failed to adequately supervise her. The driver was found to be 50% at fault. The child's own parents were determined to be 30% at fault for failure to adequately supervise him. The court has adopted the pure comparative negligence doctrine, with joint-and-several liability, in place of the common-law rules relating to plaintiff's fault. In addition, the common-law doctrines relating to intra-family liability have been abrogated.

How much, if anything, is the child's representative entitled to recover from the driver?

(A) $30,000.

(B) $50,000.

(C) $100,000.

(D) Nothing.

[Q7072]

GO ON TO THE NEXT PAGE

19. A corporation designed and built a processing plant for the manufacture of an explosive chemical. An engineer was retained by the corporation to design a filter system for the processing plant. She prepared an application for a permit to build the plant's filter system and submitted it to the state's Department of Environmental Protection (DEP). As required by DEP regulations, the engineer submitted a blueprint to the DEP with the application for permit. The blueprint showed the entire facility and was signed and sealed by her as a licensed professional engineer.

    After the project was completed, a portion of the processing plant exploded, injuring the plaintiff. During discovery in an action by the plaintiff against the engineer, it was established that the explosion was caused by a design defect in the processing plant that was unrelated to the filter system designed by the engineer.

    In that action, will the plaintiff prevail?

    (A) Yes, if the engineer signed, sealed, and submitted a blueprint that showed the design defect.

    (B) Yes, because all of the plant's designers are jointly and severally liable for the defect.

    (C) No, because the engineer owed no duty to the plaintiff to prevent the particular risk of harm.

    (D) No, if the engineer was an independent contractor of the corporation.

    [Q3032]

20. An electrical engineer designed an electronic game. The engineer entered into a licensing agreement with a toy company under which the company agreed to manufacture the game according to the engineer's specifications and to market it and pay a royalty to the engineer.

    A child, whose parents had purchased the game for her, was injured while playing the game. The child recovered a judgment against the toy company on the basis of a finding that the game was defective because of the engineer's improper design.

    In a claim for indemnity against the engineer, will the toy company prevail?

    (A) Yes, because as between the engineer and the toy company, the engineer was responsible for the design of the game.

    (B) Yes, because the toy company and the engineer were joint tortfeasors.

    (C) No, because the toy company, as the manufacturer, was strictly liable to the child.

    (D) No, if the toy company, by a reasonable inspection, could have discovered the defect in the design of the game.

    [Q4052]

21. [The basic facts are the same as in Question 12, but the question asked here is different.] A bright nine-year-old child attended a day care center after school. The day care center was located near a man-made duck pond on the property of a corporation. During the winter, the pond was used for ice skating when conditions were suitable. At a time when the pond was only partially frozen, the child sneaked away from the center and walked out onto the ice covering the pond. The ice gave way, and the child fell into the cold water. He suffered shock and would have drowned had he not been rescued by a passerby. At the time of the incident, the pond was clearly marked with signs that stated, "THIN ICE - NO SKATING." When the child left the day care center, the center was staffed with a reasonable number of qualified personnel, and the center's employees were exercising reasonable care to ensure that the children in their charge did not leave the premises. The jurisdiction follows a rule of pure comparative negligence.

    In a suit brought on the child's behalf against the corporation, who is likely to prevail?

(A) The child, because the corporation owes a duty to keep its premises free of dangerous conditions.

(B) The child, because the pond was an attractive nuisance.

(C) The corporation, because the danger of thin ice may reasonably be expected to be understood by a nine-year-old child.

(D) The corporation, because the day care center had a duty to keep the child off the ice.

[Q7093]

22. A mother rushed her eight-year-old daughter to the emergency room at a hospital after the daughter fell off her bicycle and hit her head on a sharp rock. The wound caused by the fall was extensive and bloody.

The mother was permitted to remain in the treatment room, and held the daughter's hand while the emergency room physician cleaned and sutured the wound. During the procedure, the mother said that she was feeling faint and stood up to leave the room. While leaving the room, the mother fainted and, in falling, struck her head on a metal fixture that protruded from the emergency room wall. She sustained a serious injury as a consequence.

If the mother sues the hospital to recover damages for her injury, will she prevail?

(A) Yes, because the mother was a public invitee of the hospital.

(B) Yes, unless the fixture was an obvious, commonly used, and essential part of the hospital's equipment.

(C) No, unless the hospital's personnel failed to take reasonable steps to anticipate and prevent the mother's injury.

(D) No, because the hospital's personnel owed the mother no affirmative duty of care.

[Q3036]

23. A driver, returning from a long shift at a factory, fell asleep at the wheel and lost control of his car. As a result, his car collided with a police car driven by an officer who was returning to the station after having responded to an emergency. The police officer was injured in the accident. The police officer sued the driver in negligence for her injuries. The driver moved for summary judgment, arguing that the common-law firefighters' rule barred the suit.

Should the court grant the motion?

(A) No, because the firefighters' rule does not apply to police officers.

(B) No, because the police officer's injuries were not related to any special dangers of her job.

(C) Yes, because the accident would not have occurred but for the emergency.

(D) Yes, because the police officer was injured on the job.

[Q7006]

GO ON TO THE NEXT PAGE

24. A customer ate a spicy dinner at a restaurant on Sunday night. He enjoyed the food and noticed nothing unusual about the dinner.

Later that evening, the customer had an upset stomach. He slept well through the night, went to work the next day, and ate three meals. His stomach discomfort persisted, and by Tuesday morning he was too ill to go to work.

Eventually, the customer consulted his doctor, who found that the patron was infected with a bacterium that can be contracted from contaminated food. Food can be contaminated when those who prepare it do not adequately wash their hands.

The customer sued the restaurant for damages. He introduced testimony from a health department official that various health code violations had been found at the restaurant both before and after the customer's dinner, but that none of the restaurant's employees had signs of bacterial infection when they were tested one month after the incident.

The restaurant's best argument in response to the customer's suit would be that

(A) no one else who ate at the restaurant on Sunday complained about stomach discomfort.

(B) the restaurant instructs its employees to wash their hands carefully and is not responsible if any employee fails to follow these instructions.

– (C) the customer has failed to establish that the restaurant's food caused his illness.

(D) the customer assumed the risk of an upset stomach by choosing to eat spicy food.

[Q3090]

25. A homeowner owned a large poisonous snake which had been defanged and was kept in a cage. A storm damaged the homeowner's house and the snake's cage, allowing it to escape. During the cleanup after the storm, a volunteer worker came across the snake. The worker tried to run away from the snake and fell, breaking his arm.

In a suit by the worker against the homeowner based on strict liability in tort to recover for his injury, will the worker prevail?

(A) No, because the snake's escape was caused by a force of nature.

(B) No, because the worker should have anticipated an injury during his volunteer work.

(C) Yes, because the homeowner did not take adequate precautions to secure the snake.

– (D) Yes, because the worker's injury was the result of his fear of the escaped snake.

[Q7075]

26. A married couple purchased a new mobile home from a retailer of such homes. The mobile home was assembled by a manufacturer and had an "HVAC" (heating, ventilating, and air conditioning) system designed by that manufacturer. The HVAC system contained both a furnace and an air conditioner, neither of which was made by the manufacturer — the furnace was made by a heating company and the air conditioner was made by a cooling company. The manufacturer selected and installed the furnace and the air conditioner into the overall HVAC unit. The furnace and the air conditioner were each controlled by an independent thermostat installed by the manufacturer. Because of the manner in which the manufacturer designed the HVAC system, the first time the system was operated by the couple, cold air was vented into the couple's bedroom to keep the temperature at 68°F. The cold air then activated the heater thermostat, and hot air was pumped into the bedroom of the couple's six-month-old child. The temperature in the child's room reached more than 170°F before the child's mother became

aware of the condition and shut the system off manually. As a result, the child suffered permanent physical injury.

The child, through a duly appointed guardian, has asserted claims against the manufacturer, the heating company, and the cooling company (but not the retailer), all of which claims are based on strict liability in tort. The child will probably recover against

(A) the manufacturer only, because the ventilating system was defectively designed by it.

(B) the heating company only, because it was the excessive heat from the furnace that caused the child's injuries.

(C) the manufacturer and the heating company only, because the combination of the manufacturer's design and the heating company's furnace caused the child's injuries.

(D) the manufacturer, the heating company, and the cooling company, because the combination of the manufacturer's design, the heating company's furnace, and the cooling company's air conditioning unit caused the child's injuries.

[Q4044]

27. A secretary worked in an office in a building occupied partly by her employer and partly by a retail glass store. The two areas were separated by walls and were in no way connected, except that the air conditioning unit served both areas and there was a common return-air duct.

The glass store began remodeling, and its employees did the work, which included affixing a plastic surfacing material to counters. To fasten the plastic to the counters, the employees purchased glue, with the brand name Stick, that was manufactured by a glue manufacturer, packaged in a sealed container by that glue manufacturer, and retailed to the glass store by a paint company.

In the course of the remodeling job, one of the glass store's employees turned on the air conditioning and caused fumes from the glue to travel from the glass store through the air conditioning unit and into the secretary's office. The glass store employees did not know that there was common ductwork for the air conditioners. The secretary was permanently blinded by the fumes from the glue.

The label on the container of glue read, "DANGER. Do not smoke near this product. Extremely flammable. Contains Butanone, Tuluol, and Hexane. Use with adequate ventilation. Keep out of the reach of children."

The three chemicals listed on the label are very toxic and harmful to human eyes. The glue manufacturer had received no reports of eye injuries during the ten years that the product had been manufactured and sold.

If the secretary asserts a claim against the paint company, the most likely result is that she will

(A) recover, if she can recover against the glue manufacturer.

(B) recover, because the secretary was an invitee of a tenant in the building.

(C) not recover unless the paint company was negligent.

(D) not recover, because the glue came in a sealed package.

[Q4049]

GO ON TO THE NEXT PAGE

28. The plaintiff, who was an asbestos insulation installer from 1955 to 1965, contracted asbestosis, a serious lung disorder, as a result of inhaling airborne asbestos particles on the job. The asbestos was manufactured and sold to the plaintiff's employer by an asbestos manufacturer. Because neither the asbestos manufacturer nor anyone else discovered the risk to asbestos installers until 1966, the manufacturer did not provide any warnings of the risks to installers until after that date.

    The plaintiff brought an action against the asbestos manufacturer based on strict liability in tort for failure to warn. The case is to be tried before a jury. The jurisdiction has not adopted a comparative fault rule in strict liability cases.

    In this action, an issue that is relevant to the case and is a question for the court to decide as a matter of law, rather than for the jury to decide as a question of fact, is whether

    (A) a satisfactory, safer, alternative insulation material exists under today's technology.

    (B) the defendant should be held to the standard of a prudent manufacturer who knew of the risks, regardless of whether the risks were reasonably discoverable before 1966.

    (C) the defendant should reasonably have known of the risks of asbestos insulation materials before 1966, even though no one else had discovered the risks.

    (D) the asbestos insulation materials to which the plaintiff was exposed were inherently dangerous.

    [Q3023]

29. For ten years, a vacationer and his neighbor have owned summer vacation homes on adjoining lots. A stream flows through both lots. As a result of a childhood swimming accident, the vacationer is afraid of water and has never gone close to the stream. The neighbor built a dam on her property that has completely stopped the flow of the stream to the vacationer's property.

    In a suit by the vacationer against the neighbor, will the vacationer prevail?

    (A) Yes, if the damming unreasonably interferes with the use and enjoyment of the vacationer's property.

    (B) Yes, if the neighbor intended to affect the vacationer's property.

    (C) No, because the vacationer made no use of the stream.

    (D) No, if the dam was built in conformity with all applicable laws.

    [Q3041]

30. The personnel director of an investment company told a job applicant during an interview that the company was worth millions of dollars and that the company's portfolio would triple in the next several months. The applicant was very excited about the company's prospects and accepted an offer to work for the company. Two days later, the applicant read in the newspaper that the investment company had filed for bankruptcy reorganization. As a result of reading this news, the applicant suffered severe emotional distress but he immediately found another comparable position.

    Is the applicant likely to prevail in his action for negligent misrepresentation?

    (A) No, because the applicant did not suffer any physical injury or pecuniary loss.

    (B) No, because the personnel director's statement was purely speculative.

GO ON TO THE NEXT PAGE

(C) Yes, because the applicant relied on the personnel director's misrepresentations about the investment company.

(D) Yes, because the personnel director should have foreseen that his misrepresentations would cause the applicant to be upset.

[Q7040]

31. A chemical engineer had no financial interest in or connection with a particular chemical company. The engineer noticed that the company's most recent publicly issued financial statement listed, as part of the company's assets, a large inventory of a certain special chemical compound. This asset was listed at a cost of $100,000, but the engineer knew that the ingredients of the compound were in short supply and that the current market value of the inventory was in excess of $1,000,000. There was no current public quotation of the price of the company's stock. The book value of the company's stock, according to the statement, was $5 a share; its actual value was $30 a share.

Knowing these facts, the engineer offered to purchase from a seller (an individual who had no connection with the company) at $6 a share the 1,000 shares of the company's stock owned by the seller. The seller and the engineer had not previously met. The seller sold the stock to the engineer for $6 a share.

If the seller asserts a claim based on misrepresentation against the engineer, will the seller prevail?

(A) Yes, because the engineer knew that the value of the stock was greater than the price she offered.

(B) Yes, if the engineer did not inform the seller of the true value of the inventory.

(C) No, unless the engineer told the seller that the stock was not worth more than $6 a share.

(D) No, if the company's financial statement was available to the seller.

[Q4045]

32. An associate professor in the pediatrics department of a local medical school was denied tenure. He asked a national education lobbying organization to represent him in his efforts to have the tenure decision reversed. In response to a letter from the organization on the professor's behalf, the dean of the medical school wrote to the organization explaining truthfully that the professor had been denied tenure because of reports that he had abused two of his former patients. Several months later, after a thorough investigation, the allegations were proven false and the professor was granted tenure. He had remained working at the medical school at full pay during the tenure decision review process and thus suffered no pecuniary harm.

In a suit for libel by the professor against the dean of the medical school, will the professor prevail?

(A) No, because the professor invited the libel.

(B) No, because the professor suffered no pecuniary loss.

(C) Yes, because the dean had a duty to investigate the rumor before repeating it.

(D) Yes, because the dean's defamatory statement was in the form of a writing.

[Q7050]

GO ON TO THE NEXT PAGE

33. A customer ordered some merchandise from a store. When the merchandise was delivered, the customer decided that it was not what he had ordered, and he returned it for credit. The store refused to credit the customer's account, continued to bill him, and, after 90 days, turned the account over to a bill collector for collection. The bill collector called at the customer's house at 7 p.m. on a summer evening while many of the customer's neighbors were seated on their porches. When the customer opened the door, the bill collector, who was standing just outside the door, raised an electrically amplified bullhorn to his mouth. In a voice that could be heard a block away, the bill collector called the customer a "deadbeat" and asked him when he intended to pay his bill to the store. The customer, greatly angered, slammed the door shut.

    If the customer asserts a claim based on defamation against the bill collector, will the customer prevail?

    (A) Yes, if the bill collector's remarks were heard by any of the customer's neighbors.

    (B) Yes, because the bill collector's conduct was extreme and outrageous.

    (C) No, unless the bill collector knew that the customer owed no money to the store.

    (D) No, unless the customer suffered some special damage.

    [Q4065]

34. A well-known movie actor was drinking Vineyard wine at a nightclub. A bottle of the Vineyard wine, with its label plainly showing, was on the table in front of the actor. An amateur photographer asked the actor if he could take his picture and the actor said, "Yes." Subsequently, the photographer sold the photo to the bottler of Vineyard wine. The bottler, without the actor's consent, used the photo in a wine advertisement in a nationally circulated magazine. The caption below the photo stated, "[The actor] enjoys his Vineyard wine."

    If the actor sues the bottler to recover damages as a result of the bottler's use of the photograph, will the actor prevail?

    (A) No, because the actor consented to being photographed.

    (B) No, because the actor is a public figure.

    (C) Yes, because the bottler made commercial use of the photograph.

    (D) Yes, unless the actor did, in fact, enjoy his Vineyard wine.

    [Q3192]

ANSWERS TO TORTS QUESTIONS

1. **A** The only plausible action would be for battery, the intentional infliction of a harmful or offensive bodily contact. Since it's clear that the passenger did not intend to make a "harmful" contact, the question is whether he intended to make an "offensive" contact. A bodily contact is offensive if and only if it "offends a reasonable sense of personal dignity." Rest. 2d, §19. The contact here does not meet this standard for offensiveness, because the woman gave no indication that she did not want to be subjected to the ordinary touches that are part of life in a crowded society. In the absence of such an indication from her, the passenger was entitled to believe that the woman implicitly consented to a light tap to get her attention, i.e., that such an attention-getting tap would not "offend a reasonable sense of personal dignity." Therefore, the passenger did not commit battery. (Nor did he commit negligence, since negligence requires an unreasonable risk of harm, which was not present in these circumstances when viewed from the perspective of the facts known to the passenger.)

   (B) is wrong because, while this answer correctly states that the woman cannot prevail, it misstates the legal basis for this conclusion. It is true that if the woman was suing for *assault*, she would have to prove that she thought that she was about to be touched in order to win. But the elements of a *negligence* or a *battery* action could be established without any reference to whether she had an apprehension of this or any other sort, so the lack of apprehension cannot explain the fact of non-liability. (Instead, the non-liability for negligence or battery is due to the reasons given in choice (A) above.)

   (C) is wrong because the fact that the touching was intentional does not make the touching actionable, either as battery or anything else. It's true that battery (the most likely tort on these facts) is the intentional infliction of a harmful or offensive bodily contact, so the fact that the passenger intentionally touched the woman sounds like it might lead to liability. But the defendant must not only intend the touching, he must intend a touching that, viewed from the perspective of one in his position, would be regarded as harmful or offensive. For the reasons given in choice (A), the passenger did not have cause to regard his touch as being harmful or offensive here.

   (D) is wrong because serious injury is neither necessary nor sufficient to support either battery or negligence, although some damage would be required to recover in negligence. For battery, the defendant must not only make a touching that turns out to be harmful or offensive (which the touching here arguably was because of the resulting pain to the woman), the defendant must *intend* a touching that, viewed from the perspective of one in his position, would be regarded as harmful or offensive. Here, one in the passenger's position would not expect the touch to be either harmful or offensive, so the requirement of an "intentional or offensive touching" is not met.

   [Q7063]

2. **D** Intentional force that exceeded the player's consent would be an offensive contact constituting a battery. An action for battery has three elements: (1) defendant's act bringing about a harmful or offensive contact with plaintiff's person; (2) defendant's intent to bring about such contact or to create the apprehension of immediate contact; and (3) causation. For the plaintiff to prevail in an action for battery he'd have to prove an offensive contact. Roughness up to the level to which the players as a group impliedly consented would not be deemed harmful or offensive. But consent would not be a defense if the defendant intentionally used more than the consented-to level of force.

   (A) is wrong because what is at issue is not the fact of intentional contact, but the level of contact consented to by the players in the game. Apparent consent is that which a reasonable person would infer from plaintiff's conduct. Thus, for example, somebody who voluntarily engages in a body contact sport impliedly consents to the normal contacts inherent in playing it. If the defendant intended to strike the plaintiff, but in a way that was consistent with the play of the game, then the plaintiff's consent would be found to be implied by his participation in the game and his use of the same tactics.

(B) is wrong because it ignores the significance of the plaintiff's consent. What would otherwise be a harmful or offensive contact will not be actionable if it was consented to. Because the plaintiff's participation in the rough game, and his use of the same tactics, would be found to constitute implied consent to a certain level of roughness, the mere fact that the defendant intended to cause, say, an offensive contact that was consistent with the general game-play would not expose him to liability.

(C) is wrong because it ignores the possibility that the defendant may have exceeded the scope of the players' implied consent. It's true that if the defendant acted merely with the same level of roughness as previously manifested by various players in the game (including the plaintiff), the plaintiff would be deemed to have consented to it. But the defendant may have used more than the level of force to which plaintiff would be found to have consented. In that event, the implied-consent doctrine wouldn't apply, and the defendant could be liable.

[Q3017]

3. **D** Assault occurs when, with the intent to induce such apprehension, the defendant induces in the plaintiff a reasonable apprehension that a harmful or offensive contact with the plaintiff will occur. When the defendant makes the plaintiff fear for a harmful or offensive bodily contact upon a third person, this does not constitute assault of the plaintiff no matter how closely connected the plaintiff and the third person are. Rest. 2d, §26. Since the mother did not fear contact with herself, she was not assaulted.

(A) is wrong because the defendant's conduct did not induce the mother to apprehend contact with herself.

(B) is wrong because the doctrine of transferred intent does not apply on these facts. Transferred intent can apply in an assault case, where D intends to put X in fear of imminent contact, and in fact puts P in fear that P will suffer such a contact — D has assaulted P. Rest. 2d, §32(2). But the doctrine doesn't apply here for two reasons: (1) the defendant did not intend to cause an apprehension of harmful contact in the scout (or any person); and (2) the mother was not in fact put in fear of a contact with herself.

(C) is wrong because it cites a fact that is irrelevant. If the defendant's conduct had given the mother reason to apprehend contact with herself, this would be assault of the mother, and it would not matter whether she had perceived contact with her daughter the scout.

[Q5018]

4. **C** Consent — plaintiff's willingness — is a complete defense to most intentional tort actions. Consent is implied if the reasonable person would infer from the plaintiff's conduct and the surrounding circumstances that the plaintiff is willing for the defendant's act to occur. The fact that the defendant and the plaintiff had been enjoying each other's jokes for years could result in the inference that the plaintiff was willing to have a joke like this one played upon him. Although it is not certain that a court would come to this conclusion, the argument in (C) is the only one listed which could support the defendant's defense.

(A) is wrong because as long as the plaintiff has an apprehension of an imminent harmful or offensive contact, it does not matter that what the plaintiff fears is a contact from a third person or a force of nature rather than from the defendant. See Rest. 2d, §25, and Illustr. 1 thereto (D liable for assault for making a noise that tricks P into thinking he is about to be bitten by a rattlesnake).

(B) is wrong because if the defendant's act is intended to put the plaintiff in apprehension of an immediate bodily contact and succeeds in so doing, it does not matter that that act would not have put a person of ordinary sensitivity or courage in such apprehension. Rest. 2d, §27.

(D) is wrong because, although it is true that knowledge that a particular result is substantially certain to occur is deemed the equivalent of intent to bring about the result, the fact that the defendant was not substantially certain that the plaintiff would be injured will not help the defendant. That's because what must be intended for assault is merely either the creation of a harmful or offensive bodily contact (not an injury), or the creation of an apprehension of such contact. Here, a bite from a real spider would be harmful or offensive, so the defendant intended to bring about in the plaintiff an apprehension of a harmful or offensive contact (the bite) despite the fact that the defendant knew that no such bite would occur. Since the defendant intended to put the plaintiff in apprehension of being bitten, the fact that the defendant neither intended to injure the plaintiff nor knew with substantial certainty that the plaintiff would be injured is irrelevant.

[Q5112]

5. **D** First, we have to decide whether the landlord committed trespass. Trespass to land occurs when the defendant intentionally enters land in the "possession" of another. A tenant has possession of the premises, even though he does not have outright ownership. Conversely, a landlord of leased premises, even though she owns the premises, does not have possession of them. So the landlord here committed trespass when he entered the student's premises. As to remedies: there is evidence supporting compensatory damages (emotional distress, the removal of the faucets) and punitive damages (malicious intent, ill will). Because the lease is still in effect and the trespasses are repeated and ongoing, injunctive relief should also be available.

(A) is wrong because the student is in legal possession of the apartment and thus has an interest that can be vindicated in a trespass action, as further described in Choice (D) above.

(B) is wrong because: (1) damage is not necessary to establish a cause of action in trespass; and (2) in any case, the removal of the faucets was damage to the property.

(C) is wrong because these facts demonstrate a pattern of ongoing malicious behavior, so the law student is unlikely to be limited to compensatory damages. In addition to compensatory damages for emotional distress and the removal of the faucets, the student is entitled to punitive damages (demonstrated by the landlord's malicious intent and ill will). And because the lease is still in effect and the trespasses are repeated and ongoing, injunctive relief should also be available.

[Q7088]

6. **C** If the driver was negligent, then a suit based on ordinary negligence could succeed, since the driver's negligence would have placed the owner and the owner's child in the zone of danger, and then caused emotional distress. So if the driver was negligent, the owner would prevail, making this aspect of Choice (C) correct. If the driver was not negligent, the owner's suit could of course not successfully be based on negligence. In that event, the suit would have to be based on trespass. However, trespass requires an intentional entry onto the plaintiff's property. Here, where the driver came onto the owner's property only as the result of a skid, the required "intentional entry" would not be found. (By the way, even if the driver intentionally chose to enter onto the owner's property to avoid hitting the child, the doctrine of private necessity would supply a defense to trespass.)

(A) is wrong because the fact that the entry was unauthorized does not settle the issue of whether the driver is liable. As further explained in the analysis of Choice (C) above, the driver could be liable only if negligent. The fact that the entry was "unauthorized" doesn't prove that driver was negligent. For instance, if the driver's behavior leading up to the moment he hit the brakes was non-negligent (e.g., he wasn't speeding, and was paying proper attention), the fact that the entry was not authorized by the owner would be irrelevant, and indeed the driver would not be liable in that scenario.

(B) is wrong because the presence of serious emotional distress is irrelevant if the driver violated no duty. The mere fact that the plaintiff suffered serious emotional distress does not make the defendant liable — the defendant must have violated some independent duty to the plaintiff. So the owner would have to establish either that: (1) the driver committed the tort of negligence (in which case severe emotional distress in the absence of physical injury would not be a barrier to recovery, given that the owner was in the "zone of danger"); or (2) the driver committed trespass. Since, as detailed in the treatment of Choice (C), neither of these torts is necessarily established by the facts, Choice (B)'s focus on the distress cannot be a complete answer to why or whether the owner would win.

(D) is wrong because the child's exercise of reasonable care is irrelevant to the outcome. First, let's assume the owner's suit is brought in negligence. If so, the fact that the child was or wasn't careful is irrelevant. If the child *was* careful, the driver still may or may not have behaved with reasonable care. If the child *wasn't* careful, the same is true — the driver might have been, or might have not been, careful. If the driver wasn't careful, the child's negligence would not prevent the driver's conduct from giving rise to liability — one of the common ways for a driver to be negligent is to fail to be attentive to other people's, especially children's, negligence. (Nor would the child's lack of care be imputed to the owner.) Now, let's assume that the owner's suit is brought in trespass. Again, the fact that the child was or wasn't careful would be irrelevant. Either way, the driver's conduct was not an intentional and unprivileged entry onto the owner's premises (as described in Choice (C)). So Choice (D)'s focus on the carefulness of the child is completely irrelevant no matter what the legal theory of the owner's suit.

[Q3149]

7. **B** The tort of conversion is the interference with a person's possessory rights in a chattel that is so serious as to warrant that defendant pay full value for the chattel. Under these facts, the neighbor borrowed the homeowner's chain saw without permission, thereby interfering with the homeowner's possessory rights. The facts state that the saw broke (as opposed to becoming slightly damaged or in need of minor repair), so we can take this as a serious interference as opposed to a minor one. Under the law governing conversion, the neighbor is responsible for the full value of the saw (but can keep it). In other words, the law of conversion applies the rule, familiar from retailing, that "You break it, you own it."

(A) is wrong because it incorrectly states the damages for the tort of conversion. Here, "actual damages" would or might amount to less than the full value of the homeowner's chattel, the saw (since the saw could presumably be fixed for less than the value of the saw pre-breakage). The essence of conversion is that it is a "forced sale" of the chattel to the defendant. In other words, the homeowner is entitled to the full value of the saw before it was taken, not just the actual damage amount needed to return it to the condition it was in before the neighbor took it.

(C) is wrong because it incorrectly suggests a defense to the tort of conversion. The tort of conversion is the interference with a person's possessory rights in a chattel that is so serious as to warrant that defendant pay full value for the chattel. It is not a defense that the defendant was acting for plaintiff's benefit. Had the neighbor been using the saw to, say, save the homeowner's life in an emergency, the defense of necessity might apply. But here, where the neighbor was initially acting to further his own interests, and then "helping" the homeowner in a non-emergency situation, the defense would not apply.

(D) is wrong because an intent to keep the chattel is not a necessary element in conversion. A person who makes a temporary but serious interference with another's chattel, in a way that causes substantial damage to the chattel, has committed conversion despite his intended return (or indeed his actual return) of the chattel soon after the taking. (For instance, if D takes P's car for a joy ride and seriously damages it, the fact that D promptly returns the wrecked car to P is no defense.)

[Q3003]

8. **B** The landowner has used deadly force, so the standards for using it are tougher than for using non-deadly force. A person is privileged to use deadly force (defined as force intended or likely to cause death or serious bodily harm) against another when the person believes that: (1) the other is about to inflict upon him an intentional contact or other bodily harm; and (2) the person is thereby being put in peril of death, serious bodily harm, or sexual assault, which can safely be prevented only by the immediate use of such deadly force. Rest. 2d, §65(1). Furthermore, even where deadly force would otherwise be permissible in self-defense, no amount of force (deadly or otherwise) may be permitted in excess of that force which the person reasonably believes to be necessary for his protection. Rest. 2d, §70. Since the hunter's shotgun was being pointed at the landowner, Choice (B) correctly applies these two rules, since the landowner would be privileged to use self-defense if and only if he reasonably believed that the hunter would fire, and that no lesser amount of force would safely prevent that firing. Notice also that there is no real issue of the possibility of retreat here, because the shotgun is pointed at the landowner, and a shotgun has a significant range; therefore, the landowner would reasonably believe that he could not retreat in safety — he might be shot in the back. (The range of the gun matters, because even in those courts imposing a duty to retreat outside of one's own dwelling, retreat is only required if it can be done so with apparent safety, and that is not the case here.)

(A) is wrong because it overstates the landowner's right to protect his property against trespass. A landowner *does* have the right to use force to prevent or terminate another's intrusion upon the owner's land, if (1) the owner reasonably believes that the intrusion cannot be prevented by lesser force; and (2) the owner has first asked the other to leave and he has refused, or the owner reasonably believes that such a request will be useless or dangerous. Rest. 2d, §77. So based on this formulation, Choice (A) could be right. However, where the intruder does not threaten death or serious bodily harm to the owner or another who is on the premises, the owner *may not use deadly force*, i.e., force intended or likely to cause death or serious bodily harm. Rest. 2d, §79. This choice, insofar as it asserts that the landowner was entitled to fire his pistol merely to cause the hunter to leave the premises if this couldn't be done with lesser force, is therefore wrong — a landowner is required to summon the authorities rather than use deadly force to repel an intruder who does not pose a danger of death or serious bodily harm to the occupants.

(C) is wrong because the fact that the landowner made the first use of force is irrelevant in this case. At the beginning of the encounter, the landowner asked the intruder to leave and the intruder refused; that was enough to entitle the landowner to use non-deadly force to repel the intruder if no lesser degree of force recently seemed as though it would suffice (see Choice (A) above for why this is true). The landowner's use of a gentle push met this requirement. (Even if the push went beyond what was privileged, it is still the case that after the hunter escalated the encounter by using deadly force, the landowner would have been privileged to use deadly force in self-defense if no lesser force seemed as though it would suffice.)

(D) is wrong because the fact that the landowner waited to make the first use of even non-deadly force against the hunter until after the hunter was already completely on the property is irrelevant; an owner is entitled to try to persuade the intruder to leave voluntarily, and does not thereby forfeit his right to use an appropriate level of non-deadly force if the persuasion fails.

[Q5052]

9. **A** Defense of property is a defense to an intentional tort — one may use *reasonable* force to prevent trespass, or other interference with one's land or chattels. However, deadly force (i.e., force that is likely to cause death or serious bodily harm) cannot be used except to prevent an intrusion that is likely to cause death or serious injury to the inhabitants. When a property owner uses force indirectly, by means of an automatic mechanical device like the one here, the case is judged by the

same standards as if the owner were acting directly. Consequently, if a live person in the owner's position would not reasonably have believed that the intruder posed a serious risk of death or serious injury to the inhabitants, use of the deadly-force mechanical device would not be privileged. By this standard, even though the salesman was an outright trespasser, because he did not pose a threat of death or serious bodily harm the homeowner was only entitled to use reasonable, non-deadly force to deter him.

(B) is wrong because even if the intent is only to deter, deadly force cannot be used against trespassers who do not pose a threat of death or serious injury to the inhabitants, as is more fully explained in the analysis of Choice (A).

(C) is wrong because deadly force cannot be used against non-dangerous trespassers, even if a warning is given. As is described more fully in the treatment of Choice (A), deadly force cannot be used against trespassers who do not pose a threat of death or serious injury to the inhabitants. This rule is true even if the owner gives a warning against entry. (In any event, the warning here did not even specify that serious force, posing the risk of bodily injury or death, would be used, so it's doubly unlikely to immunize the homeowner from liability.)

(D) is wrong because even if the homeowner did reasonably fear that intruders would come to harm him or his family, the salesman himself did not pose such a danger. When an owner uses an automatic mechanical device to protect against intruders, the situation is judged by the same standards as if the owner were personally applying the force. Therefore, the mechanical device can supply deadly force (force likely to cause death or serious bodily injury) only if the owner could do so personally on the particular occasion in question. An owner could use such deadly force only if the owner reasonably feared, in that particular situation, that the intruder posed a risk of death or serious bodily harm to the owner or other inhabitants. Here, one in the homeowner's position would have realized that the intruder was unlikely to pose such harm, and was instead a salesman. Since the homeowner would not have been entitled to use deadly force "by hand" against the salesman (e.g., by shooting him), he is not protected when his automatic device applies deadly force.

[Q3195]

10. **C** One who enters the realty of another to retrieve a chattel which got there through no fault of her own has a qualified privilege to do so, but must compensate the landholder for any actual damage which results.

(A) is wrong because, while the trucker had a qualified privilege to go on to the landowner's land to retrieve the gravel, it was required to pay for any damage caused by the retrieval operation. Therefore, limiting the landowner's recovery to nominal damages would not be adequate compensation.

(B) is wrong because liability for the initial spill would have to be premised on either trespass, negligence, or the conducting of an abnormally dangerous activity. There is no trespass liability here, because trespass requires that the defendant had intended to make contact with the property that belongs to the plaintiff. Here, since the contact (the spilling of gravel onto the plaintiff's property) occurred by accident rather than by the intent of the trucker, this requirement of intent is not satisfied. Nor does negligence liability apply, because we are told that the blowout was not due to any fault on the part of the trucker. Liability based on abnormally dangerous activity does not apply because the transporting of gravel is not an abnormally dangerous activity. Therefore, the trucker has no liability for the initial spill.

(D) is wrong because the trucker, although he correctly exercised a qualified privilege to recapture his chattels, must pay for the damage caused by the recapture operation, as further described in Choice (C) above.

[Q5075]

11. **B** The action here would have to be brought in negligence (not, for instance, in strict liability, since there's no indication that the banana was defective). The only way the grocer could be found negligent is if it knew or should have known that the peel was on the ground, and had time to remove it before the customer passed by. There *are* slip-and-fall scenarios in which the mere fact that the accident happened is enough to trigger *res ipsa loquitur*. For instance, if the customer slips on an old and discolored peel, that might make for a case of *res ipsa*, since there is no way such a peel could be found on a grocer's floor without it having been present long enough for the grocer to have had a duty to remove it. But the condition of the peel here does not indicate that it has been on the ground for any significant period of time. Therefore, there is not enough evidence — either direct evidence or via the operation of *res ipsa* — to support a jury verdict that the store staff was negligent in failing to remove it before the customer's fall.

(A) is wrong because, while this answer correctly states that the judge should not let the case go to the jury, it misstates the legal basis for this conclusion. In slip-and-fall cases, even if a customer was negligent, he could recover some of his damages under a system of pure comparative negligence if a jury determined that the grocer was also negligent. So although it is true that the customer had an obligation to watch where he stepped, his failure to fulfill that obligation would not prevent the case from going to the jury.

(C) is wrong because it cites a mostly irrelevant fact. Strict products liability is not applicable here because the banana was not defective. So the suit would have to be based on negligence. While it's true that the plaintiff would have to show, by a preponderance of the evidence, that the peel came from a banana offered for sale by the grocer, such a showing would not be enough to entitle the plaintiff to get to the jury. Instead, the plaintiff would also have to show that it was more likely than not that the grocer behaved negligently by not removing the peel, and that's the piece that's missing on these facts.

(D) is wrong because foreseeability alone is not sufficient to establish that the grocer was negligent. The plaintiff must also offer evidence that the grocer fell below the standard of care, i.e., that he failed to adopt the precautions that a reasonably prudent person in his situation would adopt to avoid the foreseeable risk. There is no such evidence here, as explained in the discussion of Choice (B).

[Q7083]

12. **C** For the day care center to be liable, its liability would have to be premised upon either intent, negligence, or strict liability. There is no indication of an intent by the day care center to harm the child, nor is there anything that would impose strict liability. So liability would have to be based upon negligence. But a defendant cannot be liable for negligence unless the defendant failed to use a level of care that would be reasonable in the circumstances. The facts stipulate that the center's personnel used reasonable care to prevent a child from sneaking out, so there was no negligence by the center.

(A) is wrong, because day care centers are not strictly or absolutely liable for all injuries that occur to children under their care. The center's negligence must be established. Under the facts as described, there is no evidence of lack of reasonable care, and the day care center will prevail.

(B) is wrong because the mere fact that the center is located near a pond is not in itself evidence of negligence. It might mean that reasonable care requires extra-vigilant supervision, but the facts specify that the center staff was in fact exercising "reasonable care." Accordingly, the day care center will prevail.

(D) is wrong because the child's status as a trespasser would only be relevant in litigation against an owner or possessor of the land where the accident occurred. Since the suit is against the center, not the corporation that owned the land containing the pond, the child's status as trespasser is irrelevant.

[Q7094]

13. **C** For the pedestrian to recover, she will have to show negligence on the part of the car owner. The pedestrian has two shots at this: (1) negligence per se; and (2) garden-variety negligence. As to negligence per se, before the standard of care in a statute can be the basis for a claim of negligence per se, it must be the case that the ordinance was drafted at least in part for the purpose of protecting against the particular hazard that occurred. Rest. 2d, §286(d). This requirement is not satisfied here, because we're told that the purpose of the statute was solely to expedite the flow of car traffic, not to protect against the formation of the ice. With respect to garden-variety negligence, the pedestrian has simply come forward with no evidence that the accident was caused (i.e., the ice was caused) by any failure on the part of the car owner to use reasonable care under the circumstances. (Indeed, if the car owner had complied with the statute by washing the car in a private driveway instead of the street, this would not have reduced the risk of accumulating ice on pedestrian walkways and might even have increased that risk.) Accordingly, the car owner's motion should be granted.

(A) is wrong because negligence creating the risk of an icy surface cannot be inferred from the mere fact that the car owner allowed the water to accumulate; the cold snap was "sudden and unexpected." Because there is no reasonable inference of negligence and no evidence of negligence (the statute is irrelevant because it does not speak to the risk that materialized in this case), the car owner's motion should be granted.

(B) is wrong because the statutory violation is not even evidence of negligence here. The statute was not enacted to reduce the risk of accumulating ice on the public walkways. Indeed, if the car owner had complied with the statute by washing the car in a private driveway, this would not have reduced the risk of accumulating ice on pedestrian walkways and might even have increased that risk. Therefore, violation of the statute has no probative value on the issue of whether the car owner was negligent.

(D) is wrong because, as is discussed further in Choice (C) above, the statute was enacted solely to reduce a particular safety risk (congested traffic lanes) that neither materialized nor caused the pedestrian's injury, so the negligence per se doctrine does not apply, and the statutory violation is irrelevant.

[Q7020]

14. **A** Under the doctrine of "negligence per se," where a legislature has enacted a statute that is intended to prescribe the standard of conduct of a reasonable person in a particular situation, an excused violation of that standard that leads to the harm will constitute a prima facie showing of negligence if certain requirements are met (e.g., that the statute was intended to guard against the type of harm, and to protect the class of persons, at issue in the present case). So if the statutory violation were the only evidence regarding negligence that had been presented on either side, the plaintiff would win. But notice that the above formulation refers to an "*unexcused*" violation of the statute. Here, the decedent's estate, by demonstrating that the decedent had an unforeseeable heart attack while otherwise driving reasonably, has established that the statutory violation was excused. See, e.g., Rest. 2d, §288A(2)(a) (giving an excuse for a statutory violation where "the violation is reasonable because of the actor's incapacity"). Since this evidence of excuse is undisputed, and since there is no other evidence of negligence, the decedent's estate wins.

(B) is wrong because, while this answer correctly states that the decedent's estate will prevail, it misstates the legal basis for this conclusion. The plaintiff's evidence that the decedent violated the statute by crossing over into her lane of traffic *does* establish a prima facie case of negligence. (That is, if it were the only evidence of negligence in the case, plaintiff would be entitled to go to the jury.) Nevertheless, the decedent's estate successfully rebutted the plaintiff's evidence by providing an uncontested explanation of how the accident happened that is inconsistent with a finding of negligence (that the decedent's unforeseeable heart attack made her unable to comply with the statute, or indeed with any standard of care). Keep in mind that when a statement says that the plaintiff has or has not "established a prima facie case for liability," the statement is referring merely to the facts presented by the plaintiff in the plaintiff's case, not referring to the overall set of proven facts after both sides have rested. So it can happen — as it did here — that the plaintiff establishes a prima facie case in her own case, but that the defendant then produces counterproof to rebut that prima facie case, entitling the defendant to a verdict (perhaps even a directed verdict that takes the case away from the jury).

(C) is wrong, because while it may or may not be true that accidents of this type do not ordinarily happen in the absence of negligence, that is beside the point. This choice is suggesting the applicability of *res ipsa loquitur,* one requirement for which is that the accident be of a type that ordinarily does not happen in the absence of negligence. There are two problems with the use of *res ipsa* here: (1) it is far from clear that median-crossing accidents "do not ordinarily happen in the absence of negligence" (there are a lot of heart attack, seizure, and other involuntary median-crossing scenarios, perhaps amounting to a majority); and (2) even where the "does not usually happen without negligence" requirement is met, the doctrine will not be applied where there is direct and unrebutted evidence that something other than the defendant's negligence was the cause (and here, that evidence exists in the form of the heart attack evidence).

(D) is wrong because the plaintiff's evidence that the decedent violated the statute and crossed over into her lane of traffic establishes only a prima facie case of negligence. The decedent's estate successfully rebutted the plaintiff's evidence — and thus made the negligence per se doctrine inapplicable — by providing an undisputed explanation of how the accident happened that is inconsistent with a finding of negligence.

[Q7059]

15. **C** The doctrine of *res ipsa loquitor* ("the thing speaks for itself ") permits the jury to infer negligence without the plaintiff's having produced any direct evidence of negligence. There are two main requirements: (1) the event must be of a kind which ordinarily does not occur in the absence of negligence; and (2) other causes, including the conduct of the plaintiff and third persons, must be sufficiently eliminated by the evidence. Rest. 2d, §328D. These requirements are satisfied here: (1) commercial airline flights normally do not crash into mountains in the absence of negligence; and (2) other causes have been essentially eliminated (for instance, the fact that the weather was good eliminates poor weather as the cause). Some courts add two additional elements for *res ipsa*: (3) that the instrument that caused the injury have been in the exclusive control of the defendant; and (4) that there be no direct evidence of how the defendant behaved. These two additional requirements, if the jurisdiction applies them, are also easily satisfied, since the airline was in control of the plane, and since there is no direct evidence of what went wrong. Therefore, *res ipsa* applies, and its effect is to permit the jury to infer: (1) that the defendant was negligent, and (2) that this negligence caused the accident.

(A) is wrong because, as described in Choice (C) above, the doctrine of *res ipsa* permits the jury to infer that the crash was caused by the airline's negligence, even in the absence of direct evidence from the plaintiff about the cause.

(B) is wrong because, while *res ipsa* requires that the plaintiff show that the event was of a kind which "ordinarily" does not occur except through the fault of someone, the plaintiff is *not* required to show that the event couldn't possibly have been due to a cause not involving the defendant's fault (as the phrase "negating the possibility" implies). All plaintiff has to show is that, by a preponderance of the evidence (i.e., *more likely than not*), the airline's negligence was to blame, and the fulfillment of the "ordinarily does not occur without negligence" requirement for *res ipsa* satisfies this more-likely-than-not element of the plaintiff's prima facie case.

(D) is wrong because it misstates the rules for common carriers. Common carriers (including airlines) are required to exercise a very high degree of care toward their passengers and guests, which is to say they are liable for even slight negligence. But they do not have strict liability.

[Q3161]

16. **A** A negligent tortfeasor is not generally liable for the criminal acts of third parties made possible by his negligence, but there is an exception when the tortfeasor should have realized the likelihood of the crime at the time of his negligence. The issue of foreseeability is generally a question for the jury. In this case, there had been many thefts from the construction area during the course of construction. Accordingly, there was enough evidence to support a jury verdict for the plaintiff, but it was not so overwhelming as to require the judge to take the rare step of granting summary judgment for the plaintiff.

(B) is wrong because the issue of foreseeability is generally a question for the jury. In this case, there had been many thefts from the construction area during the course of construction. The jury should be asked to consider whether the failure to place warning lights could foreseeably create a situation in which a damaged vehicle would be left vulnerable to theft.

(C) is wrong because, while it is true that a negligent tortfeasor is not generally liable for the criminal acts of third parties made possible by his negligence, there is an exception when the tortfeasor should have realized the likelihood of the crime at the time of his negligence. In other words, third-party criminal acts are not "superseding" when they were reasonably foreseeable to one in the defendant's position. The issue of foreseeability is generally a question for the jury, and that's true here, where there had been many thefts from the construction area during the course of construction. Accordingly, there is enough evidence to support a jury finding that the theft was foreseeable, so the defendant's motion for summary judgment should be denied.

(D) is wrong because, while the fact that the goods would not have been stolen but for the construction company's negligence answers the question whether that negligence was a cause-in-fact of the thefts, it doesn't answer the question whether that negligence was the proximate cause of the thefts. The construction company's negligence was the proximate cause of the thefts if and only if the third-party criminal acts were reasonably foreseeable to one in the construction company's position. And such issues of foreseeability are generally a question for the jury, so that a grant of summary judgment for a plaintiff on that basis is rare. In this case, there remains a jury question as to whether the pattern of past thefts from the construction site made the theft of the goods from the delivery truck foreseeable.

[Q7032]

17. **A** A person who is engaged in the *business of selling products*, and who sells a *defective product*, is subject to liability for harm to persons or property caused by the defect. Rest. 3d (P.L.) §1. One type of defect is a "*design* defect." A design defect occurs "when the foreseeable risks of harm posed by the product could have been reduced or avoided by the adoption of a *reasonable alternative design* by the seller or other distributor, or a predecessor in the commercial chain of distribution, and the omission of the alternative design renders the product *not reasonably safe*." Rest. 3d (P. L.) §2(b). The plaintiff has made a prima facie showing that satisfies these requirements for strict liability, since a reasonable jury could find that: (1) the defendant was engaged in the business of selling or distributing cars; (2) the fact that the Rapido's motor may stall if the engine has not had an extended warm-up is a design defect since a reasonable alternative design (which didn't need an extended warm-up to avoid stalling) was available and would have reduced this risk; (3) the omission of this alternative design made the car not reasonably safe; and (4) the defect (the stalling motor and ensuing accident) caused harm to the plaintiff (his shock, which resulted in a heart attack). The plaintiff can thus make her prima facie case, so the defendant's motion should

be denied.

(B) is wrong because the "crashworthiness" of the car was not at issue on these facts. "Crashworthiness" in a vehicle is the attribute of being able to withstand a collision without posing an unacceptably large risk of injury to the passengers. Non-crashworthiness can certainly be a type of defect. However, on the facts as alleged by the plaintiff here, the injury to her occurred from the "shock of the crash," not from any failure of the vehicle to appropriately withstand the collision. (In other words, the facts indicate that even in a perfectly crashworthy vehicle, the plaintiff would probably have had the same shock and thus the same heart attack.) Consequently, even if a reasonable jury could find that the vehicle was "defective" because it was non-crashworthy (something not at all clear on these facts), the jury would probably not be entitled to find that the defect of non-crashworthiness was the legal cause of the injury. In that event, the defendant would still win on its motion. So although the conclusion (the defendant loses on the motion) is correct, the explanation of why it loses is not correct.

(C) is wrong because it was foreseeable that cars with engines that stall could be in accidents, so the elderly man's failure to stop was not superseding. An intervening cause is a force that takes effect after the defendant's negligence and which contributes to that negligence in producing the plaintiff's injury. Some, but not all, intervening causes are sufficient to prevent the defendant's negligence from being considered the proximate cause of the injury. Intervening causes of this kind are usually called "superseding causes" because they supersede or cancel the defendant's liability. An intervening cause that was "foreseeable" as something that might combine with a defect to cause an injury will generally not be deemed to be superseding cause. Here, it was perfectly foreseeable that a car that stalled due to a defect would be extra likely to be hit from the rear. Therefore, being hit from the rear was a foreseeable (and thus non-superseding) intervening cause given a "defective-because-likely-to-stall" engine.

(D) is wrong because the defendant "takes the plaintiff as he finds him." Where the defendant's negligence causes an aggravation of plaintiff's existing physical or mental illness, defendant is liable for the damages caused by the aggravation, which is to say, the tortfeasor takes the victim as he finds him. So here, this rule means that the defendant cannot escape liability by arguing that a person of normal sensitivity would not have suffered a heart attack under these circumstances.

[Q3146]

18. **C** Under joint-and-several liability, the entire amount can be collected from any one of the defendants. That defendant, in turn, can seek to recover a proportional share of the damages from the other defendants. The fact that there is no imputed negligence means that the parents' lack of care does not reduce the child's recovery.

(A) is wrong because, while this might be a correct computation of the driver's pro rata share of damages, it is not correct under comparative negligence with joint-and-several liability. Under joint-and-several liability, the entire amount can be collected from any one of the defendants. That defendant, in turn, can seek to recover a proportional (rather than a pro rata) share of the damages from the other defendants.

(B) is wrong because, although this answer would be correct if liability were only several, here liability is joint and several. Under joint-and-several liability, the entire amount can be collected from any one of the defendants. That defendant, in turn, can seek to recover a proportional share of the damages from the other defendants.

(D) is wrong because, while this might be the rule under a traditional contributory negligence regime where the negligence of the parent is imputed to the child and bars all recovery, it is not the rule under the regime here (no imputation, plus joint-and-several liability). Under joint-and-several liability, the entire amount can be collected from any one of the defendants. And with no imputing of liability, the parents' fault is not imputed to the child, so that parental fault does not reduce the child's recovery from the driver.

[Q7072]

19. **C** This is the correct choice, because the explosion was caused by a design defect in a part of the plant unrelated to the filter system designed by the engineer. The only plausible basis for the suit here would have to be negligence. (Although the making of explosive chemicals may have been an "abnormally dangerous activity" — triggering strict liability — the engineer was not herself carrying out that manufacturing activity, and only the person carrying out the ultrahazardous activity has strict liability for it.) To be liable in negligence, the engineer would have to have had a duty to avoid a particular type of harm, and then to have failed to use reasonable care in carrying out that duty. If the engineer had worked on the design that contained the defect, she certainly could have been held liable in negligence. But since the engineer dealt only with the filtering system, she never undertook any duty to ascertain the safety of the other aspects of the plant design. Consequently, nothing she did (or didn't do) could possibly have constituted a failure to use reasonable care in the discharging of a duty.

(A) is wrong because the engineer does not become liable for a design defect merely by including that defect in her blueprints. The facts state that the engineer was retained to design a filter system. Her duty was to protect people from unreasonable risk of injury arising from her design. The only way to show the design for the filter system was to include the rest of the plant in which the filter system was to be installed. Showing the rest of the plant, including the design defect, does not make her liable for all injuries arising for all design defects in the plant, absent an affirmative requirement to review or inspect those other parts of the blueprints. There is no principle that would impose on an engineer such an affirmative duty to review the safety of parts of blueprints for which the engineer has had no responsibility.

(B) is wrong because joint-and-several liability does not apply on these facts. Where two or more tortious acts combine to proximately cause an indivisible injury to a plaintiff, each tortfeasor is jointly and severally liable for that injury. Under these facts the engineer committed no tort. Merely including a part of the defectively designed plant in her drawings absent a requirement that she knew or should have known of the defect does not make her liable in tort for the defect. Without the engineer's having committed a tort leading to the plaintiff's injury, there can be no joint-and-several liability.

(D) is wrong because the fact that the plaintiff brought suit against the engineer personally means that it doesn't matter whether the engineer was an independent contractor or not. Had Plaintiff brought suit against *the corporation*, then perhaps the engineer's status with the corporation — that is, whether she was an employee or an independent contractor — might be relevant to the corporation's liability. However, the facts state that the plaintiff brought the action against the engineer individually. The engineer's liability will depend solely on whether the engineer behaved negligently, and that would be so (or not so) regardless of whether the corporation employed her or merely engaged her.

[Q3032]

20. **A** While the facts here don't state it explicitly, the child's claim had to be in strict liability, since she recovered from the toy company for the engineer's improper design. (If the child's claim had been for negligence, the toy company could only have been held liable for its *own* negligence, not the engineer's improper design.) Indemnity applies to strict products liability in such a way that subsequent suppliers (those closer to the ultimate user) can seek indemnity from those earlier in the supply chain, so that whoever was responsible for the defect is ultimately liable for it. Thus when a secondary "downstream" tortfeasor (here, the toy company) pays a judgment due to the tort of the primary "upstream" tortfeasor (here, the engineer), the secondary tortfeasor can recover indemnity

— full reimbursement — from the primary tortfeasor.

(B) is wrong because it mischaracterizes the facts. Joint tortfeasors are tortfeasors who act "in concert" (with an express or implied agreement) to produce a single result. Under these facts, the engineer and the toy company didn't act in concert; it was the engineer's improper design that created the risk. As a result, they weren't joint tortfeasors. Even if they *were,* this *wouldn't* mean that the toy company would prevail against the engineer – at most, in some states he could recover from the engineer some portion of the damages as "contribution." And contribution would not match up with these facts, under which the toy company's claim is based on *indemnity,* as opposed to contribution.

(C) is wrong because its conclusion doesn't follow from its premise. When a "downstream" seller (one closer to the ultimate user) incurs strict liability for a defective product, that seller is entitled to indemnity from the upstream person who introduced the defect by, for instance, creating a defective design. (See the further discussion of the indemnity mechanism in Choice (A) above.) So this choice reaches the wrong conclusion from the correct premise: because the toy company was strictly liable (but not a primary tortfeasor), it *can* recover from the engineer.

(D) is wrong because in a strict product liability case, a downstream party does not lose its right to indemnification from an upstream party (as further described in Choice (A) above) by the mere fact that the downstream party could have discovered the defect by a reasonable inspection and did not do so. That is, the party who introduced the defect — here, the engineer — has to ultimately foot the bill, and can't escape the bill by the fact that the party seeking indemnity failed to catch the introducer's error.

[Q4052]

21. **C** As a general rule, a landowner owes no duty to a trespasser to make her land safe. There are several exceptions, but none of those exceptions applies here. The exception that comes closest to applying is that an owner may have a duty of reasonable care to a trespassing child, if the owner has maintained an "attractive nuisance." But for reasons described in the analysis of Choice (B) below, this exception does not apply here.

(A) is wrong because the duty of a landowner to trespassers to keep the property free of dangerous artificial conditions exists only where the owner has reason to know that trespassers are in dangerous proximity to the condition and that they are unlikely to appreciate the risk. Even then, the duty is only to exercise reasonable care to warn trespassers of the danger, which was done here.

(B) is wrong because, while it is true that an owner may be liable to a trespasser if the owner has maintained an "attractive nuisance," the condition here was not an attractive nuisance. For a condition on land to be considered an attractive nuisance, there must be evidence that the possessor had reason to know that children were likely to trespass, as well as evidence that the plaintiff did not appreciate the risk involved. No such evidence is mentioned in the facts; for instance, there is no suggestion that children often stray from the day care center, and there is no reason to believe the child was not aware of the danger (since we're told he was a "bright nine-year-old" and that the danger was well-marked).

(D) is wrong because, while, this answer correctly states that the corporation will prevail, it misstates the legal basis for this conclusion. Even if the day care center had a duty to keep children from the ice, the corporation could also be liable if it was negligent. That is, if A is negligent as to a risk, the fact that B was also negligent as to the same risk is unlikely to save A from liability.

[Q7093]

22. **C** An invitee is a person who enters onto the premises in response to an express or implied invitation of the landowner. The landowner owes the invitee a general duty to use reasonable and ordinary care in keeping the property safe for the benefit of the invitee. That duty includes the duty to

inspect and correct hidden dangers and defects. Under these facts, the mother accompanied the daughter, a minor patient. That makes the mother an invitee, since she entered the premises under the hospital's implied invitation. At issue then is whether the hospital used reasonable and ordinary care to keep the property safe. The mere fact that the mother injured herself on a protruding fixture does not establish that the hospital failed to use due care to protect one in the mother's position. (For instance, the fixture may have been necessary to the functioning of the emergency room, and there may have been nothing that could reasonably have been done to make it safer for one who happened to faint near it.) On the other hand, it's certainly possible that inspection of the fixture would have shown that its shape and/or size posed an unreasonable risk to passersby, one which could have been easily corrected by, say, use of padding. This choice is the only one, therefore, that turns on the relevant issue: whether the hospital's personnel took, or failed to take, reasonable steps to safeguard invitees like the mother from dangers posed by the fixture.

(A) is wrong because, while the mother was indeed an invitee, as such the hospital only owed her a general duty of reasonable and ordinary care, including the duty to inspect the premises and see to it that they were reasonably safe. So the only way the hospital would be liable for damages suffered by the mother was if it did not exercise ordinary care. To the extent that this choice suggests that the mother automatically wins because she was an invitee — that a landowner has in effect strict liability to invitees who are injured by a condition of the land — it's simply wrong as a matter of law.

(B) is wrong because whether the fixture on which the mother injured herself in her fall was obvious, commonly used, and an essential part of the hospital's equipment does not go to the level of care the hospital owed the mother, or to whether the hospital failed to exercise that level of care. For example, suppose that the fixture was *non-obvious* and rarely-used. As long as the device did not pose an unreasonable danger to those around it, the hospital would still not be liable, because the hospital would not have failed to use reasonable care in connection with the device. Conversely, even if the fixture *was* obvious, commonly-used, and essential, the hospital may have negligently failed to protect passersby from it (e.g., by putting padding around it, if this could be done without interfering with the device's function).

(D) is wrong because the hospital *did* owe the mother the duty of care owed to an invitee, which includes affirmative aspects. A landowner owes its invitee a general duty to use reasonable and ordinary care in keeping the property safe for the benefit of the invitee, a duty which includes the obligation to *inspect* the property so as to identify and correct hidden dangers. So, for instance, if inspection would have showed that the fixture's shape or location posed an unreasonable risk of injury to passersby, the hospital owed the mother the affirmative duty of finding and correcting the condition (e.g., by installing protective padding).

[Q3036]

23. **B** The common-law "firefighters' rule" says that when firefighters or police officers are injured during the course of the job, they normally have no claim against the person whose conduct created the peril. Dobbs, §285. Not all states follow the firefighters' rule. But even among those that do, the doctrine is generally limited to risks that are inherent in, and special to, that particular occupation. Dobbs, §286. This limit means that the doctrine will not apply here because being struck by a car in normal traffic is not one of the special risks inherent to dangerous police work. So the driver can be held liable under ordinary negligence principles. (Also, many courts say that the firefighters' rule applies only where the negligently-created peril was *responsible for the officer's presence at the scene*, and that approach, too, would cause the rule not to apply here, since the officer was not responding to the risk caused by the driver and was instead present at the scene by coincidence.)

(A) is wrong because, although this answer correctly states that the driver's motion should be denied, it misstates the legal basis for this conclusion. The firefighters' rule, although named with reference to firefighters, also covers police officers. They, too, are public servants at risk of injury by the perils that they have been employed to confront.

(C) is wrong because but-for causation is not sufficient to support the firefighters' rule defense here. As further described in the analysis of choice (B) above, the firefighters' rule applies to bar liability only when the risk that materialized was one of the unique risks inherent to the officer's dangerous work. Here, the fact that the officer was returning from an emergency when she was struck was just a coincidence. So the driver could still be held liable for his negligence because being struck by a car in normal traffic is not one of the special risks inherent in dangerous police work.

(D) is wrong because it overstates the scope of the firefighters' rule. The firefighters' rule only bars claims for injuries that result from risks that are unique or special to the plaintiff's inherently dangerous work. Thus where, as here, the officer is injured on the job, but by a risk that was not part of what makes the officer's job inherently dangerous, the firefighters' rule will not apply, and the driver can be held liable under garden-variety negligence principles.

[Q7006]

24. **C** Plaintiff bears the burden of proving by a preponderance of the evidence that defendant actually caused his injury, just as he must bear the burden of proving the other parts of his prima facie case. Under these facts, the customer cannot produce any real evidence that the restaurant caused him to become sick. At best the customer can introduce facts that raise a mere suspicion that the restaurant was the cause — he can show that he had an upset stomach later in the evening and that various health code violations had been found at the restaurant. What he cannot show is that the meal was the but-for cause of his becoming ill. In response to the customer's facts, the restaurant can show that the customer had three meals after eating in their restaurant, any of which could have caused his infection. The restaurant could also argue that the bacterium causing the customer's illness could have come from the customer's own hands. While this "no causation" defense might not work, it is the restaurant's best chance of those defenses listed.

(A) is wrong because the fact that no one else became ill creates only an inference that the restaurant was not the cause. The fact that no one else got sick certainly doesn't prove that the restaurant wasn't the cause — perhaps one employee failed to wash his hands, prepared the one dish eaten by the customer, then washed them. In any event, the restaurant is better off making the much more general argument (listed in Choice (C)) that the customer is required to make an affirmative showing that the restaurant's negligence caused the illness, and that he has failed to carry this burden by a preponderance of the evidence.

(B) is wrong because the restaurant is responsible for the acts of its employees while in the course of their duties, even if they disregard instructions. Under the doctrine of respondeat superior, an employer is vicariously liable for the negligent acts of its employees, done within the scope of the employment. The fact that the employee has disobeyed rules formulated by the employer is not a defense. Thus as long as there was evidence that an employee failed to wash her hands and then prepared a dish eaten by the customer, the fact that this happened in violation of the restaurant's instructions would not prevent respondeat superior from applying against it.

(D) is wrong because assumption of risk would not apply here. The assumption of the risk doctrine bars a plaintiff from recovery if he voluntarily consented to take the chance that the harm in question would occur. Here, the customer may have assumed the risk of an upset stomach caused by spicy food, but he did not assume the risk of becoming ill because of a bacterium in contaminated food, and his claim is that the latter is what occurred.

[Q3090]

25. **D** An owner of a wild animal or an abnormally dangerous animal is strictly liable for harm caused by

that animal's dangerous nature. Part of what makes wild animals dangerous is that third persons who encounter the animal may well experience acute fear, whether that fear is well-founded or not as to the particular animal. Rest. 2d, §507, Comm. g and Illustr. 1. Here, even though the snake was defanged, the worker had no reason to know this. Therefore, his injury was caused by a foreseeable aspect of the animal's wild and dangerous nature, namely, its tendency to cause fear of being bitten.

(A) is wrong because owners of dangerous animals are strictly liable even when the harm would not have occurred but for the operation of a force of nature.

(B) is wrong because an owner of a wild animal or an abnormally dangerous animal is strictly liable for harm caused by that animal's dangerous nature. The contributory negligence of the worker would not be a defense to strict liability, and in any case there is nothing in the facts to indicate that the worker would have reason to foresee the risk of a poisonous snake.

(C) is wrong because, while this answer correctly states that the worker will prevail, it misstates the legal basis for this conclusion. There is probably not enough evidence here to support a finding of negligence. In any event, whether the owner did or did not take precautions that would be "adequate" (i.e., that would constitute reasonable care), this won't matter — the whole point of strict liability for keeping wild animals is that if the wild animal causes harm in a way that is related to its wildness, the plaintiff does not have to show negligence by the owner. Nor does it matter that the snake was defanged; the worker had no reason to know this, and his injury falls within the risk run by the homeowner because it was caused by the worker's foreseeable reaction to seeing an escaped snake.

[Q7075]

26. **A** The manufacturer is the only one of the three potential defendants who can be liable in strict liability. A person who is engaged in the business of selling products, and who sells a defective product, is subject to liability for harm to persons or property caused by the defect. Rest. 3d (P.L.) §1. One type of defect is a "design defect." A design defect occurs "when the foreseeable risks of harm posed by the product could have been reduced or avoided by the adoption of a reasonable alternative design by the seller or other distributor, or a predecessor in the commercial chain of distribution, and the omission of the alternative design renders the product not reasonably safe." Rest. 3d (P.L.) § 2(b). Here, the manufacturer will be strictly liable because it satisfies the required elements for strict liability: (1) it was in the business of selling products; (2) it sold the product that caused the harm here (the HVAC system); and (3) the HVAC system was "defectively designed," since a better HVAC system was a reasonably available alternative design that could have reduced or avoided the harm, making the omission of such alternative something that rendered the product not reasonably safe.

Neither the heating company nor the cooling company is liable under this test, since neither sold the defectively-designed product (the HVAC system). It's true that the heating company and the cooling company sold *components* that went into the defective HVAC system. But their components were not themselves defective at the time of sale, and these defendants did not do anything that contributed to the "downstream" design defect introduced by the manufacturer (e.g., they didn't give the manufacturer instructions that induced the manufacturer to design the ventilating system in a defective manner). So they cannot be said to have "sold" a "defectively-designed product)."

Since (B), (C), and (D) all treat either the heating company or the cooling company as liable, these choices are wrong for the reasons described in the discussion of Choice (A) above.

[Q4044]

27. **A** This choice is correct because: (1) it correctly implies that the only basis on which the glue manu-

facturer could be liable is on a strict product liability theory; and (2) it correctly asserts that if the glue manufacturer is strictly liable, then the paint company must be as well. Let's take these steps one at a time. As to (1), the glue manufacturer won't be found negligent, since it had no reason to believe that the product posed eye dangers, and since it warned of any danger (e.g., from lack of ventilation) of which it was aware. So if the glue manufacturer were liable, it would have to be on a product liability basis. As to (2), if the glue manufacturer were strictly liable, it would have to be because it sold a defectively dangerous product. If the product was defectively dangerous, then the paint company, as a "downstream" re-seller, would have exactly the same liability, since anyone who sells a defectively dangerous product is strictly liable for it. So there's no way the glue manufacturer could be liable without the paint company's also being liable.

(B) is wrong because it doesn't matter whether the secretary was an invitee of a tenant in the building or not. The recovery here would have to be on a strict product liability basis (see the analysis of Choice (A) for why), and any person who is injured by a defect in a defective product can recover against any seller of that product, whether the plaintiff was an invitee at the time of the injury or not. (Indeed, even if the secretary had been a trespasser, she could have recovered against the paint company in strict product liability.)

(C) is wrong because it ignores the possibility that the paint company is strictly liable as a non-negligent seller of a dangerously defective product.

(D) is wrong because it ignores the possibility that the paint company as a seller of a dangerously defective product would be strictly liable even though the product came in a sealed package. Sellers of dangerously defective products are strictly liable for the harm caused by the defect, and that is true even though the seller behaved with all possible care. So the fact that the product came in a sealed package — thus preventing the paint company from recognizing or altering the danger even if it wanted to — is irrelevant.

[Q4049]

28. **B** The suit has been brought on a failure-to-warn theory. The facts stipulate that the dangers that the plaintiff says should have been warned of were not known or knowable at the time of the plaintiff's exposure. Therefore, the judge must at the outset answer a pure question of law: Does a defendant who is selling dangerous substances have a duty to warn of their dangerousness if that dangerousness is unknown at the time? Choice (B) encapsulates this issue, since if (and only if) the defendant is held to have a duty to warn of these not-yet-known dangers can a reasonable jury possibly find that the defendant is liable for failing to warn. It's not clear how the judge should rule, but it's clear that this is the central issue in the case. (By the way, Rest. 3d (P.L.), §2(c), seems to answer "no" to the question posed by Choice (B), since the Restatement imposes only a duty to warn of "foreseeable risks," which seems equivalent to the question's "risks [that] were reasonably discoverable" at the time.)

(A) is wrong because (1) the issue is irrelevant to plaintiff's failure-to-warn theory, and (2) in any event, this is a question of fact, to be left to the jury. Plaintiff has sued on a failure-to-warn theory. Therefore, even if no satisfactory, safe alternative exists even today, there could still be a duty to warn of these unavoidable dangers. (One in plaintiff's position would be entitled to conclude that in view of the dangers, he should take a different job.) Consequently, the existence of a satisfactory alternative is simply not relevant to the claim. In any event, even if this issue were relevant, the answer would be a pure question of fact, not law.

(C) is wrong because (1) the issue posed may not even be a relevant issue; and (2) the issue is in any event a question of fact. As to (1), the judge could quite plausibly decide (as a matter of law, and as described in Choice (B)), that the plaintiff should be held to have had a duty to warn of not-yet-discoverable risks. If the judge so held, then the issue here (whether D in fact knew of the risks) would be legally irrelevant. As to (2), in any event, what any defendant should reasonably have known at a particular moment is inevitably a factual issue, properly left to the jury.

(D) is wrong because (1) "inherent dangerousness" is probably not an issue; and (2) even if it were, this would be a factual issue to be left to the jury. The concept of "inherent dangerousness," to the extent that it's relevant in a product-liability suit, generally refers to the issue of "unavoidable danger." That is, if a product has some social utility, and is "unavoidably dangerous" (or as it is sometimes put, "inherently dangerous"), the defendant may be able to argue that the product is not "defective." (That's because the idea of a "defect" involves something that is "wrong" or "needlessly dangerous," and something that is unavoidably hazardous does not meet this standard.) Here, the case has been brought on a failure-to-warn theory. So even if asbestos is "inherently dangerous" (and thus not defective), this fact would not spare the defendant from having a duty to warn of its inherent dangers (assuming there is a duty to warn of not-yet-knowable dangers). So the inherent dangerousness of the product would be irrelevant. In any event, even if inherent dangerousness were a relevant issue, this would be a matter of fact, not law, and thus properly left to the jury.

[Q3023]

29. **A** A landowner who causes a substantial, unreasonable interference with a neighbor's use or enjoyment of his property without a valid defense is liable for private nuisance. Most courts apply this rule in the case of watercourses, holding that an upstream owner may not completely block the flow of water if this would unreasonably interfere with a downstream owner's use and enjoyment of the latter's property.

(B) is wrong because the neighbor's desire to affect the vacationer's property is not an element of the tort of private nuisance. As described in the treatment of Choice (A) above, private nuisance is the unreasonable interference with another's use and enjoyment of the latter's property. Choice (B) is wrong mostly because it fails to factor in whether there has been an unreasonable interference with the vacationer's use and enjoyment of his property. For instance, if the damming was the only way to avoid flooding of the neighbor's property, and the harm it posed to the vacationer's use and enjoyment was very small, a court would conclude that the damning was not "unreasonable," and the vacationer would lose, even though the neighbor "intended" (in the sense of knowing with substantial certainty) that the vacationer's property would be "affected" (in the sense that water would no longer flow through it).

(C) is wrong because the tort nuisance covers use and *enjoyment*, not just use. A landowner who causes a substantial, unreasonable interference with a neighbor's use or enjoyment of his property without a valid defense is liable for private nuisance. The fact that the vacationer never goes "close" to the stream is not inconsistent with her having sustained an unreasonable interference with her "use and *enjoyment*" of her property. For instance, it's very possible that the vacationer used to like to view, from an upstairs window, the stream running through her property, and that she now has much less pleasure from the waterless view. Consequently, her "use and enjoyment" have been substantially impaired, even though in a narrow sense she never "made use" of the stream.

(D) is wrong because compliance with this type of statute would not preclude liability for nuisance. A landowner who causes a substantial, unreasonable interference with a neighbor's use or enjoyment of his property without a valid defense is liable for private nuisance. Many nuisances are not in violation of any particular law, since "positive law" (statutes, ordinances, and the like) do not purport to be the sole source of legal obligations. (For instance, a factory might get all required local permits, but might still be a private nuisance because it's unreasonably loud and noisy.) Therefore, the fact that the dam satisfied the relevant affirmative laws when it was built does not foreclose the possibility of a successful nuisance suit.

[Q3041]

30. **A** The situations in which a plaintiff can recover for purely emotional distress caused by negligence are limited, and this is not one of them. Recovery for negligent misrepresentation is usually limited to pecuniary loss unless there was a risk of physical harm. In this case, the applicant found a comparable position promptly, so he suffered no pecuniary harm from the personnel director's misrepresentation, and therefore cannot recover for the non-pecuniary harm of emotional distress.

(B) is wrong because, while this answer correctly states that the applicant will not prevail, it misstates the legal basis for this conclusion. It is not the case that the director's statement is purely speculative. Some of the information conveyed to the job applicant was factual; it was clearly intended to assure the applicant that the company was in fact at the time economically strong, and to induce reliance. Therefore, the information was sufficiently concrete that it could serve as the basis for a negligent misrepresentation action.

(C) is wrong because, while reliance is essential for recovery in negligent misrepresentation, it is not sufficient. (For instance, the reliance must be reasonable.) The biggest problem is that this choice does not reflect the fact that while there are situations in which a plaintiff can recover for purely emotional distress caused by negligence, this is not one of them. Recovery for negligent misrepresentation is usually limited to pecuniary loss unless the misrepresentation also involved a risk of physical harm. In this case, the applicant found a comparable position promptly, so he suffered no pecuniary harm from the personnel director's misrepresentation.

(D) is wrong because recovery for negligent misrepresentation does not extend to all foreseeable damages. The applicant cannot prevail because recovery for negligent misrepresentation is usually limited to pecuniary loss, unless the misrepresentation produced a risk of physical harm. Here, there was never any risk of physical harm to the applicant. Since the applicant found a comparable position promptly, he suffered no pecuniary harm from the personnel director's misrepresentation, and therefore is not permitted to recover for his non-pecuniary harm (from emotional distress).

[Q7040]

31. **C** The central problem with these facts is that they don't indicate an active misrepresentation by the engineer, and there's no duty on the engineer to disclose the true value of the stock. Such a duty only arises where, for instance, there is a specific query about the matter, a special (e.g., fiduciary) relationship exists, or there are other circumstances meriting disclosure (e.g., a half-truth, subsequent information which makes prior statement misleading, or knowledge of undisclosed facts basic to a transaction). None of these apply to these facts; thus, for there to be liability, an option would have to add facts *creating* liability. That's what Choice (C) does, by adding a misrepresentation — that the stock is not worth more than $6. This qualifies because the fact pattern now satisfies all the requirements of liability for intentional misrepresentation: (1) defendant's misrepresentation of a material past or present fact; (2) defendant's knowledge of falsity or reckless disregard for falsity; (3) defendant's intent to induce plaintiff's reliance; (4) plaintiff's actual, justifiable reliance; and (5) damages. Here, the misrepresentation about value obviously satisfies (1), and without that misrepresentation about value, requirement (1) would not be satisfied.

(A) is wrong because the general rule is that liability for misrepresentation requires some form of active concealment or active misleading, not just mere failure to disclose a material fact. There are a number of exceptions (e.g., the telling of a half-truth, or the existence of a fiduciary relationship between the parties). But no exception applies on these facts, so the engineer's silence about the material fact doesn't constitute an actionable misrepresentation.

(B) is wrong for the same reason Choice (A) is wrong: liability for misrepresentation requires some form of active concealment or active misleading, not just mere failure to disclose a material fact. There are a number of exceptions, but none applies here.

(D) is wrong because the availability of the financial statement would not be relevant to the seller's claim. Even if the financial statement was not available to the seller, the engineer would not be liable for here mere failure to disclose a material fact that she knew, for the reasons described in the discussion of Choice (C) above.

[Q4045]

32. **A** The professor can state a prima facie case of defamation, but he cannot prevail because the dean has a valid defense based on his reasonable belief that the professor invited him to speak. See Rest. 2d, §583 ("The consent of another to the publication of defamatory matter concerning him is a complete defense to his action for defamation.") By authorizing his agents to investigate his case, the professor apparently consented to limited publication in response to their inquiries. By the way, ill will on the part of the dean, even if it existed, would be irrelevant to this defense.

(B) is wrong because, while this answer correctly states that the professor will lose, it misstates the legal basis for this conclusion. Some jurisdictions may require evidence of pecuniary loss for oral statements that are not slander per se, but this is a written statement. Under the common law applicable to libel (written defamations), damages to the professor's reputation would be presumed, allowing him to recover even if he sustained no provable pecuniary loss.

(C) is wrong because the tort of defamation does not turn on whether an investigation, reasonable or not, has been conducted. It is true that defamation is not a strict liability tort, and requires at least negligence by the defendant (and indeed requires knowledge of falsity or reckless disregard of the truth if the plaintiff is a public figure). So the dean's failure to investigate might constitute negligence, thereby supplying the requisite mental state. But even with the mental-state requirement satisfied, the professor would lose on the grounds of consent, as further detailed in the discussion of Choice (A).

(D) is wrong because the fact that the statement was in writing does not affect the outcome here. Even if the statement were oral, the professor could recover for slander if the dean were shown to have behaved negligently (e.g., by not investigating the rumor) and if no defense applied. But a defense does apply, namely the defense of consent, as further detailed in Choice (A).

[Q7050]

33. **D** Where the defendant's statement is oral rather than written, any defamation action would have to be for slander rather than libel. The plaintiff is not entitled to recover for slander unless either: (1) the slander falls within one of four "slander per se" categories; or (2) plaintiff has shown "special damage" (which means economic or pecuniary harm). The four slander per se categories are accusations of: (1) a criminal offense; (2) a "loathsome" disease (i.e., a sexually transmitted disease); (3) a matter incompatible with the plaintiff's business, trade, profession or office; and (4) serious sexual misconduct. Rest. 2d, §570. Calling the plaintiff a "deadbeat" doesn't fall into any of these categories (at least if the plaintiff is a consumer rather than a businessperson, as is the case here). Therefore, since the statement is slander rather than libel, and since it's not slander per se, the customer can win only if he shows that he has suffered some "special damage," i.e., economic harm.

(A) is wrong because, although it mentions an element that will be necessary to the customer's recovery ("publication" to a third person), it omits any discussion of special harm, which is required for this slander-not-per-se action as discussed in Choice (D) above.

(B) is wrong because, although the fact that the conduct was extreme and outrageous (if indeed it was) would be relevant to an action by the customer for intentional infliction of emotional distress, it is not relevant to an action for defamation, which is what the question is asking you about.

(C) is wrong because the customer might be able to win even if the bill collector did not know that the customer didn't really owe any money to the store. Even under Supreme Court First Amendment-based restrictions, states are permitted to give a private (i.e., non-public-figure) plaintiff the right to win if the plaintiff can show that the defendant made a defamatory falsehood and behaved at least negligently with respect to the statement's truth. Therefore, assuming that the customer did not in fact owe the store anything (something that is not really clear from the facts), the customer can win even if the bill collector didn't know that the customer owed nothing, but negligently believed that the customer owed money. (The customer's problem is that he would have to show special damage, i.e., pecuniary harm, as detailed in the discussion of Choice (D) above.)

[Q4065]

34. **C** To establish a prima facie case for invasion of privacy by appropriation of plaintiff's picture or name, only one element needs to be proved: that there was an unauthorized use by defendant of plaintiff's picture or name for commercial advantage. Under these facts the actor consented to an amateur photographer taking his picture as he sat drinking Vineyard wine at a nightclub. He did not consent to the bottler's using his photo for commercial purposes. The bottler's advertisement in a nationally circulated magazine was intended for the bottler's commercial advantage.

(A) is wrong because the actor's consent was to the amateur photographer, not to the bottler's commercial use. To establish a prima facie case for invasion of privacy by appropriation of plaintiff's picture or name, only one element needs to be proved: that there was an unauthorized use by defendant of plaintiff's picture or name for commercial advantage. Here, the actor's consent was specifically to an amateur photographer. The scope of the actor's consent was to a single amateur photograph. He did not consent to the bottler's using that photograph for its commercial advantage. Therefore, his "consent" would not negate the bottler's liability.

(B) is wrong because public figures retain the right not to have their image utilized for commercial advantage. It's true that the actor was a well-known movie star and so would be considered a public figure. While this fact might conceivably be relevant in other kinds of invasion of privacy claims, or in some defamation claims, it is irrelevant to the claim here, as to which the only element that needs to be proved is that there was an unauthorized use by defendant of plaintiff's picture or name for commercial advantage. Therefore, the actor's status as a public figure does not exonerate the bottler.

(D) is wrong because a person's enjoyment of a product does not convey the rights to commercial use of an image of the person using the product. To establish a prima facie case for invasion of privacy by appropriation of plaintiff's picture or name, only one element needs to be proved: that there was an unauthorized use by defendant of plaintiff's picture or name for commercial advantage. Truth is therefore not a defense to this appropriation form of invasion of privacy. Thus although it's true that the actor enjoyed Vineyard wine, this fact did not give the bottler the right to make commercial use of the actor's image, or to say, for commercial purposes, that the actor liked the wine.

[Q3192]